LAW, CRIME AND LAW ENFORCEMENT

ORGANIZED CRIME

ASPECTS AND GLOBALIZED ELEMENTS

LAW, CRIME AND LAW ENFORCEMENT

Additional books in this series can be found on Nova's website
under the Series tab.

Additional E-books in this series can be found on Nova's website
under the E-book tab.

CRIMINAL JUSTICE, LAW ENFORCEMENT AND CORRECTIONS

Additional books in this series can be found on Nova's website
under the Series tab.

Additional E-books in this series can be found on Nova's website
under the E-book tab.

LAW, CRIME AND LAW ENFORCEMENT

ORGANIZED CRIME

ASPECTS AND GLOBALIZED ELEMENTS

FREDERICK B. HALL
AND
FRANCIS C. MARTIN
EDITORS

nova publishers
New York

Library of Congress Cataloging-in-Publication Data

ISBN: 978-1-62618-415-2

Published by Nova Science Publishers, Inc. † New York

CONTENTS

PREFACE

In the last two decades, organized crime has grown more complex, posing evolving challenges for U.S. federal law enforcement. These criminals have transformed their operations in ways that broaden their reach and make it harder for law enforcement to combat them. They have adopted more-networked structural models, internationalized their operations, and grown more tech savvy. They are a significant challenge to U.S. law enforcement. This book examines a broad conceptualization of organized crime in its narrative discussion of criminal activity. The analysis includes groups engaged in sustained criminal enterprises, such as, but not limited to: drug traffickers, mafia families, smugglers, violent gangs, and fraudsters. These operations may or may not have a transnational dimension to them, but they directly impact U.S. persons, businesses, and/or interests.

Chapter 1 - In the last two decades, organized crime has grown more complex, posing evolving challenges for U.S. federal law enforcement. These criminals have transformed their operations in ways that broaden their reach and make it harder for law enforcement to combat them. They have adopted more-networked structural models, internationalized their operations, and grown more tech savvy. They are a significant challenge to U.S. law enforcement.

Modern organized criminals often prefer cellular or networked structural models for their flexibility and avoid the hierarchies that previously governed more traditional organized crime groups such as the Cosa Nostra. Fluid network structures make it harder for law enforcement to infiltrate, disrupt, and dismantle conspiracies. Many 21st century organized crime groups opportunistically form around specific, short-term schemes and may outsource portions of their operations rather than keeping it all "in-house."

Globalization has revolutionized both licit and illicit commerce. Commercial and technological innovations have reduced national trade barriers, widened transportation infrastructure, and bolstered volumes of international business. The Internet and extensive cellular telephone networks have fostered rapid communication. Integrated financial systems, which allow for easy global movement of money, are exploited by criminals to launder their illicit proceeds. Estimates suggest that money laundering annually accounts for between 2% and 5% of world GDP. Simultaneously, borders are opportunities for criminals and impediments to law enforcement.

Organized criminals have expanded their technological "toolkits," incorporating technology-driven fraud into their capabilities. Their operations can harm U.S. citizens without ever having a physical presence in the country. These illicit activities include cyber intrusions into corporate databases, theft of individual consumer credit card information, fencing of stolen merchandise online, and leveraging technology to aid in narcotics smuggling. Further, criminal organizations—which have historically burrowed into and exploited local ethnic communities— can now rely on Internet connectivity and extensive, international transportation linkages to target localities around the globe.

Since the terrorist attacks of September 11, 2001, there has been a shift in law enforcement attention and resources toward counterterrorism-related activities and away from traditional crime fighting activities including the investigation of organized crime. Although the effects of organized crime may not be seen in a consolidated attack resulting in the physical loss of life, they are far-reaching—impacting economic stability, public health and safety, as well as national security.

In July 2011, the Obama Administration issued its *Strategy to Combat Transnational Organized Crime.* It addresses the fact that federal investigation of organized crime matters has not historically been a centralized effort. Regardless, there still is no single agency charged with investigating organized crime in the way the Federal Bureau of Investigation (FBI) has been designated the lead investigative agency for terrorism. Further, resources to tackle this issue are divided among many federal agencies. As such, Congress may exert its oversight authority regarding the federal coordination of organized crime investigations via the 2011 strategy. Policymakers may also debate the efficacy of current resources appropriated to combat organized crime.

Chapter 2 - Organized retail crime (ORC) involves the large-scale theft of everyday consumer items and potentially has much broader implications. Organized groups of professional shoplifters, or "boosters," steal or fraudulently obtain merchandise that is then sold, or "fenced," to individuals and retailers through a variety of venues. In an increasingly globalized society, more and more transactions take place online rather than face-to-face. As such, in addition to relying on physical resale markets, organized retail thieves have turned to online marketplaces as means to fence their ill-gotten goods.

ORC exposes the United States to costs and harms in the economic, public health, and domestic security arenas. The exact loss from ORC to the retail industry is unknown, but estimates have ranged from $15 billion to $37 billion annually. The economic impact, however, extends beyond the manufacturing and retail industry and includes costs incurred by consumers and taxes lost by the states. The theft and resale of stolen consumable or health and beauty products such as infant formula (that may have been repackaged, relabeled, and subjected to altered expiration dates) poses potential safety concerns for individuals purchasing such goods from ORC fences. In addition, some industry experts and policy makers have expressed concern about the possibility that proceeds from ORC may be used to fund terrorist activities.

Current efforts to combat ORC largely come from retailers, online marketplaces, and law enforcement alike. Retailers responding to the 2010 National Retail Security Survey spent an average of 0.46% of their annual sales on loss prevention measures. These loss prevention costs are ultimately borne by consumers in the form of higher prices on goods. Also, online marketplaces report taking various measures to combat the sale of stolen and fraudulently obtained goods on their websites, including educating sellers and consumers, monitoring suspicious activity, and partnering with retailers and law enforcement. Combating retail theft has traditionally been handled by state law enforcement under state criminal laws. Some, however, have begun to question whether state laws—which vary in the quantity of monetary losses that constitute major theft—are adequate to combat ORC. While many agree that ORC is a national problem, there is debate over the federal government's role in deterring ORC and sanctioning various actors that may be involved in committing or aiding these crimes. One policy issue facing Congress is whether criminalizing organized retail crime in the *U.S. Code* would allow for more effective investigation and prosecution of these criminals. Congress may also wish to consider whether regulating resale marketplaces (online markets, in particular), to require such entities to increase information sharing with retailers and law enforcement, would strengthen investigations and prosecutions of ORC as well as decrease the prevalence of retail thieves relying on legitimate online marketplaces to fence stolen goods.

Chapter 3 - Violence has been an inherent feature of the trade in illicit drugs, but the violence generated by Mexico's drug trafficking organizations (DTOs) in recent years has been unprecedented and remarkably brutal. The tactics—including mass killings, the use of torture and dismemberment, and the phenomena of car bombs—have led some analysts to speculate whether the violence has been transformed into something new, perhaps requiring a different set of policy responses. According to government and other data, the best estimates are that there were slightly more than 50,000 homicides related to organized crime from December 2006 through December 2011. Some analysts see in this year's data about Mexico's organized crime-related homicides the possibility that the violence may have peaked or reached a plateau, if it has not begun to decline. Many observers maintain that the steep increase in organized crime-related homicides in recent years is likely to trend down far more slowly.

In December 2006, Mexico's newly inaugurated President Felipe Calderón launched an aggressive campaign against the DTOs—an initiative that has defined his administration—that has been met with a violent response from the DTOs. Of the seven most significant DTOs operating during the first five years of the Calderón Administration, the government successfully removed key leaders from each of them, through arrests or by death in arrest efforts. However, these efforts add to the dynamic of change—consolidation or fragmentation, succession struggles, and new competition—that generates more conflict and violence among competing criminal groups. In the last six years, fragments of some of the DTOs have formed new criminal organizations, while two DTOs have become dominant and polarized rivals: the Sinaloa DTO in the western part of the country and Los Zetas in the east. In addition, the DTOs have increasingly diversified into other criminal activities, now posing a multi-faceted organized criminal challenge to governance in Mexico.

U.S. citizens have also been victims of the security crisis in Mexico. In March 2010, three individuals connected to the U.S. consulate in Ciudad Juárez, two of them U.S. citizens, were killed by a gang working for one of the major DTOs operating in that city. In February 2011, two U.S. Immigration and Customs Enforcement (ICE) agents were shot, one fatally, allegedly by Los Zetas, one of Mexico's most violent DTOs. In the U.S. Congress, these events have raised concerns about the stability of a strategic partner and neighbor. Congress is also concerned about the possibility of "spillover" violence along the U.S. border and further inland. The 112th Congress has held several hearings on DTO violence, the efforts by the Calderón government to address the situation, and implications of the violence for the United States. Members have maintained close oversight of U.S.-Mexico security cooperation and related bilateral issues. This report provides background on drug trafficking in Mexico: it identifies the major DTOs; examines how the organized crime "landscape" has been altered by fragmentation; and analyzes the context, scope, and scale of the violence. It examines current trends of the violence, analyzes prospects for curbing violence in the future, and compares it with violence in Colombia.

Chapter 4 - The *Strategy to Combat Transnational Organized Crime* applies all elements of national power to protect citizens and U.S. national security interests from the convergence of 21st century transnational criminal threats. This *Strategy* is organized around a single unifying principle: *to build, balance, and integrate the tools of American power to combat transnational organized crime and related threats to national security—and to urge our foreign partners to do the same.* The end-state we seek is to reduce transnational organized crime (TOC) from a national security threat to a manageable public safety problem in the United States and in strategic regions around the world. The *Strategy* will achieve this end-state by pursuing five key policy objectives:

1) Protect Americans and our partners from the harm, violence, and exploitation of transnational criminal networks.
2) Help partner countries strengthen governance and transparency, break the corruptive power of transnational criminal networks, and sever state-crime alliances.
3) Break the economic power of transnational criminal networks and protect strategic markets and the U.S. financial system from TOC penetration and abuse.
4) Defeat transnational criminal networks that pose the greatest threat to national security by targeting their infrastructures, depriving them of their enabling means, and preventing the criminal facilitation of terrorist activities.
5) Build international consensus, multilateral cooperation, and public-private partnerships to defeat transnational organized crime.

The *Strategy* also introduces new and innovative capabilities and tools, which will be accomplished by prioritizing within the resources available to affected departments and agencies.

A new Executive Order will establish a sanctions program to block the property of and prohibit transactions with significant transnational criminal networks that threaten national security, foreign policy, or economic interests.

A proposed legislative package will enhance the authorities available to investigate, interdict, and prosecute the activities of top transnational criminal networks.

A new Presidential Proclamation under the Immigration and Nationality Act (INA) will deny entry to transnational criminal aliens and others who have been targeted for financial sanctions.

A new rewards program will replicate the success of narcotics rewards programs in obtaining information that leads to the arrest and conviction of the leaders of transnational criminal organizations that pose the greatest threats to national security.

An interagency Threat Mitigation Working Group will identify those TOC networks that present a sufficiently high national security risk and will ensure the coordination of all elements of national power to combat them.

In: Organized Crime
Editors: F. B. Hall and F. C. Martin
ISBN: 978-1-62618-415-2

Chapter 1

ORGANIZED CRIME: AN EVOLVING CHALLENGE FOR U.S. LAW ENFORCEMENT*

Jerome P. Bjelopera and Kristin M. Finklea

SUMMARY

In the last two decades, organized crime has grown more complex, posing evolving challenges for U.S. federal law enforcement. These criminals have transformed their operations in ways that broaden their reach and make it harder for law enforcement to combat them. They have adopted more-networked structural models, internationalized their operations, and grown more tech savvy. They are a significant challenge to U.S. law enforcement.

Modern organized criminals often prefer cellular or networked structural models for their flexibility and avoid the hierarchies that previously governed more traditional organized crime groups such as the Cosa Nostra. Fluid network structures make it harder for law enforcement to infiltrate, disrupt, and dismantle conspiracies. Many 21st century organized crime groups opportunistically form around specific, short-term schemes and may outsource portions of their operations rather than keeping it all "in-house."

Globalization has revolutionized both licit and illicit commerce. Commercial and technological innovations have reduced national trade barriers, widened transportation infrastructure, and bolstered volumes of international business. The Internet and extensive cellular telephone networks have fostered rapid communication. Integrated financial systems, which allow for easy global movement of money, are exploited by criminals to launder their illicit proceeds. Estimates suggest that money laundering annually accounts for between 2% and 5% of world GDP. Simultaneously, borders are opportunities for criminals and impediments to law enforcement.

Organized criminals have expanded their technological "toolkits," incorporating technology-driven fraud into their capabilities. Their operations can harm U.S. citizens without ever having a physical presence in the country. These illicit activities include cyber intrusions into corporate databases, theft of individual consumer credit card information, fencing of stolen merchandise online, and leveraging technology to aid in narcotics smuggling. Further, criminal organizations—which have historically burrowed

* This is an edited, reformatted and augmented version of Congressional Research Service, Publication No. R41547, dated January 6, 2012.

into and exploited local ethnic communities— can now rely on Internet connectivity and extensive, international transportation linkages to target localities around the globe.

Since the terrorist attacks of September 11, 2001, there has been a shift in law enforcement attention and resources toward counterterrorism-related activities and away from traditional crime fighting activities including the investigation of organized crime. Although the effects of organized crime may not be seen in a consolidated attack resulting in the physical loss of life, they are far-reaching—impacting economic stability, public health and safety, as well as national security.

In July 2011, the Obama Administration issued its *Strategy to Combat Transnational Organized Crime*. It addresses the fact that federal investigation of organized crime matters has not historically been a centralized effort. Regardless, there still is no single agency charged with investigating organized crime in the way the Federal Bureau of Investigation (FBI) has been designated the lead investigative agency for terrorism. Further, resources to tackle this issue are divided among many federal agencies. As such, Congress may exert its oversight authority regarding the federal coordination of organized crime investigations via the 2011 strategy. Policymakers may also debate the efficacy of current resources appropriated to combat organized crime.

INTRODUCTION

In the last two decades, organized crime has grown more complex, posing evolving challenges for U.S. federal law enforcement. This is largely because these criminals have transformed their operations in ways that broaden their reach and make it harder for law enforcement to define and combat the threat they pose. Globalization and technological innovation have not only impacted legitimate commerce, but they have simultaneously revolutionized crime. In response to these forces, organized criminals have adopted more-networked structural models, internationalized their operations, and grown more tech savvy. Criminals have become more elusive. They see international borders as opportunities while law enforcement views them as obstacles. Criminals have expanded their range of tools and targets as well. Meanwhile, law enforcement "plays by yesterday's rules and increasingly risks dealing only with the weakest criminals and the easiest problems," according to the Strategic Alliance Group, a partnership of seven law enforcement agencies from five nations.[1]

Motivated by money, organized crime fills needs not met by licit market structures and/or exploits businesses, consumers, and nations for profit. Organized criminals have capitalized on commercial and technological advances that have bolstered communication and international business. They use innovative methods of moving illegal proceeds around the world. Some nations have also witnessed the creation of ties between powerful business figures, politicians, and criminals.

Modern organized criminals may prefer cellular or networked structural models for their flexibility and avoid the hierarchies governed by elaborate initiation rituals that were favored by their predecessors. Fluid network structures make it harder for law enforcement to infiltrate, disrupt, and dismantle conspiracies. Many 21st century organized crime groups opportunistically form around specific, short-term schemes. Further, these groups may outsource portions of their operations rather than keeping all of their expertise "in-house."

In July 2011, to address these and other issues, the Obama Administration issued its *Strategy to Combat Transnational Organized Crime* (*2011 Strategy*). It described transnational organized crime (TOC) networks as a strategic threat to national security, laid out a definition of transnational organized crime, and set forth five policy objectives and six categories of priority actions in an attempt to devise a cohesive federal response to transnational organized crime.[2] Complicating all of this, since the terrorist attacks of September 11, 2001 (9/11), there has been a shift in law enforcement attention and resources more toward counterterrorism-related activities and away from traditional crime fighting activities—including the investigation of organized crime.

This report provides an analysis of how organized crime has capitalized on globalization by using borders as opportunities, relying on fast-paced technological change, and adapting its organizational structures. It illustrates how these transformations can impact U.S. persons, businesses, and interests. The report includes a discussion of how U.S. law enforcement conceptualizes organized crime in the 21st century and concludes by examining potential issues for Congress, including the extent to which organized crime is a national security threat (partly to be tackled by U.S. law enforcement agencies), congressional oversight regarding the federal coordination of organized crime investigations, and the utility of current resources appropriated to combat organized crime.

This report employs a broad conceptualization of organized crime in its narrative discussion of criminal activity. In other words, the analysis includes groups engaged in sustained criminal enterprises, such as—but not limited to—drug traffickers, mafia families, smugglers, violent gangs, and fraudsters. These operations may or may not have a transnational dimension to them (which is a requirement under the guidelines of the 2011 Strategy), *but they directly impact U.S. persons, businesses, and/or interests. While this conceptualization may be broader than the definition laid out in the* 2011 Strategy, *it incorporates a range of criminality that may inform Congress in future legislation impacting organized crime. The cases and examples discussed in this report are not intended to set definitional boundaries for organized crime.*

ORGANIZED CRIME ADAPTING TO GLOBALIZATION

Organized crime targeting the United States has internationalized and its structures have flattened. The popular image of mobsters employing elaborate initiation rituals and strict codes of conduct to control crews that assail their own communities is outmoded. Today, nimble, adaptive, loosely structured small groups with global reach harm consumers, businesses, and government interests on a daily basis. Commercial and technological innovations are behind this transformation. They have helped to reduce national trade barriers, widen transportation infrastructure, and bolster volumes of international business. Smugglers have taken advantage of growing international commerce to hide illicit trade. The Internet and extensive cellular telephone networks have fostered rapid communication, simultaneously revolutionizing licit and illicit commerce. For example, integrated financial systems allow for easy global movement of money. Estimates suggest that money laundering annually accounts for between 2% and 5% of world GDP.[3] Criminal organizations targeting the United States operate in many of the world's nations. Areas wracked by social disorder, inadequate policing, and poor governance offer opportunities for organized crime to take root.[4] These groups exploit diaspora communities in the United States as cover for their operations, situating elements of their global operations among immigrant enclaves.

Organized crime groups are becoming more entrepreneurial or market focused, reacting to changes in both illicit and licit economies.[5] Of course, they are still heavily involved in activities such as narcotics trafficking and money laundering (which have been greatly impacted by globalization), but organized criminals are increasingly involved in less "traditional" high-tech operations encompassing identity theft, counterfeiting of goods, and various types of fraud.

Borders and Organized Crime

Modern organized criminals prey upon weaknesses in international transportation and customs security regimens.[6] Border policing efforts have attempted to keep pace with the expansion of international commerce. Organized criminals attempting to smuggle goods, people, or information across borders also face enhanced border security regimens resulting from the terrorist attacks of 9/11. Regardless, specialized criminal networks smuggle items such as narcotics, counterfeit goods, stolen goods, and bulk cash, as well as humans, around the world and into the United States. They have hidden their contraband within the growing volume of legitimate global trade. Prior to the global recession, between 1995 and 2008 the volume of global containerized traffic tripled.[7] Drug traffickers move large loads of cocaine, eventually destined for U.S. markets, from South America to Mexico via containerized shipping. International counterfeiters use containers to smuggle their fake goods into the United States. As Moisės Naím has succinctly put it, most illicit trade involves copycats, smugglers, and traffickers.[8] While individuals can and do engage in these activities, a good deal can be attributed to organized crime.

Copycats and Smugglers

Criminal groups engage in counterfeiting and smuggling across and within the borders of the United States. This activity includes a wide range of products and influences the lives of everyday Americans, U.S. businesses, and government.

Counterfeiting and Piracy

Counterfeiting highlights the nexus between globalization and the modernization of organized crime. Although it is difficult, if not impossible, to determine how deeply immersed organized criminals are in this activity, at least one study has suggested serious involvement.[9] Further, in a recent speech before the International Intellectual Property Summit, Attorney General Holder reinforced the need for the international law enforcement community to combat "the international networks of organized criminals now seeking to profit from IP [intellectual property] crimes."[10]

In areas such as film piracy, counterfeiting does not necessarily involve high entry costs or large legal penalties when compared to more conventional criminal activity such as drug trafficking.[11] It is also potentially very lucrative. With little infrastructure—a high-speed Internet connection, scanner, and copier and off-the-shelf software—criminals around the globe can easily imitate the branding and packaging that accompanies products, let alone copy the products themselves.[12] Counterfeiting and pirating goods[13] involves the violation of intellectual property rights (IPR),[14] essential to creative and high-tech industries particularly reliant on copyrights, trademarks, and patents to protect innovation. Counterfeiting and piracy potentially harm legitimate businesses and consumers, sapping profits and brand value and flooding markets with inferior and even dangerous products masquerading as legitimate goods. Aside from enforcement outlays, the activity also costs governments tax revenue and may slow economic growth by driving down incentives to innovate.[15]

Between FY2005 and FY2008, the yearly domestic value[16] of IPR-related law enforcement seizures of contraband in the United States leaped from $93 million to $273 million. In FY2009, the domestic value of seizures dropped 4%.[17] This is likely due to the global recession. Products originating in China—both Mainland China and Hong Kong—accounted for over 85% of these IPR seizures in FY2008 and FY2009.[18] Two 2010 operations in the United States together netted $240 million in counterfeit materials. The hauls included fake Rolex watches, Coach handbags, pirated DVDs, and fake pharmaceutical products. Much of the material came from China.[19]

Auto Theft Rings

Another example of organized criminals viewing borders as opportunity involves auto theft. Although international automobile theft has existed almost as long as cars have been around,[20] the integration of worldwide markets and expansion of international shipping have greatly impacted it by facilitating international transport of stolen automobiles. Assessing the level of such activity is very difficult since few metrics for it exist. Regardless, today's international automobile theft rings benefit from the high levels of cargo container traffic ushered in by globalization. These groups profit by stealing vehicles in the United States and shipping them abroad, where they are sold. Such illicit operations react to global demand for luxury vehicles, and in some instances are extremely responsive to market forces. They trawl large U.S. metropolitan areas that have assortments of vehicles and rely on rail or port facilities to move stolen vehicles abroad.[21]

In June 2010, law enforcement officials announced indictments of 17 participants in an alleged scheme that pilfered 450 cars annually in New York, New Jersey, and Connecticut. According to law enforcement officials, the group, described as a "steal to order" outfit by New York State Attorney General Andrew Cuomo, filled specific requests from U.S. customers and others in Senegal and netted up to $25,000 per car. The group supposedly relied on specialists who could reprogram car keys to match a vehicle's specific code, exporters, and two car dealership employees, among others. The ring allegedly stored vehicles in four Bronx, NY, garages and loaded those destined for Senegal into shipping containers, concealing the cars behind furniture.[22]

Human Smuggling and Trafficking

Criminal organizations are taking advantage of an unprecedented era of international migration, including illegal migration to the United States.[23] However, since 2007 illegal immigration to the United States has declined.[24] This may be attributable, in part, to dwindling job opportunities resulting from the global recession and increased immigration enforcement activity along the U.S. Southwest border.[25] Nonetheless, criminal organizations continue to capitalize on the desire of unauthorized immigrants to enter the United States. Networks of human smugglers and others— including Mexican drug trafficking organizations (DTOs) that have broadened their money-generating activities to include human and weapon smuggling, counterfeiting, kidnapping for ransom, and extortion—bring unauthorized immigrants across the border and into the United States.[26] In one well-known case, Cheng

Chui Ping—also known as "Sister Ping"—sentenced in March 2006, had led an international human smuggling ring that was responsible for smuggling Chinese villagers to the United States between the early 1980s and April 2000. In a 2006 press release, the Department of Justice (DOJ) described her as "one of the first, and ultimately most successful, alien smugglers of all time."[27] At the start, Ping's smuggling ring brought small numbers of villagers to the United States via aircraft, using fake immigration documents. She turned from exclusive reliance on air transit to include the use of maritime shipping as her operation matured. This way, Ping likely exploited increasing volumes of international seaborne cargo engendered by globalization to mask her illegal movement of human beings. She eventually developed the capability to smuggle hundreds of victims at a time via cargo ships, where the villagers could be stashed below the deck until they reached their U.S. destination and eventually paid her exorbitant smuggling fees.[28] Criminals who smuggle individuals into the United States may also turn the smuggling into a trafficking situation by increasing the immigrants' debts owed once they have been smuggled to the United States. The smugglers/traffickers may then require their victims to work for a period of time to pay off the debts.[29]

Organized crime exploits individuals through both labor and sex trafficking. In 2006, the FBI reported that human trafficking generates about $9.5 billion for organized crime annually.[30]

However, as the Government Accountability Office (GAO) has noted, estimates regarding the global scale of human trafficking are questionable;[31] as such, any estimates regarding the proceeds generated through these crimes may not be representative of their true scope. These criminal organizations target both U.S. citizens and foreign nationals who are drawn to visions of better lives in the United States.

International borders often play a central role in the dynamics involved in forced labor and sex trafficking. In many instances, victims likely perceive borders and border security regimens as insurmountable barriers via legitimate means, requiring them to turn to illicit methods of transit offered by traffickers. Organized criminals prey on victims' powerful desires to live or work in other countries. While the following two cases may not have been prosecuted by DOJ as traditional "organized crime," the networks involved highlight some of the dynamics involved in labor and sex trafficking. In August 2010, federal law enforcement announced an indictment of six individuals for participation in an alleged conspiracy to exploit Thai nationals through forced labor in the United States. The defendants allegedly enticed workers to the United States by offering opportunities for lucrative jobs. Once in the United States, the approximately 400 Thai workers had their passports confiscated, were threatened with economic harm and deportation, and were forced to work on farms in Washington and Hawaii.[32] In another case, four individuals from the United States, Mexico, and Guatemala were sentenced in April 2010 for involvement in a sex trafficking organization that targeted young Mexican women. They lured these women to the United States on the promise of better lives or legitimate employment. Once the women were brought to the United States, they were instead physically threatened, beaten, intimidated, and forced to engage in commercial sex.[33] DOJ has also reported an uptick in Asian organized crime groups becoming involved as pimps or brokers in domestic human sex trafficking. Although the increase is noted for Asian organized crime groups, involvement in sex trafficking is certainly not limited by ethnic or geographic origin; these criminals collaborate with other, non-Asian groups to further their sex trafficking enterprises.[34]

Drug Trafficking

In the last decade, cocaine has become a truly global commodity dependent on illicit market fluctuations. Traffickers now can leverage wide, international distribution networks to ride out pressures or changes that may make their traditional illicit markets less hospitable. According to media reports, some Colombian and Mexican cocaine suppliers have shifted sizeable amounts of product using containerized shipping—hiding their illicit material within the daily globalized flow of legitimate seaborne international commerce.[35] And some of the Mexican Gulf Cartel's smuggling activity involving European markets has used the United States as a transshipment point.[36]

When it comes to the internationalization of cocaine markets, not all the news involves the growth of supply, however. Global demand for cocaine has partly impacted U.S. bound supplies of the drug. Cocaine availability levels in the United States have decreased since 2006. Diversion of cocaine to European and Latin American markets by Colombian and Mexican drug cartels has fueled this downturn in availability, as have coca eradication efforts, large seizures, law enforcement pressure on Mexican cartels, and violent inter-cartel rivalries.[37]

While the story of globalized drug smuggling impacting the United States often revolves around Colombian and Mexican cartels specializing in drugs such as cocaine, marijuana, heroin, and methamphetamine, criminal groups trafficking narcotics come in all sizes and handle a variety of drugs. Because of the ease of international communications, travel, and transportation networks inherent in globalization, drug trafficking groups need not be directly tied to the large cartels to have significant worldwide reach. Even relatively small groups can forge far-flung supply and transportation links.

The FBI's operation Black Eagle tracked a small Albanian network of alleged criminals based in northern New Jersey who were indicted in March 2009.[38] The network purportedly had domestic ties to Chicago, Detroit, and Texas, as well as international links to Macedonia and Albania. At one point, the group of opportunists supposedly conspired to smuggle 100 kilograms of heroin from Albania to the United States. According to the FBI, the group planned to use a Balkan front company to conceal the heroin in containerized shipments of furniture bound for the United States. The heroin was purportedly to come from Afghanistan, likely via Turkey and into Albania. There was no clear cut leadership in the loosely knit group. The heroin deal was going to be one last score before some of the criminals "retired," according to the FBI. They were also likely involved with stealing and selling pharmaceuticals, illegal gambling, dealing ecstasy, and theft of retail goods.[39]

In another case involving a relatively small group, Phuong Thi Tran pleaded guilty in February 2010 for her involvement in what has been described in press reports as an Asian drug trafficking ring that smuggled ecstasy pills and other drugs into the United States from Canada, where they were manufactured. Tran, who lived in Canada, is originally from Vietnam and served as the group's ringleader. She oversaw an operation that smuggled millions of ecstasy pills into the United States between 2002 and 2008, when she was arrested.[40]

Money Laundering

Making ill-gotten gains appear legitimate is critical to the success of organized criminals. For many criminals, the movement of money—either as bulk cash or digital transactions—across international borders plays an integral role in this process. They use many techniques to launder money, often exploiting legitimate financial structures to mask the illegal origins of their profits. Money laundering includes three fundamental steps: (1) placement, the introduction of illicit funds into licit financial systems; (2) layering, the movement (often international) of illicit funds through a variety of business structures to obscure its origins; and (3) integration, the use of illicit funds that at this stage appear legitimate in lawful business transactions.[41] It is impossible to determine with any accuracy how much money is laundered by organized criminals whose operations impact the United States. However, U.S. government estimates suggest that Mexican and Columbian drug trafficking organizations earn between $18 billion and $39 billion annually from sales in the United States.[42] Annually, perhaps between $20 billion and $25 billion in bank notes is smuggled across the Southwest border into Mexico.[43] How much of this is profit and then laundered is unclear.[44] While bulk cash smuggling is an important means by which criminals move illegal profits from the United States into Mexico, they have increasingly turned to stored-value cards[45] to move money. With these cards, criminals are able to avoid the reporting requirement under which they would have to declare any amount over $10,000 in cash moving across the border.[46] Aside from bulk cash smuggling and stored-value cards, Mexican traffickers move and launder money by using digital currency accounts, e-businesses that facilitate money transfers via the Internet, online role-playing games or virtual worlds that enable the exchange of game-based currencies for real currency, and "mobile payments through cell phones that provide traffickers with remote access to existing payment mechanisms such as bank and credit card accounts and prepaid cards."[47]

Organized criminals also use the globalized international financial system in the layering stage of money laundering. The United States is impacted by this from at least two directions. Criminals operating abroad can exploit U.S. structures to launder money while those operating domestically can wash their illicit profits abroad in an attempt to avoid U.S. law enforcement. Large financial markets such as New York, where criminal activity is potentially hidden within voluminous legitimate business, are used by criminals. Criminals use banks and businesses to launder money in offshore locations with strict privacy laws such as Panama, the Cayman Islands, or the Isle of Man. In these locales, law enforcement struggles to determine the true ownership of assets.[48]

International or domestic shell companies can be used for money laundering. They are legal entities that have no independent operations or assets of their own and largely exist only on paper. Shell companies have legitimate purposes, for example, "they may be formed to obtain financing prior to starting operations."[49] Regardless, DOJ has identified U.S.-based shell companies as especially difficult to investigate because "lax company formation laws [allow] criminals [to] form [them] quickly and cheaply and obtain virtual anonymity."[50]

Organized criminals likely rely on the veneer of legitimacy conferred by U.S.-based shell companies, which in many instances allow criminals to conceal their ownership.[51] Most U.S. states do not require owner information when companies are formed or even on annual or biennial reports.[52] Individuals can distance themselves from the actual formation of specific shell companies by using company formation agents (registered agents) to establish them. Shell companies enable criminals to move money around the globe through legitimate bank accounts without attracting law enforcement scrutiny. With relative ease, a criminal organization can open multiple shell companies worldwide and systematically distance ill-gotten gains from their criminal origins, leaving behind a hard-to-untangle web of accounts, legitimate corporations, and transactions.[53] Both Mexico's Sinaloa Cartel and alleged

Eurasian organized crime figure Semion Mogilevich have likely used U.S. shell companies to launder money.[54]

Organized Crime and Technological Change

Organized criminals have expanded their technological "toolkits." They have adapted to incorporate technology-driven fraud into their capabilities.[55] Their operations can harm U.S. citizens without ever having a physical presence in the country. Organized crime groups engage in a wide variety of tech savvy mass marketing frauds. Even traditional arenas of criminal activity such as illegal gambling have been transformed by the Internet. For example, illegal gambling has been a staple in the Cosa Nostra's criminal diet for decades. In recent years, they have branched out into Internet gambling,[56] which debuted in the mid 1990s.[57] Operation Heat, an investigation by the New Jersey Division of Criminal Justice, led to the arrest of Brian Cohen, who allegedly facilitated the Lucchese family's offshore gambling activities. According to law enforcement officials, the family earned billions of dollars via offshore Internet activity that included a website and a Costa Rican wire room that handled transactions, both managed by Cohen.[58]

Mass Marketing Fraud

The International Mass-Marketing Fraud Working Group defines mass marketing fraud as

> Fraud schemes that use mass-communications media—including telephones, the Internet, mass mailings, television, radio, and even personal contact—to contact, solicit, and obtain money, funds, or other items of value from multiple victims in one or more jurisdictions.[59]

Mass marketing fraud involves a wide range of criminal activity that has been transformed by globalization and technological change. It can be perpetrated by individuals, small groups, or sophisticated criminal enterprises. Parsing out exactly how much of this activity can be attributed to organized criminals is tricky, but experts suggest that "fraudulent mass marketing operations are increasingly transnational, interconnected, and fluid."[60] "Boiler room" scams, one iteration of the fraud with a long history, entail groups of fraudsters making high-pressure deceptive merchandise pitches and misleading service offers to unwitting customers around the world. Recently, criminals have innovated based on tried-and-true boiler room schemes by outsourcing some activity to specialists, internationalizing their operations, and adopting sophisticated concealment strategies for their communications capabilities and locations.

The Cosa Nostra and other organized criminals use boiler rooms.[61] In June 2010, the FBI raided an alleged boiler room operation involving Anthony Guarino, a purported Bonnano family soldier. According to law enforcement officials, the boiler room hoodwinked elderly investors into buying shares of companies, and 40% of the money taken in was handed over to the boiler room operators as commissions.[62]

Technology Transforms Advance Fee Fraud (AFF)

Since the 1970s, technological advancements have revolutionized advance fee fraud (AFF) operations—a form of mass marketing fraud used by criminal organizations and individual fraudsters. Today, these schemes often involve criminals appealing for money via unsolicited (spam) emails. These emails typically request an initial cash payment from recipients. The initial cash payment supposedly facilitates the disbursement of a much larger sum of money to the email recipients.[63] The later sum never arrives. A recent AFF email scam attempting to dupe people into believing they had been contacted by the FBI's Detroit Field Office asked email recipients to forward $14,300 in return for the release of over $18 million to their accounts. In one of the emails associated with this scheme, the fraudsters suggest that "the International clamp down on Terrorist [sic]" has frozen the larger pot of money.[64]

Also known as "419 scams" after a section in the Nigerian criminal code, the broad outlines of the modern version of AFF originated in Nigeria during the 1970s and early 1980s, and perhaps even earlier. AFF's original incarnation may stretch back to the 1500s in the "Spanish Prisoner" scheme. Wealthy English business owners were asked to help pay for a rescue mission to save someone held captive in Spain. In return, they would supposedly receive part of the vast alleged reward payment. Of course, it never came.[65] In the late 1970s and early 1980s, Nigerian fraudsters became known for mailing unsolicited letters requesting monetary assistance in transferring frozen or hidden funds out of West African countries. When fax machines became commonplace, perpetrators quickly reached many more victims with less effort. The Internet and email further revolutionized AFF operations.

Today, these schemes are global, emanating from many other countries.[66] The spamming networks involved often have short lives focusing on specific schemes.[67] Recent estimates suggest that AFF networks may have swindled over $2 billion from U.S. companies and citizens in 2009.[68] In July 2011, six defendants were sentenced for running an AFF scam that duped U.S. sweepstakes participants into believing that they had won substantial cash prizes. This money would have purportedly been sent to the victims once they paid the required taxes and fees. Ultimately, there was no lottery prize, and the fraud netted about $2 million.[69] Estimates indicate that today's AFF networks only need to dupe 1% of the people or businesses they reach to turn a profit.[70]

Cyberspace, Electronic Information, and Organized Crime

As the history of AFF may indicate, organized criminals have adapted to the digital age by becoming expert at stealing information stored and shared electronically. Many are adept at manipulating and defrauding victims in the virtual world. All of this covers a range of activity including cyber intrusions into corporate databases, the theft of individual consumer credit card information, and a wide variety of fraudulent online activity. The criminal groups operating in cyberspace can be broken into two categories: (1) part-timers—those who leverage digital information to enhance other activities, and (2) full-timers—those who solely commit and specialize in online or digital crimes.[71] While this is a helpful distinction to draw for discussion purposes, it is difficult to attribute specific volumes of criminal activity to each category of actors. General statistics suggest that organized criminals from both categories play a large role in online data theft. For instance, in selected data breaches investigated by Verizon and the U.S. Secret Service (USSS) involving businesses around the globe during 2009, 85% of compromised computer records were attributed to organized crime. As 94% of all compromised records in this study were in the financial services sector, many of those records targeted by organized criminals were likely from financial organizations as well.[72]

Online Identity Theft and Sophisticated Credit Card Fraud

Organized criminals are involved in stealing the identities of online consumers and have engaged in technologically advanced credit card fraud. These illicit ventures pilfer from the bank accounts of ordinary citizens and often cast a wide net to maximize the number of victims.

Some organized crime groups have stolen money from victims on intenet auction sites such as eBay. For example, on March 13, 2010, Georgi Boychev Georgiev, a Bulgarian national pleaded guilty in U.S. federal court to laundering money for a transnational criminal network involved in eBay fraud. The scam did not physically exist in the United States, but it accrued more than $1.4 million from U.S. victims in 2005 and 2006. The network posted fraudulent advertisements on eBay and used a ruse dubbed "eBay Secure Traders" to bilk people out of cash that was wired directly into Eastern European bank accounts.[73] In another case from April 2010, Romanian law enforcement, the FBI, and USSS cooperated in the dismantling an alleged eBay fraud ring that purportedly involved 70 individuals from what have been described in media sources as three different organized cybercrime groups. According to news reports, the scheme included hijacking the eBay accounts of legitimate consumers and then using the hijacked accounts to stage fake sales of non-existent merchandise on eBay. Fraudsters purportedly scammed bidders from Spain, Italy, France, New Zealand, Denmark, Sweden, Germany, Austria, Canada, Switzerland, and the United States, generating $1 million in profits since 2006.[74]

Eurasian criminals in California are engaging in identity theft in which they leverage technological savvy, old-school organized crime strategies, and Internet connectivity to reap thousands of dollars in profits. In 2009 in the city of Redondo Beach in Southern California, Armenian or Russian criminals allegedly targeted a gas station with an Armenian owner (exploiting their own ethnic group). They placed one of their crew members as an employee at the station, where he implanted high-tech skimming devices at gas pumps to steal customer credit card information, victimizing more than 1,000 individuals, including Redondo Beach police officers. The employee quit work and the group made off with more than $300,000 from people's accounts.[75] Another case, this time in the Las Vegas area in 2008, involved an alleged Armenian criminal group that reportedly skimmed more than 1,000 credit and debit cards using insiders at restaurants, bars, and smoke shops. In some instances, the crew manufactured its own cards using stolen information.[76] Losses approached $1.5 million.[77] In 2009, Las Vegas authorities also uncovered a skimming scheme complete with a credit card manufacturing lab.[78] This crew used skimmers that captured information from magnetic strips on credit cards as well as pin numbers using a camera.[79]

In March 2010, Albert Gonzalez, the leader of the largest identity theft and retail hacking ring prosecuted by the United States, was sentenced to 20 years in prison.[80] Through "wardriving"—a technique in which individuals drive around in a car with a laptop computer and search for unsecured wireless networks—the ring hacked into credit card payment systems at retailers including TJX Companies, BJ's Wholesale Club, OfficeMax, Boston Market, Barnes & Noble and Sports Authority, and stole more than 40 million credit and debit card numbers. Gonzalez also provided malware to hackers to aid them in evading anti-virus programs and firewalls in order to access companies' networks and payment systems.

The conspirators, located in the United States, Ukraine, and Estonia, laundered their illicit proceeds through banks in Eastern Europe.

Organized Retail Crime and Online Fencing

While not necessarily viewed as "organized crime" by U.S. law enforcement agencies, as its name implies organized retail crime (ORC), or organized retail theft, bears some of the hallmarks of organized criminal activity. ORC typically refers to large-scale retail theft and fraud by organized groups of professional shoplifters, or "boosters."[81] ORC involves a host of retail crimes ranging from retail, manufacturing, distribution, and cargo theft to gift card fraud, receipt fraud, and ticket switching.[82] The organized crime rings resell illegally acquired merchandise in a variety of fencing operations such as flea markets, swap meets, pawn shops, and, more recently, online marketplaces. Most stolen merchandise is sold to a low-level fence, commonly called a "street fence." Street fences will either sell these goods directly to the public or will sell the merchandise to mid-level fences who run "cleaning operations" that remove security tags and store labels as well as repackage stolen goods so they appear as though they came directly from the manufacturer. This "cleaning" may even involve changing the expiration date on perishable goods such as over-the-counter medication and infant formula.

Globalization and technological innovation have allowed more and more transactions to take place online rather than face-to-face. This holds true for retail crime, where thieves have turned to "e-fencing"—using the Internet and online marketplaces as means to fence ill-gotten goods.[83] This has increased criminals' anonymity, global reach, and profitability. Online markets allow criminals to easily distribute stolen goods across the nation and around the globe. E-fencing has also proven to be more profitable to criminals than has fencing at physical locations. While criminals may profit about 30 cents on the dollar (30% of the retail price) by selling goods at physical fencing locations, they can make about 70 cents on the dollar via e-fencing.[84]

A criminal network based in Baltimore serves as an example of an operation that integrated traditional as well as more technologically advanced fencing techniques. As of September 2010, at least 10 defendants, including the owners of pawn shops implicated in the scheme, had pleaded guilty to roles in this organized retail crime ring.[85] In this conspiracy, boosters stole products, including over-the-counter medications, health and beauty aids, gift cards, DVDs, and tools, from retailers such as Target, Safeway, Wal-Mart, and Kohl's. Several pawn shops bought these stolen goods from boosters, cleaned them, and then transported them to other locations for resale. Some co-conspirators used online marketplaces such as eBay and Amazon.com to fence the stolen goods. In all, the case involved about $20 million in stolen goods.

Bulk Narcotics Smuggling and Technology

Technological advances have transformed cocaine and other narcotics trafficking. In the early 1990s, Colombian traffickers—moving narcotics to the United States and elsewhere around the globe—began experimenting with semisubmersible maritime smuggling vessels, which at first were likely too impractical, costly, and risky to operate. Hybrids of traditional submarines and boats, these craft have small above-water profiles—about 18 inches. Increased law enforcement seizures of cocaine shipments carried by more traditional surface vessels encouraged traffickers to adopt semisubmersible technology.[86] Colombian traffickers likely co-opted experts from the legitimate world to develop this technology. Most often, semisubmersibles are used to move product from coastal areas to boats waiting on the open seas. While their current use likely responds in part to interdiction pressures, it also reflects the global availability of expertise, designs, and materials. Vast illicit global cocaine markets have also made such endeavors possible, producing huge profits for traffickers that are then tilled into technology to circumvent law enforcement. But semisubmersibles, which account for 27% of the maritime movement of cocaine toward the United States, themselves are not immune to capture.[87] Since 2006, law enforcement has regularly seized semisubmersible cocaine smuggling vessels from Colombian drug traffickers on the high seas or in clandestine shipyards hidden in coastal mangrove swamps. The Drug Trafficking Vessel Interdiction Act of 2008 (P.L. 110-407) enhanced the federal government's ability to prosecute traffickers operating submersible and semisubmersible vessels by making it a federal crime to operate, embark on, or conspire to operate these vessels in international waters with the intent to avoid detection.

In early July 2010, police in Ecuador seized a fiberglass submarine designed to operate *fully submerged* at a depth of 65 feet. The diesel-powered, twin-screw sub, a marked step forward in technology, was likely intended to transport cocaine on the high seas and could carry 10 tons of cocaine on a 10-day voyage. This vessel represented a large improvement over the semisubmersibles that have been regularly seized from traffickers since 2006.[88]

Mexican drug traffickers have increasingly relied upon ultralight aircraft[89] to smuggle drugs across the Southwest border into the United States. These small planes can fly as low as tree level and are less easily detected than the larger aircrafts that were used by the traffickers prior to 2007.[90] While some traffickers may land the ultralights on the U.S. side of the border to pass off drug loads to distributors, others attach drop baskets that can carry over 300 pounds of marijuana or other drugs. These drop baskets release packages of drugs that will fall to the ground when a lever in the aircraft is activated, and then local gangs or traffickers can pick up and distribute the drugs. In May 2009, a low-flying ultralight aircraft carrying about 275 pounds of marijuana, estimated to be worth $220,480, crashed in Yuma, AZ. The pilot escaped, but two suspected coconspirators were arrested.[91]

Cross-Border Tunnels

Mexican drug traffickers rely on the use of underground, cross-border tunnels to smuggle drugs from Mexico into the United States. Tunneling, while not in and of itself a new tool—having been used for hundreds of years during conflicts and for escapes—has increased not only in prevalence but in sophistication.[92] Early tunnels were rudimentary, "gopher hole" tunnels dug on the Mexican side of the border, traveling just below the surface, and popping out on the U.S. side as close as 100 feet from the border. Slightly more advanced tunnels began to rely on existing infrastructure, which may be shared by neighboring border cities such as the tunnel shared by Nogales, AZ, in the United States and Nogales, Sonora, in Mexico. These interconnecting tunnels may tap into storm drains or sewage systems in order to move drugs even further than smugglers could move them by digging tunnels alone. The most sophisticated tunnels can have rail, ventilation, and electrical systems. In January 2006 in Otay Mesa, CA, a tunnel, stretching nearly three-quarters of a mile in length and traveling over 85 feet below the surface of the earth, was discovered, where more than two tons of marijuana was seized.[93] The tunnel had lighting, ventilation, and groundwater drainage systems. In November 2010, the San Diego Tunnel Task Force—created in 2003 as a partnership between the U.S. Immigration and Customs Enforcement (ICE), DEA, and the U.S. Border Patrol working along with state law enforcement and Mexican counterparts—uncovered a 600-yard passageway stretching from Tijuana to Otay Mesa. About 30 tons of marijuana, with an estimated street value of about $20 million, were seized in the United States and Mexico.[94] About a year later, the task force unearthed two other tunnels in Otay Mesa within a two-week period. One of them stretched 612 yards and had electric rail cars, lighting, reinforced walls, and wooden floors.[95]

U.S. law enforcement uses various tactics and simultaneously faces numerous challenges in detecting these cross-border tunnels. About 125 tunnels have been discovered since the 1990s— primarily in Arizona and California—and more than 75 of these have been found since 2006.[96] One such method of tunnel detection is the use of ground penetrating radar (GPR).[97] However, this technology is limited by factors including soil conditions, tunnel diameter, and tunnel depth. Law enforcement may also use sonic equipment to detect the sounds of digging and tunnel construction and seismic technologies to detect blasts that may be linked to tunnel excavation. U.S. officials have acknowledged that law enforcement currently does not have technology that is reliably able to detect sophisticated tunnels.[98] Rather, tunnels are more effectively discovered as a result of human intelligence and tips rather than technology.

Exploitation of Ethnic Diaspora Communities

Criminal organizations structured along ethnic lines sometimes base their operations in immigrant communities.[99] They use these enclaves to provide cover for their dealings and occasionally also exploit their ethnic compatriots. Historically, criminal groups have burrowed into local ethnic communities, but now this is enhanced by the fact that they can leverage Internet connectivity and extensive, international transportation linkages from localities around the globe. A number of recent cases highlight these issues.

In October 2010, a total of 73 individuals were indicted in the largest single Medicare fraud ever charged.[100] As described by DOJ, the Mirzoyan-Terdjanian organization, an Armenian criminal group, ran fake clinics in 25 states, but had its leadership based in Los Angeles and New York City,[101] two areas with large immigrant populations from the former Soviet Union, (e.g., Glendale, in the Los Angeles region, is home to 200,000 Armenian Americans). According to the president of the Los Angeles chapter of the Armenian-American Chamber of Commerce, this community is exploited by a handful of criminals who were "raised under communist rule in the former Soviet republic of Armenia, where exploiting a corrupt government was seen as fair game."[102]

Organized Crime and Health Care Fraud

Acting Deputy Attorney General Gary G. Grinder has stated that "the emergence of international organized crime in domestic health care fraud schemes signals a dangerous expansion that poses a serious threat to consumers"[1] The health care system as well as both public and private assistance programs have been targets of individual scammers and organized criminals alike.

Criminals steal the identities—or create fake identities—of medical providers, clinics and businesses, and patients. According to the most recent data, in FY2009 U.S. Attorneys opened 1,014 health care fraud investigations, encompassing 1,786 defendants.[1] Aside from the Mirzoyan-Terdjanian organization indicted by DOJ, other criminal networks—Eurasian and Nigerian groups—involved in large-scale health care fraud in Los Angeles have recently been caught by U.S. law enforcement. According to news reports, organized crime has turned to targeting Medicare and Medicaid for profit.[1] It is very likely that the groups in Los Angeles favored stealing doctor and patient identities for fraudulent billing over more violent and less lucrative criminal activity. One expert has suggested, "[Health care fraud is] lucrative and it's safe for them [organized criminals]. Why rob a bank and risk getting shot when you can click a mouse and bill Medicare or Medicaid, basically lie on some forms and make millions of dollars doing so."[1]

Members of the Mirzoyan-Terdjanian group allegedly billed Medicare for more than $163 million in fraudulent medical services. They reaped about $35 million in profits.[103]

The case involves the stolen identities of both doctors and Medicare beneficiaries and the creation of at least 118 spurious medical clinics across at least 25 states, all part of a largely "virtual" operation. FBI Assistant Director in Charge Janice K. Fedarcyk described the organization as

> completely notional. There were no real medical clinics behind the fraudulent billings, just stolen doctors' identities. There were no colluding patients signing in at the clinics for unneeded treatments, just stolen patient identities. The whole doctor-patient interaction was a mirage. But the money was real, while it lasted.[104]

The indictment in the case also linked Armen Kazarian to the scheme. Arrested in Los Angeles, Kazarian, an Armenian residing in the United States, had substantial influence in the criminal underworld as a *vor v zakone,* a Russian term meaning "thief-in-law."[105]

Kazarian had reputedly lied to federal authorities to obtain asylum after emigrating to the United States in 1996.106In the course of the scheme, Kazarian mediated disputes for the Mirzoyan-Terdjanian group and allegedly threatened to assault and kill an associate. In July 2011, Kazarian pled guilty to racketeering in the case.[107]

The indictment suggests that members of the organization, many of them Armenian nationals or immigrants, sent criminal proceeds to Armenia, purchasing real estate and operating businesses with the funds.[108]

Organized Crime and Health Care Fraud

Acting Deputy Attorney General Gary G. Grinder has stated that "the emergence of international organized crime in domestic health care fraud schemes signals a dangerous expansion that poses a serious threat to consumers"[1] The health care system as well as both public and private assistance programs have been targets of individual scammers and organized criminals alike. Criminals steal the identities—or create fake identities—of medical providers, clinics and businesses, and patients. According to the most recent data, in FY2009 U.S. Attorneys opened 1,014 health care fraud investigations, encompassing 1,786 defendants.[1]

Aside from the Mirzoyan-Terdjanian organization indicted by DOJ, other criminal networks—Eurasian and Nigerian groups—involved in large-scale health care fraud in Los Angeles have recently been caught by U.S. law enforcement. According to news reports, organized crime has turned to targeting Medicare and Medicaid for profit.[1] It is very likely that the groups Los Angeles favored stealing doctor and patient identities for fraudulent billing over more violent and less lucrative criminal activity. One expert has suggested, "[Health care fraud is] lucrative and it's safe for them [organized criminals]. Why rob a bank and risk getting shot when you can click a mouse and bill Medicare or Medicaid, basically lie on some forms and make millions of dollars doing so."[1]

In June 2010, DOJ charged five Ukrainian brothers with extortion and conspiring to engage in a pattern of racketeering activity. This far-flung operation based out of Philadelphia and Ukraine had allegedly trafficked about 30 Ukrainians into the United States via Mexico, exploiting them in cleaning crews operating in stores, private residences, and office buildings in Pennsylvania, New York, New Jersey, Maryland, and Washington, DC. According to DOJ, the brothers failed to pay their victims, threatened them with violence, physically abused them, and housed them in overcrowded quarters. One of the brothers is accused of raping a trafficked woman on several occasions.[109] The victims of this scheme likely trusted the brothers as immigrants who had ties to the United States and were willing to help others start new lives in the country.

In another case, at least five Chinese citizens involved in operating Asian massage parlors in Kansas were sentenced between April and October of 2009 for their roles in exploiting Chinese women in the United States.[110] The defendants recruited women from China to work in the United States as masseuses. They then confiscated the women's identification documents and used these documents to fraudulently wire proceeds from illegal activities back to China. They forced the women to work for 14 hours every day, locked them inside the massage parlors to sleep at night, and forced them to perform sexual services for the male patrons of the massage parlors.

West African criminal networks specializing in AFF operate in many nations including the United States, where members have assimilated into local ethnic communities. Many West African fraudsters based outside of their home countries direct proceeds back to organizations in their homelands. More recently, it appears that some of these diaspora-based criminals are operating independently and retaining their ill-gotten gains.[111]

Changing Structures

The traditional image of organized crime involves elaborate hierarchies, behavioral codes, and initiation rituals. Some criminal organizations like the Cosa Nostra retain a strong element of hierarchy. However, in the last 20 years the criminal underworld has likely moved away from rigid hierarchical organizational structures and toward decentralized and more flexible "network" models. One scholar has argued that the public is still wedded to hierarchical archetypes particularly when conceptualizing how smugglers operate:

> Still infused with images of cartels and syndicates—rigid, top-down organizations—we are not accustomed to thinking of flexible, even unchartable networks of

intermediaries that operate across many borders and provide different services. Some are permanently linked and others vary in their composition, activities, and geographical scope depending on markets and circumstances. Thus, brokers and agents with access to multiple suppliers, conveyors, and buyers are more significant in the drug trade than are old-fashioned "kingpins." For all these brokers, expanding into new product lines, legal or illegal is just a logical business step.[112]

As discussed elsewhere, criminals (much like legitimate businesses) have internationalized their operations, particularly in the last two decades. The fast movement of people, goods, and information stimulated by globalization and technological change has encouraged decentralization and outsourcing. Networks are especially suited for this type of environment.[113] Global businesses and criminal organizations now give critical roles to individuals or groups outside of an organization's core that are often physically separated by thousands of miles. In some cases, such as Colombian drug trafficking organizations, law enforcement successes against criminal hierarchies may have encouraged the adaptation of networks.[114] Criminals conduct more business offshore because of the efficiencies offered by the Internet and advances in the world's transportation and communication infrastructures.[115] In the underground economy, these changes have encouraged the abandonment of exclusivity implied by the elaborate codes of behavior, ethnic bonds, and rigid hierarchy that once typified organized crime.[116]

Networked structures shield organized criminals from law enforcement efforts.[117] Beyond its immediate duties, one element or node in a network can have little understanding of the entire network's criminal activity. It is possible for a network to operate without a single constituent part knowing the entire scheme. In larger networks with clear cut leaders, layers of peripheral nodes likely do not know who directs them. Disruption of peripheral network elements by law enforcement may alert core players to shut down the enterprise.[118]

Network Models

Illicit networks broadly follow two models. "Hub and spoke" networks involve peripheral nodes tied to a leadership core. Core players initiate schemes, settle conflicts, and provide guidance to others. In this model, activity moves from core to peripheral players while the peripheral entities do not interact with one another. "Chain" networks involve the flow of information or movement of criminal goods from node to node in linear fashion without a discernable center of gravity or central command.[119] They often lack obvious individual focal points for policing efforts.

Networks can quickly adapt to changing market conditions or the elimination of nodes by law enforcement by quickly recruiting replacement specialists. Unlike hierarchies such as the Cosa Nostra, networks have few membership requirements, initiation rituals, or loyalty tests. These organizations can also shift allegiances easily, opportunistically drawing in participants for specific tasks.[120]

Blurring of Forms

Some powerful criminal groups that still favor traditional hierarchical structures featuring distinct lines of authority simultaneously exhibit networked characteristics as well, especially a flattening of leadership arrangements and outsourcing of some activities to criminals outside their immediate command and control structures. For example, in the United States hierarchical Mexican drug cartels rely on networks to handle aspects of trafficking. Violent

U.S. gangs transport wholesale quantities of narcotics into the United States and procure weapons for some cartels.[121] Prison gangs, for instance, are highly structured, and both national- and regional-level prison gangs have formed alliances with Mexican DTOs. For example, the Barrio Azteca prison gang—operating primarily in southwestern Texas and southeastern New Mexico—has partnered with the Juárez cartel and generates much of its money from smuggling marijuana, heroin, and cocaine across the Southwest border.[122] Similarly, one author of a broad study of criminal organizations in Mexico, Brazil, and Colombia has noted that these groups embody characteristics of what he dubs the "Godfather Model"—rigid hierarchy—and the "Facebook Model"—dynamic network.[123]

Advantage: Networks Challenge Law Enforcement

The shift to networked structures may suggest that criminals are more elusive than ever as the illicit world evolves rapidly, while law enforcement "plays by yesterday's rules and increasingly risks dealing only with the weakest criminals and the easiest problems."[124] According to one study, when combating agile drug cartels, a number of impediments hobble law enforcement officials. Most broadly, the hierarchical authority embodied in bureaucratic structures complicates the decision-making process.[125] Additionally, law enforcement potentially faces

> interagency coordination problems that further complicate, and decelerate, decision making, comprehensive legal and bureaucratic constraints to action, and ambiguous incentive structures that undermine some agents' willingness to share information—and others' commitment to winning the war on drugs.[126]

Yet another challenge for law enforcement investigating more-networked organized criminal groups may arise from constraints in extraterritorial jurisdiction. While some criminal actors in a network may conduct business offshore or overseas and federal law enforcement does have extraterritorial jurisdiction to investigate and prosecute individuals who criminally violate U.S. interests abroad, this jurisdiction does not necessarily cover all crimes committed by organized crime groups.[127] Further, jurisdictional issues can present substantial diplomatic and practical challenges for law enforcement.

Disadvantage: Networks Have Exploitable Weaknesses

Some of the strengths suggested by network structure can also be interpreted as weaknesses. Their inherent compartmentalization potentially impedes efficient information sharing, as key players keep peripheral actors in the dark about important aspects of complex schemes. This suggests that highly networked organizations more effectively engage in simpler criminal conspiracies.

Decentralization can undermine the development of strategy and slow down decision making. It may also encourage excessive risk taking by peripheral actors who are not controlled by hierarchical roles rooted in rules enforced by the organization. Decentralization possibly also nurtures challengers who compete with core leaders and foster organizational instability.[128] Maintaining networks also likely requires "time-consuming" effort geared toward "building and fostering relationships."[129]

Corruption

Some criminal networks co-opt or attract participants from the licit realm, using their specialized skills to provide "logistical advantages."[130] These skills are especially valuable in a globalized, high tech era in which technology is critical in overcoming geographical barriers that once slowed international trade. Corrupt individuals maintain their status in above-board business or governmental jobs, providing criminals with clean assets, closely guarded information, specialized access, sensitive information, or resources. Corrupt licit-realm actors also potentially lend criminal enterprises a sense of legitimacy.[131] Because of globalization, it is likely harder to disprove a criminal's claims that he is a legitimate businessman, especially if the proof lies overseas or in multiple jurisdictions. The efforts of organized criminals to draw into their organizations legitimate persons can be described from three broad perspectives: grass-roots, private sector criminal infiltration of businesses; co-optation of powerful business leaders; and public corruption.

"Ground-Level" Exploitation of Private Businesses

Non-executive employees or self-employed individuals can provide criminal organizations with highly specialized capabilities in our highly networked age. The possibilities for co-opted private sector specialists are plentiful. The three examples below suggest this.

- Viktar Krus operated a network that illegally brought foreign workers into the United States. He relied on legitimate facilitators such as Beth Ann Broyles, an Illinois immigration attorney who prepared fraudulent immigration petitions for the organization. Broyles claimed that she initially did not know that she was involved in criminal activity. When she eventually discerned that she was, Broyles rationalized her participation by believing that she was actually somehow assisting immigrants. She was among two dozen co-defendants who worked in Krus's network. Additionally, Krus likely relied on bribing hotel employees to inflate the number of workers they needed to hire. Between 2003 and 2008, he used at least 10 shell companies and evaded millions of dollars in taxes while bringing in 3,800 immigrants, many illegally, to work in the service sector and industrial jobs in the Norfolk, VA, region and elsewhere around the United States. He grossed $34 million, forced people to live 12-15 to an apartment, garnered fees from their wages, and charged legitimate businesses $10 per hour for their labor. Krus received a seven-year prison sentence for conspiracy, tax fraud, visa fraud, and money laundering.[132]
- According to DOJ, the Tran organization, a criminal group that cheated approximately 27 casinos in the United States and Canada out of more than $7 million, bribed card dealers and supervisors at casinos to advance its scheme. In what has been dubbed "the largest cheating ring of all time,"[133] corrupt dealers rigged their shuffles during mini-baccarat and blackjack games. The group also used technologically advanced tools such as hidden transmitters and custom software to predict the order in which cards would reappear during games.[134] The organization began its operations in 2002, and the initial indictment was returned against the group in May 2007.[135]

- DOJ's Organized Crime and Racketeering Section helped prosecute Victor Kaganov in connection with an illegal money transmitting business he allegedly ran in Oregon. In March 2011, Kaganov pled guilty to operating an illegal money transmitting business.[136] DOJ has not publicly linked Kaganov, who was indicted in March 2010, to any organized crime figures. However, Kaganov purportedly opened multiple shell corporations in Oregon on behalf of Russian clients. He used the shells to shuttle more than $172 million via more than 4,200 wire transactions "in and out of the United States to more than 50 countries," according to DOJ.[137] His supposed criminal activity highlights services that organized criminals could potentially use to launder money.

Big Business and Organized Criminals

In his Annual Threat Assessment for 2010, then-Director of National Intelligence Dennis Blair noted that government, organized crime, intelligence services, and big business figures are growing increasingly close in their interactions. He stated,

> an increasing risk from Russian organized crime is that criminals and criminally linked oligarchs [powerful Eurasian businessmen who rose to power in the immediate post-Soviet period] will enhance the ability of state or state-allied actors to undermine competition in gas, oil, aluminum, and precious metals markets.[138]

However, based on open source information, it is often difficult to determine with any degree of certainty whether oligarchs or other powerful international entrepreneurs with interests in U.S. markets or investors have criminal connections.

Russian billionaire Oleg Deripaska exemplifies this difficulty. According to unnamed U.S. federal officials cited in news reports, Deripaska has struggled to maintain a U.S. visa because of his alleged ties to organized crime.[139] Prior to the global financial crisis, he possessed a $28 billion fortune and was the ninth-wealthiest person in the world.[140] He obtained a U.S. visa in 2005, but it was revoked soon thereafter.[141] According to press reporting, in 2009 the FBI set up two U.S. visits by Deripaska for undisclosed reasons on a limited entry permit from the Department of Homeland Security (DHS).[142] Claims of criminal connections have publicly dogged him for years. But Deripaska has never been convicted of a crime and has strongly denied all accusations.[143] His difficulty getting a U.S. visa may have kept some U.S. bankers from participation in an initial public offering (IPO) involving his aluminum company, UC Rusal.[144] The IPO occurred in January 2010 on the Hong Kong stock exchange.[145]

Like Deripaska, Stanley Ho, a billionaire casino magnate from Macau, has routinely denied accusations of ties to organized crime. According to media reports, U.S. officials have long suspected Ho had links to Chinese criminal groups known as triads.[146] These suspicions recently resurfaced and involved his daughter, Pansy, and a casino venture in Macau. Pansy and Nevada-based MGM Resorts International (MGM)[147] jointly operate the MGM Macau, which opened in December 2007.[148]

Pansy Ho's co-ownership of MGM Macau emerged as an issue for New Jersey gaming regulators because MGM also possessed a 50% share in Atlantic City's Borgata Hotel Casino and Spa. According to New Jersey law, MGM had to prove "by clear and convincing evidence, its 'good character, honesty and integrity' on a continuing basis" to maintain its

50% share in the Borgata.[149] In essence, the company and its partners had to be found suitable to operate in New Jersey.

It appears that MGM's direct ties to the Ho family were troubling to New Jersey regulators. In May 2009, the New Jersey Division of Gaming Enforcement (DGE) published a report based on its own investigation of MGM's partnership with Pansy Ho in Macau. The DGE report recommended that both Pansy and Stanley Ho be found "unsuitable persons" by the New Jersey Casino Control Commission.[150] The DGE noted the elder Ho's "continued business ties to persons associated with organized crime" and his daughter's "direct, substantial, and continuing business and financial ties to her father."[151] In March 2010, MGM decided to sell its interest in the Borgata rather than sever ties with Pansy Ho.[152]

Corruption of Public Officials

Organized criminals corrupt public employees, especially individuals who have sensitive jobs. In many cases, criminals seek people who have skills, particular access to information, or job responsibilities that lend themselves to specific schemes. For example, some criminals whose operations depend on personal identification documents seek to inveigle employees with unique access to such information, and smugglers lure people charged with protecting borders into their operations.

In August 2010, Vitaly Fedorchuk was sentenced to 46 months in prison for leading a criminal organization in the Cleveland, OH, area that fraudulently procured Ohio driver's licenses and identification cards for foreign nationals. To do so, Fedorchuk's group relied on Sonya Hilaszek, a corrupt employee at the Deputy Registrar's Office in Parma, OH. She also pleaded guilty in the case and received a prison sentence of 33 months. DOJ accused Hilaszek of producing documents for between 300 and 500 individuals. The criminal group charged foreign nationals—many were from Ukraine or Uzbekistan and in the United States illegally—between $1,500 and $3,000 for the documents. Fedorchuk's group also allegedly cooperated with criminals in Ukraine to fraudulently obtain non-immigrant visas from the U.S. Embassy in Kyiv. They purportedly relied on corrupt Ukrainian nationals employed by the Embassy and charged $12,000 per visa.[153]

Mexican drug traffickers corrupt employees of federal agencies charged with protecting the Southwest border. The number of cases involving corruption at Customs and Border Protection (CBP) reported by the DHS Office of Inspector General have risen from 245 in FY2006 to more than 770 (projected) for FY2010.[154] In FY2009 alone, the DHS Inspector General opened 839 investigations of potential corruption regarding DHS employees. Of the 839 investigations, 576 worked for CBP, 164 for ICE, 64 for U.S. Citizen and Immigration Services (CIS), and 35 for the Transportation Security Administration (TSA).[155] While none of these figures establish exactly how many of these corruption cases are attributable to organized crime, they do suggest a growing challenge for federal law enforcement focused on combating smuggling and trafficking groups along the border. In an attempt to prevent corruption, federal investigation and law enforcement agencies may vet potential employees. For instance, in 2009 available resources allowed CBP to polygraph 10%–15% of applicants applying for border patrol positions, and of those who were polygraphed, about 60% were found *unsuitable* for service.[156]

Two cases highlight the potential for corruption by organized crime along the Southwest border. In May 2010, Martha Garnica, a former CBP technician and officer, pleaded guilty to corruption and drug and alien smuggling charges.[157] She played a significant role in smuggling operations for the Ciudad Juarez-based La Linea criminal organization.[158] In another case, Jose Raul Montano, Jr. was sentenced to 140 months in prison for bribery, cocaine trafficking, and alien smuggling while assigned as a CBP officer at the Brownsville Gateway Port of Entry (POE) in Brownsville, TX. He allowed Mexican drug traffickers and alien smugglers to illegally transport drugs and people into the United States. At the POE, Montano permitted vehicles containing illicit shipments to pass—without inspection—through the lane he worked. In return, Mexican criminals bribed him. By the time of his arrest in April 2009, he received between $8,000 and $10,000 per vehicle.[159]

ORGANIZED CRIME, A "NATIONAL SECURITY" AND "PUBLIC SECURITY" CONCERN

Clearly, organized crime can be seen as a *public security* concern, largely endangering people, businesses, and property. In fact, in 1995 the National Intelligence Council (NIC) produced a National Intelligence Estimate (NIE) on international organized crime that emphasized just this. However, the U.S. intelligence community's view of international organized crime has shifted critically in the intervening years. In early 2010, the NIC issued a second NIE on the topic. While, according to DOJ officials, most of the salient issues in the 2010 NIE are consistent with those discussed in the 1995 NIE, a key difference emerged. The 2010 NIE argues that international organized crime has evolved into a *national security* concern as well.[160] DOJ officials have described these national security threats in five broad categories: (1) penetrating or influencing state institutions—particularly in those states with weak governance; (2) threatening the global economy by infiltrating financial and commercial markets, driving out legitimate businesses, and using a variety of illegal business practices; (3) engaging in cybercrimes across a range of fraudulent activities impacting individuals, businesses, and global trust systems; (4) partnering with terrorist organizations and insurgent groups such as the Revolutionary Armed Forces of Colombia (FARC), Taliban, and Hezbollah; and (5) expanding the reach of drug trafficking such that DTOs ally with other criminal organizations—regardless of ethnic background—and with local drug distributors.

Alleged Eurasian mob boss Semion Mogilevich embodies both the public and national security dimensions of organized crime. In October 2009, the FBI placed Mogilevich on its Ten Most Wanted Fugitives list.[161] He is wanted for leading a financial scheme that defrauded investors of $150 million between 1993 and 1998. The company that he allegedly controlled at the heart of the operation, YBM Magnex, was based in Newtown, PA, and was incorporated in Canada.[162] Mogilevich was also likely involved in laundering money through YBM Magnex and a network of offshore companies.[163] By purportedly swindling investors, Mogilevich ran an operation that harmed members of the public. More broadly—and involving national security interests—the FBI and DOJ have suggested that the reputed mob boss also has his hands in Eastern European natural gas markets and that he uses his ill-gotten gains to influence "governments and their economies."[164] Russian law enforcement arrested Mogilevich in January 2008 on tax evasion charges but released him in July 2009 on an oath not to flee.[165]

Although analysts have assessed organized crime as being a threat to both public security as well as a national security, the scope of these threats cannot be fully evaluated without a clearer understanding of the scope of organized crime.

Conceptualizing Organized Crime

One of the primary challenges in conceptualizing organized crime is that it is usually not thought of as a specific crime, but rather as a large number of illicit activities committed by groups of individuals who are often so loosely connected that the members themselves do not know who their criminal associates may be. This has historically led to a lack of consistency in the way different groups—scholars, policymakers, various federal law enforcement agencies, and nation states—view what constitutes organized crime and think about how to combat it. The inconsistent conceptualization of organized crime has also made it difficult to measure its impact.[166]

The *2011 Strategy* laid out the federal government's first broad conceptualization of "transnational organized crime," focusing on it as a national security concern.[167] To what extent this definition will drive Administration policy is unclear. In evaluating the *2011 Strategy*, policymakers may exercise their oversight authority regarding both the adequacy of the Administration's definition of transnational organized crime as well as its utilization in driving counter-crime policies.

Transnational Organized Crime Defined

The *2011 Strategy* offers the following definition of organized crime:

> Transnational organized crime refers to those self-perpetuating associations of individuals who operate transnationally for the purpose of obtaining power, influence, monetary and/or commercial gains, wholly or in part by illegal means, while protecting their activities through a pattern of corruption and/or violence, or while protecting their illegal activities through a transnational organizational structure and the exploitation of transnational commerce or communication mechanisms. There is no single structure under which transnational organized criminals operate; they vary from hierarchies to clans, networks, and cells, and may evolve to other structures. The crimes they commit also vary. Transnational organized criminals act conspiratorially in their criminal activities and possess certain characteristics which may include, but are not limited to:
>
> In at least part of their activities they commit violence or other acts which are likely to intimidate, or make actual or implicit threats to do so;
>
> They exploit differences between countries to further their objectives, enriching their organization, expanding its power, and/or avoiding detection/apprehension;
>
> They attempt to gain influence in government, politics, and commerce through corrupt as well as legitimate means;
>
> They have economic gain as their primary goal, not only from patently illegal activities but also from investment in legitimate businesses; and
>
> They attempt to insulate both their leadership and membership from detection, sanction, and/or prosecution through their organizational structure.[168]

As the term "transnational organized crime" (TOC) may suggest, any definition of it should detail three elements: (1) "transnationality," (2) organization, and (3) crime. While the above TOC definition, and more generally the *2011 Strategy*'s text, hit on all three elements, key gaps in understanding the Administration's framing of TOC remain.

Transnationality

The strategy's definition addresses the concept of "transnationality" in the broadest terms, suggesting that TOC is transnational because it operates transnationally. At least three factors— none of which are discussed in the definition—may determine how transnational a group is: residence, product provenance, and supply chain complexity.[169]

Regarding residence, a TOC group's members can reside in multiple countries, clearly making it a transnational network. However, if all members reside in a single country, but a seemingly minor aspect of the group's activities is situated outside this home country, is the criminal network still considered transnational?

- Does controlling a bank account in one country while committing crimes in another make a network transnational?
- Can a group be considered transnational simply if its communications concerning criminal activity are routed outside of its home country via international communications networks?

In terms of product provenance, it seems clear that illicit trade (whether it involves people, goods, services, or information) from one country to another is a transnational activity. However, can a domestically based group be considered transnational if the illicit product it handles in the United States had a foreign origin but the group played no role in getting it across international borders?

- A street-level cocaine dealer may have never directly colluded with foreign criminals, but the cocaine he retails originated abroad. Does this automatically make him part of a TOC network?[170]

Supply chain complexity is also likely a prominent feature of TOC. This involves managing the routes that illicit products take.

- Does the complexity of a group's supply chain factor into measurement of how transnational the group is? This complexity can include elements such as the number of borders a product crosses as well as the resources a group expends to move a product. These resources can include money used for things such as bribing public officials, protecting illicit routes from other criminals, the acquisition and retention of technical expertise, and the development of tools and infrastructure to maintain the route (e.g., shell companies, front companies, drug smuggling semi-submersibles, cross-border smuggling tunnels).

These factors suggest a broader question: does the level of transnationality inherent in a network impact how the U.S. government views it as a threat? In other words, if one network is more transnational than another, is it a greater concern? Would an organized crime group with transnational ties necessarily be a larger threat than a criminal network based solely in the United States?

Organization

The TOC definition includes almost any form of organization. This is reflected in the strategy's emphasis on the organizational fluidity of TOC.[171] As this may suggest, the definition lacks precise baselines for the concept of "organization." Two baselines seem central here. The first involves routine. In essence, to qualify as "organized" does a network have to routinely cooperate? If so, what constitutes routine cooperation? The second baseline is size. How small is "organized"—can it be as basic as two individuals collaborating? Low thresholds for these two baselines—allowing TOC to include groups as small as two individuals who do not routinely interact—may render the concept of "organization" meaningless. *In other words, with low thresholds, almost any criminal activity that does not involve a sole operator could be defined as "organized."* In an attempt to clarify matters, the definition suggests that TOC groups are "self-perpetuating," but the definition does not explain what this concept entails. Seemingly, any group not construed and controlled by some external authority or environmental condition is "self-perpetuating."

Crime

The TOC definition in the *2011 Strategy* broadly describes some of the activities TOC groups can engage in to turn profits and protect themselves—violence, exploiting the "differences between countries," and gaining influence in legitimate sectors. Going beyond the definition, the strategy's text lays out 10 areas of illicit activity in which TOC poses "a growing threat to national and international security."[172] These 10 areas encompass a wide swath of federal law enforcement activity.

1) Penetration of State Institutions, Corruption, and Threats to Governance
2) Threats to the Economy, U.S. Competitiveness, and Strategic Markets
3) Crime-Terror-Insurgency Nexus
4) Expansion of Drug Trafficking
5) Human Smuggling
6) Trafficking in Persons
7) Weapons Trafficking
8) Intellectual Property Theft
9) Cybercrime
10) The Critical Role of Facilitators.[173]

It is unclear what sway the *2011 Strategy*'s definition will hold over what is practically investigated as "transnational organized crime" by federal agencies. This is because these 10 areas touch on a range of U.S. law enforcement activity that involves many federal agencies, including numerous components of both DOJ and DHS. The 10 areas clearly enumerate crimes such as drug and weapons trafficking. However, the areas can subsume other illegal activity. For example, many crimes related to financial fraud and identity theft potentially fall under "Cybercrime," "Intellectual Property Theft," or "Threats to the Economy, U.S. Competitiveness, and Strategic Markets." In the past, numerous investigative programs within the federal government have been developed to combat crimes subsumed by the 10 areas without specifically characterizing them as "organized crime." Complicating things, neither the definition nor the *2011 Strategy* lay out a methodology for somehow differentiating among TOC actors in terms of the potential impact of their crimes— namely, the threat they pose to U.S. national security or public interests. Without a methodology establishing thresholds based on severity, vastly different criminals potentially fall under the strategy's purview. A 15-year-old gang member and his friends who illegally download Hollywood movies from a foreign website is arguably a much different target for law enforcement than a powerful international mobster with vast economic resources and an army of foot soldiers. However, the strategy potentially targets both. A form of threat assessment rubric may focus federal efforts, thus focusing the groups or individuals targeted by the strategy. While the *2011 Strategy* does not articulate a threat assessment methodology, two items suggest that Administration efforts supporting the strategy involve some calculation of threat. First, an interagency "Threat Mitigation Working Group" has been given the responsibility of identifying TOC networks "present[ing] a sufficiently high national security risk."[174] Whether or not the networks identified by this working group will be the *only* ones targeted by efforts embraced under the strategy is unclear. Second, four TOC groups were listed in an annex to a new executive order issued in conjunction with the *2011 Strategy*.[175] The order established a sanctions program "to block the property of and prohibit transactions with significant transnational criminal networks that threaten national security, foreign policy, or economic interests."[176] While it is unclear exactly how or why the four groups were chosen, presumably some calculation of threat was involved.[177]

The Definition, 2011 Strategy, and Key Questions

Because the strategy's TOC definition is broad, it may be difficult to ascertain answers to a number of questions critical to policymaking (see Figure 1).

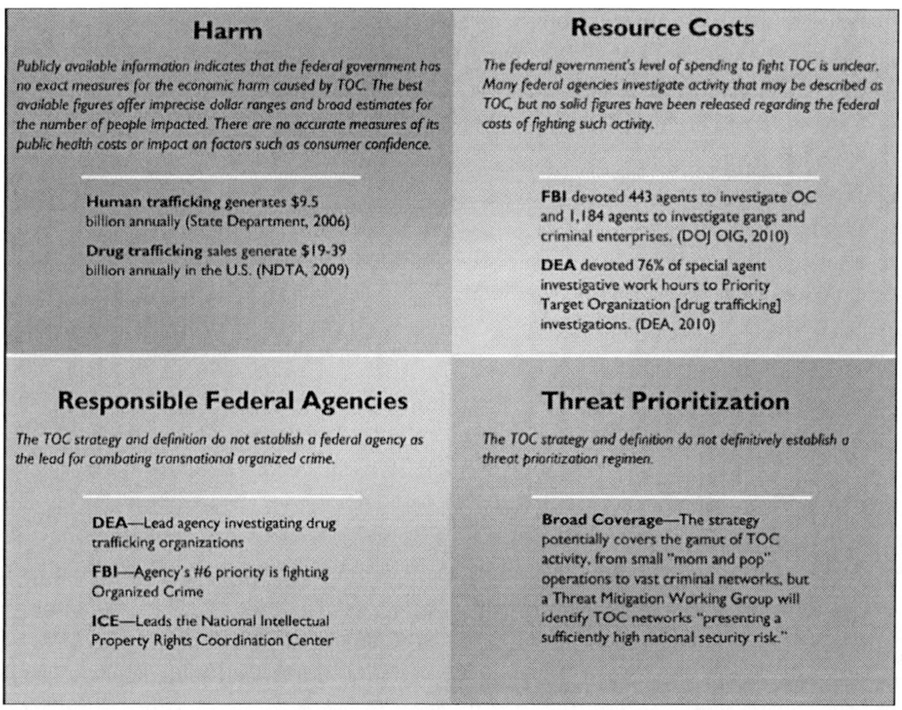

Source: CRS.

Figure 1. Transnational Organized Crime Strategy; Key Issues for Policymakers.

First, how much harm is imposed by transnational organized crime? Second, how many federal resources are directly and indirectly dedicated to combating TOC? Third, which federal agencies are primarily responsible for fighting TOC? Fourth, how are threats prioritized by the new strategy. Are national security concerns weighed against other concerns such as public security when targeting specific TOC groups? Without clear answers to these questions, it may be difficult for Congress to exercise both legislative and oversight responsibilities in order to bolster the federal government's abilities to counter organized crime.

Statutory Definition

There is no current statutory definition of organized crime. The Omnibus Crime Control and Safe Streets Act of 1968, as amended (P.L. 90-351),[178] had at one point defined organized crime as "the unlawful activities of the members of a highly organized, disciplined association engaged in supplying illegal goods and services, including but not limited to gambling, prostitution, loan sharking, narcotics, labor racketeering, and other unlawful activities of members of such organizations." This definition—repealed in the Justice System Improvement Act of 1979 (P.L. 96-157)—appears to be even broader than DOJ's or the FBI's conceptualizations. Similarly, in the Racketeer Influenced and Corrupt Organizations (RICO)[179] provisions, organized crime is described in terms of an "enterprise" and a "pattern of racketeering activity."[180] The predicate offenses for racketeering include a host of state and federal crimes listed in 18 U.S.C. § 1961.

Although RICO does not define organized crime, it provides a definition for an "enterprise." It does not, however, describe those attributes of a *criminal* enterprise that distinguish it from a legal enterprise. In addition, this provision describes organized crime more in terms of the illegal activities committed by conspirators rather than in terms of the criminal organization. As such, these statutory provisions could encompass the activities of not only organized crime groups but of terrorist groups and corrupt businesses as well. Largely describing organized crime as a list of crimes may help in the effective prosecution of these groups, but it provides little aid in developing an understanding of the groups themselves.[181] Moreover, the statutory provisions offer limited guidance regarding criminal organizations and the nature of their operational structure.

ISSUES

Defining Organized Crime in Statute

Currently, there is no statutory definition of organized crime. RICO[182] provisions describe organized crime in terms of an "enterprise" and a "pattern of racketeering activity."[183] The U.S. Code does not, however, provide guidance and information surrounding the nature of criminal organizations and their operational structure. There also appears to be a divergence between the RICO provisions and what federal law enforcement—namely the FBI—considers to be organized crime. For instance, patterns of racketeering activity specified under RICO indicate that criminal organizations may be engaged in a host of crimes including, but not limited to, an act or threat involving murder, kidnapping, gambling, arson, robbery, bribery, extortion, dealing in a controlled substance, and other illegal activities. Although drug trafficking is included in RICO's predicate offenses, law enforcement does not necessarily consider drug trafficking or DTOs to be within the purview of organized crime investigations. One reason for this may be that federal law enforcement tends to segment investigations more on the basis of the criminal violation than on the basis of the criminal actor. While legislating a federal definition of organized crime may notnecessarily solve this disconnect with law enforcement, it might lead to changes in the way law enforcement views and investigates organized crime.

A second statutory issue that Congress may consider is that of organized crime in the U.S. Criminal Code. For instance, while there is a Chapter (113B) in Title 18 that deals specifically with terrorism and related crimes, there is no centralized section that speaks specifically to organized crime.[184] Yet organized crime has been described as a leading threat to U.S. security. Though the lack of centralization of organized crime-related statutes may not impact law enforcement's abilities to investigate and prosecute organized crime, it is indicative of the approach by which the federal government views it. And, as mentioned, the harm caused by organized crime may not be clearly estimated without a common understanding of what defines organized crime. Building on this, accurately gauging the public and national security threat posed by organized crime may be complicated without a solid notion of the harm it routinely causes.

Congressional Commission

Beginning in the 1950s, congressional concern about organized crime has resulted not only in legislative efforts to combat it, but in commissions and in various series of hearings aimed at gathering information on the scope of organized crime. One of the first such efforts was the Senate Special Committee to Investigate Organized Crime in Interstate Commerce in 1950 and 1951 led by Senator Kefauver. Another example of such congressional attention is the series of Senate hearings on organized crime in 1958 and 1963 led by Senator McClellan. There was also the 1967 Commission on Crime in the United States led by Attorney General Katzenbach. More recently, and particularly since the terrorist attacks of September 11, 2001, congressional attention has shifted away from traditional crime fighting—including organized crime—toward counterterrorism.

Of the more recent hearings involving organized crime topics, focus has primarily been on threats posed by the DTOs in Mexico. While this is one of the most visible organized crime threats—not only are some of the actors exceedingly violent, but this violence is seen directly along the U.S. Southwest border—it is likely not the sole serious organized crime threat to the United States. As discussed, numerous other organized crime groups, though perhaps not as violent, commit crimes that impact the economic stability, public safety, and domestic security of the United States. As such, one option that Congress may ultimately consider is the convening of a congressional commission to evaluate the scope of organized crime. Such an evaluation might help policymakers determine whether they have provided law enforcement with the appropriate tools to combat today's threats posed by organized crime. It may also result in a clarification of how the federal government defines organized crime and consequently how investigative efforts at the federal level are organized. The

Administration has also proposed a legislative package related to the *2011 Strategy.*[185] In light of this, Congress may consider exploring the issue of transnational organized crime more extensively.

Incentives for Investigating Organized Crime

While the effects of certain, high-profile crimes—such as terrorism—are readily seen, the aftermath of organized crime is not always as striking, nor does it produce the same negative visceral reactions. Some argue that this may be one reason for the shift in law enforcement attention and resources more toward counterterrorism-related activities and further away from traditional crime fighting activities since the terrorist attacks of September 11, 2001. However, although the effects of organized crime may not be seen in a consolidated attack resulting in the physical loss of life, the effects are far-reaching. As mentioned, organized crime impacts economic stability, public health and safety, and national security. Consequently, some experts argue that there should be some form of incentive (as well as disincentive) to entice law enforcement to target more monetary and manpower resources toward investigating organized crime.[186]

One such form of incentive that Congress may consider is federal grants to state and local law enforcement for training and technical assistance to investigate and prosecute organized crime. There are several grant programs—such as the Community Oriented Policing Services (COPS) grant program[187] and the Edward Byrne Memorial Justice Assistance Grant (JAG) program[188]— through which state and local law enforcement assistance is available for a variety of purpose areas. However, these purposes do not directly specify as a purpose area the use of funds for combating organized crime. Therefore, policymakers may consider a specific grant program providing not only funding, but technical training and assistance.

Other suggestions that experts have put forward involve the use of negative peer reviews to incentivize law enforcement around the world to focus resources toward combating organized crime.[189] As discussed, various state and federal law enforcement agencies investigate organized crime in the United States. As such, one option Congress may consider could be to direct the formation of a domestic peer review system[190] for law enforcement agencies charged with investigating organized crime. Participation in some form of peer review system could be tied to law enforcement assistance and grant funding eligibility.

Implementing the National Strategy to Combat TOC

Congress may wish to consider oversight of the national strategy's implementation by federal law enforcement agencies. In part, the strategy involves many law enforcement agencies, their investigative resources, and their intelligence collection efforts. A critical issue may be the coordination of these activities.

Coordination of Domestic Efforts

As mentioned, the federal investigation of organized crime matters has not historically been a centralized effort, and even with the *2011 Strategy,* there is no single lead agency charged with investigating organized crime.[191] Specific agencies have had jurisdiction over an organized crime case based on the criminal violations involved. For instance, organized crime cases built around drug trafficking offenses have generally been investigated by the DEA, whereas those cases built around human trafficking cases are typically investigated by ICE. However, many organized crime cases may involve offenses that fall under the jurisdiction of multiple investigative agencies. For example, organized crime groups involved in crimes ranging from counterfeiting and financial institution fraud to identity crimes, computer crimes, and money laundering may be investigated by the U.S. Secret Service (USSS), FBI, ICE, and any number of other federal, state, and local law enforcement agencies. As a result of structuring organized crime investigations around the alleged crimes, it is not always clear which agency will take the lead on a particular case. This can lead to inter-agency conflicts, and if case information is not effectively communicated between agencies, each agency involved may not have a comprehensive view of the case. There are, however, several law enforcement fusion centers, such as the Organized Crime Drug Enforcement Task Force (OCDETF) Fusion Center (OFC), the International Organized Crime Intelligence and Operations Center (IOC-2), and the El Paso Intelligence Center (EPIC), that are charged with consolidating and disseminating intelligence on various organized crime matters. Additionally, different agencies across federal, state, and local levels participate in these centers.

For instance, the OFC assimilates information for the OCDETF Program, which targets major drug trafficking and money laundering organizations. Federal agencies that participate in the OCDETF Program include the DEA; FBI; ICE; Bureau of Alcohol, Tobacco, Firearms, and Explosives (ATF); U.S. Marshals; Internal Revenue Service (IRS); U.S. Coast Guard (USCG); 94 U.S. Attorneys Offices; and DOJ's Criminal and Tax Divisions. These federal agencies also collaborate with state and local law enforcement.

In May 2009, DOJ announced the creation of the IOC-2—housed at the OFC—which brings together the FBI; ICE; DEA; IRS; ATF; U.S. Secret Service; U.S. Postal Inspection Service (USPIS); U.S. Department of State, Bureau of Diplomatic Security; U.S. Department of Labor, Office of the Inspector General; and DOJ's Criminal Division in partnership with the 94 U.S. Attorneys' Offices and the U.S. Department of the Treasury, Office of Terrorism and Financial Intelligence. Unlike the OFC, the IOC-2 has yet to be funded.[192] It is charged with analyzing and resolving conflicts in information on a host of organized crime cases, not solely those that center on drug trafficking.

EPIC was originally established as an intelligence center to collect and disseminate information relating to drug, alien, and weapon smuggling in support of field enforcement entities throughout the Southwest border region. Following 9/11, counterterrorism also became part of its mission. Though these crimes are not exclusively committed by organized crime groups, they may be, and thus EPIC is involved in combating organized crime. EPIC is jointly operated by the DEA and U.S. Customs and Border Protection (CBP), and other participating agencies include ICE, USCG, U.S. Secret Service, Department of Defense (DOD), Department of the Interior, FBI, ATF, U.S. Marshals Service, Federal Aviation Administration, National Drug Intelligence Center (NDIC), IRS, National Geospatial-Intelligence Agency, Joint Task Force-North, Joint Interagency Task Force-South, Texas Department of Public Safety, Texas Air National Guard, and El Paso County Sheriff's Office.

In evaluating the most effective means to share organized crime intelligence, Congress may consider several options. One option may include increasing support for intelligence fusion centers such as the OFC, IOC-2, and EPIC. Another option could involve the creation of an interagency organization similar to the National Counterterrorism Center (NCTC), but centered around organized crime. Such an organization would be responsible for "analyzing the [organized crime] threat, sharing that information with ... partners, and integrating all instruments of national power to ensure unity of effort"[193] against organized crime. On the prosecution end, DOJ has already announced a proposed consolidation of the Organized Crime and Racketeering Section (OCRS), the Criminal Division's gang unit, and the National Gang Targeting, Enforcement, and Coordination Center (GangTECC) into a single Organized Crime and Gang Section.[194] This harmonizes the prosecution of organized crime and gang cases, which DOJ has cited as being similar.

One non-legislative option that Congress may consider regarding the coordination of federal law enforcement efforts to combat organized crime is enforcing its oversight over existing fusion centers. In June 2010, the DOJ Office of the Inspector General (OIG) issued a review of EPIC.[195] The OIG found that EPIC's users value its products, but that EPIC could benefit from improvement in fully developing the National Seizure System and coordinating the High Intensity Drug Trafficking Area (HIDTA) program, consistently coordinating with intelligence organizations across the country, maintaining and analyzing current information from all

available sources, and creating objective performance measures by which to evaluate its programs, among other things. Similarly, in November 2009 the OIG reviewed DOJ's anti-gang intelligence and coordination centers.[196] As a result of the review, the OIG determined that the National Gang Intelligence Center had not created a gang information database, as had been directed by Congress.

End Notes

[1] These law enforcement agencies include the U.S. Federal Bureau of Investigation (FBI); Drug Enforcement Administration (DEA); Immigration and Customs Enforcement (ICE); the United Kingdom's Serious Organised Crime Agency (SOCA); the Australian Crime Commission and Australian Federal Police; the New Zealand Police; and the Royal Canadian Mounted Police. See SOCA, "SOCA Working in Partnership Worldwide," http://www.soca.gov.uk/about-soca/working-in-partnership/international-partnerships. Intelligence Committee Futures Working Group, *Crime and Policing Futures*, Strategic Alliance Group, March 2008, p. 2. (Hereafter, Intelligence Committee Futures Working Group, *Futures*.)

[2] For details see *Strategy to Combat Transnational Organized Crime,* July 2011, http://www.whitehouse.gov/sites/default/files/Strategy_to_Combat_Transnational_ Organized_Crime_July_2011.pdf. (Hereafter: *Strategy to Combat Transnational Organized Crime.*)

[3] Moisés Naím, *Illicit: How Smugglers, Traffickers, and Copycats are Hijacking the Global Economy* (New York: Anchor Books, 2006) p. 16. (Hereafter: Naím, *Illicit.*)

[4] Intelligence Committee Futures Working Group, *Futures,* p. 5. See also United Nations Office on Drugs and Crime (UNODC), *The Globalization of Crime: A Transnational Organized Crime Threat Assessment,* (Vienna: UNODC, 2010), p. 221.

[5] Jharna Chatterjee, *The Changing Structure of Organized Crime Groups*, Royal Canadian Mounted Police, 2005, pp. 2, 7-8, http://dsp-psd.pwgsc.gc.ca/Collection/PS64-9-2005E.pdf. (Hereafter: Chatterjee, *The Changing Structure*.)

[6] For more on this, see Naím, *Illicit*; Melvyn Levitsky, "Transnational Criminal Networks and International Security," *Syracuse Journal of International Law and Commerce*, vol. 30, no. 2 (Summer 2003), pp. 227-240.

[7] Research and Innovative Technology Administration, Bureau of Transportation Statistics, *America's Container Ports: Freight Hubs That Connect Our Nation to Global Markets*, Department of Transportation, June 2009, pp. 7-8, http://www.bts.gov/publications /americas_container_ports/2009/pdf/entire.pdf.

[8] Naím, *Illicit*, pp. 1-8.

[9] See, for example, Gregory F. Treverton et al., *Film Piracy, Organized Crime, and Terrorism*, RAND Corporation, Santa Monica, CA, 2009, p. 27, http://www.rand.org/pubs/monographs /2009/RAND_MG742.pdf. (Hereafter, Treverton et al., *Film Piracy*.)

[10] Department of Justice, "Attorney General Eric Holder Speaks at the International Intellectual Property Summit," press release, October 18, 2010, http://www.justice.gov/iso/opa/ag /speeches/2010/ag-speech-101018.html.

[11] Treverton et al., *Film Piracy*.

[12] Treverton et al., *Film Piracy*, p. 3; Deputy Assistant Attorney General Criminal Division, Department of Justice, Jason M. Weinstein, *Statement Before the United States House of Representatives Committee on Oversight and Government Reform Subcommittee on Government Management, Organization, and Procurement*, Department of Justice, Prepared Testimony "Protecting Intellectual Property Rights in a Global Economy: Current Trends and Future Challenges," December 9, 2009, p. 2, http://oversight.house.gov/images /stories/Hearings/Government_Management/Intellectual_Property_Rights/Draft_DAAG_ Weinstein_testimony_OMB_CLEARED_with_new_date.pdf.

[13] U.S. Government Accountability Office (GAO), *Intellectual Property*, p. 5 offers the following definition: "'Pirated copyright goods' refer to any goods that are copies made without the consent of the right holder or person duly authorized by the right holder. 'Counterfeit goods' refer to any goods, including packaging or bearing without authorization, a trademark that is identical to a trademark validly registered for those goods, or that cannot be distinguished in its essential aspects from such a trademark, and that, thereby, infringes the rights of the owner of the trademark in question. According to the U.S. Food and Drug Administration (FDA), 'counterfeit drugs' are defined under U.S. law as those sold under a product name without proper authorization, where the identity of the source drug is knowingly and intentionally mislabeled in a way that suggests that it is the authentic and approved product."

[14] U.S. Government Accountability Office (GAO), *Intellectual Property: Observations on Efforts to Quantify the Economic Effects of Counterfeit and Pirated Goods*, GAO-1-423, April 2010, p. 5, http://www.gao.gov/new.items/ d10423.pdf defines intellectual property (IP) as "any innovation, commercial or artistic, or any unique name, symbol, logo, or design used commercially. IP rights protect the economic interests of the creators of these works by giving them property rights over their creations." The report describes copyright as "[a] set of exclusive rights subsisting in original works of authorship fixed in any tangible medium of expression now known or later developed, for a fixed period of time. For example, works may be literary, musical, or artistic." The report defines trademark as "[a]ny sign or any combination of signs capable of distinguishing the source of goods or services is capable of constituting a trademark. Such signs—in particular, words (including personal names), letters, numerals, figurative elements, and combinations of colors, as well as any combination of such signs—are eligible for registration as trademarks." Patents are "[e]xclusive rights granted to inventions for a fixed period of time, whether products or processes, in all fields of technology, provided they are new, not obvious (involve an inventive step), and have utility (are capable of industrial application)."

[15] U.S. Government Accountability Office (GAO), *Intellectual Property*; U.S. Chamber of Commerce, "Protecting Intellectual Property," pp. 9-15, http://www.uschamber.com/IP.htm. IPR infringement may also have some positive effects for consumers who may derive benefit from the lower costs of pirated goods. Industry may also eventually generate more sales as consumers possibly develop interest in purchasing legitimate versions of cheaper counterfeit products they have sampled.

[16] According to U.S. Customs and Border Protection, "domestic value" is the "cost of seized goods, plus the cost of shipping and importing the goods into the U.S. and an amount for profit."

[17] U.S. Customs and Border Protection, "Yearly Comparisons: Seizure Statistics for Intellectual Property Rights (FY 2005-FY2009)," January 2010, http://www.cbp.gov/xp/cgov/trade /priority_trade/ipr/seizure /seizure_stats.xml; U.S. Customs and Border Protection, U.S. Immigration and Customs Enforcement, "Intellectual Property Rights Seizure Statistics: FY 2009," October 2009, p. 2, http://www.cbp.gov/linkhandler /cgov/trade /priority_trade/ipr/seizure/ fy09_stats.ctt/fy09_stats.pdf; U.S. Customs and Border Protection, U.S. Immigration and Customs Enforcement, "Intellectual Property Rights Seizure Statistics: FY 2008," January 2009, p. 2, http://www.cbp.gov /linkhandler/cgov/ trade/priority_trade/ipr/seizure/fy08_final_stat.ctt /fy08_final_stat.pdf.

[18] U.S. Customs and Border Protection, U.S. Immigration and Customs Enforcement, "Intellectual Property Rights Seizure Statistics: FY2009," October 2009, p. 12, http://www.cbp.gov/linkhandler/cgov/trade/priority_ trade/ipr/pubs/ seizure/fy09_stats.ctt/fy09_stats.pdf; U.S. Customs and Border Protection, U.S. Immigration and Customs Enforcement, "Intellectual Property Rights Seizure Statistics: FY2008," January 2009, p. 13,

http://www.cbp.gov/ linkhandler/cgov/trade/priority_ trade/ipr/pubs/seizure/fy08_final_stat.ctt/fy08_final_stat.pdf.

[19] Keith Johnson, "U.S. Seizes Big Batches of Fake Goods," *Wall Street Journal*, April 26, 2010.

[20] See "Stolen American Autos Clog the Mexican Market," *New York Times*, February 5, 1922, http://query.nytimes.com/mem/archive-free/pdf?res=9D0DE5D71130EE3ABC4D53DFB4668389639EDE.

[21] Eva Dou, "New-York Based Theft Ring Shipped Hot Cars to Senegal," *Associated Press*, June 30, 2010.

[22] Ibid; Rob Sgobbo, Joe Jackson, and Brendan Brosh, "U.S. to Senegal Car Theft Ring Busted, Attorney General Andrew Cuomo Says," *New York Daily News*, June 30, 2010.

[23] Naím, *Illicit* p. 89; Jackie Turner and Liz Kelly, "Intersections Between Diasporas and Crime Groups in the Constitution of the Human Trafficking Chain," *British Journal of Criminology*, vol. 49, no. 2 (March 2009), p. 184.

[24] Jeffrey S. Passel and D'Vera Cohn, *U.S. Unauthorized Immigration Flows Are Down Sharply Since Mid-Decade*, Pew Hispanic Center, Report, Washington, DC, September 1, 2010, p. i, http://pewhispanic.org/files /reports/126.pdf.

[25] Miriam Jordan, "Illegal Immigration to U.S. Slows Sharply," *Wall Street Journal*, September 1, 2010, http://online.wsj.com/article/SB100014240527487038823045754657426 709 85642.html?mod=googlenews_wsj.

[26] Also, while some drug trafficking organizations may not be directly involved in human smuggling, they may tax the smugglers who wish to use the established drug trafficking routes. For details on Mexican cartels and human smuggling, see David Luhnow and Jose De Cordoba, "Mexican Military Finds 72 Bodies Near Border," *Wall Street Journal*, August 26, 2010, http://online.wsj.com/article/ SB100014240527 4870363230457545076 1550490920.html#articleTabs%3Darticle; Josh Meyer, "Drug Cartels Raise the Stakes on Human Smuggling," *Los Angeles Times*, March 23, 2009, http://articles.latimes.com /2009/mar /23/nation/ na-human-smuggling23.

[27] Department of Justice, "Sister Ping Sentenced to 35 Years in Prison for Alien Smuggling, Hostage Taking, Money Laundering, and Ransom Proceeds Conspiracy," press release, March 16, 2006, http://www.justice.gov/usao/nys/ pressreleases/March06/sister pingsentencingpr.pdf.

[28] Ibid.

[29] Department of Justice, "Hudson County Bar Owner Pleads Guilty to Role in International Human Smuggling Ring," press release, September 12, 2006, http://www.justice.gov/usao /nj/press/files/pdffiles/medr0912rel.pdf.

[30] Department of State, *Trafficking In Persons Report 2006*, June 2006, p. 13, http://www.state.gov/documents/ organization/66086.pdf.

[31] Government Accountability Office (GAO), *Human Trafficking: Better Data, Strategy, and Reporting Needed to Enhance U.S. Antitrafficking Efforts Abroad*, GAO-06-825, July 2006, http://www.gao.gov/new.items /d06825.pdf.

[32] Department of Justice, "Six People Charged in Human Trafficking Conspiracy for Exploiting 400 Thai Farm Workers," press release, September 2, 2010, http://www.justice.gov/opa/pr /2010/September/10-crt-999.html. For another case involving forced labor, see Department of Justice, "Uzbek Man Sentenced for Role in Multi-National Racketeering and Forced Labor Enterprise," press release, May 9, 2011, http://www.justice.gov /opa/pr/2011/May/11- crt-589.html.

[33] Department of Justice, "Four Defendants Sentenced to Prison in Human Trafficking Ring," press release, April 28, 2010, http://www.justice.gov/usao/gan/press/2010/04-28-10.pdf.

[34] Comments by DOJ officials at the 2010 National Conference on Human Trafficking, May 3–5, Arlington, VA.

[35] Mark Townsend, "How Liverpool Docks Became a Hub of Europe's Deadly Cocaine Trade," *The Guardian*, May 16, 2010.

[36] Michele M. Leonhart, DEA Acting Administrator, "Prepared Remarks: Project Reckoning Press Conference," September 17, 2008, http://www.justice.gov/dea/speeches /s091808.html.

[37] National Drug Intelligence Center, *National Drug Threat Assessment*, February 2010, p. 29, http://www.justice.gov/ ndic/pubs38/38661/38661p.pdf.

[38] Federal Bureau of Investigation, Newark Division, "Federal Agents Shut Down International Smorgasbord of Crime," press release, March 18, 2009, http://newark.fbi.gov/pressrel /pressrel09/nk031809.htm.

[39] Federal Bureau of Investigation, "Inside the FBI: Albanian Organized Crime," November 27, 2009, http://www.fbi.gov/inside/archive/inside112709.htm. For more on Albanian organized crime activity in the United States see Department of Justice, "Two Leaders of Violent Albanian Drug Gang Found Guilty in Manhattan Federal Court," press release, December 7, 2011, http://www.fbi.gov/newyork/press-releases/2011/two-leaders-of-violentalbanian-drug-gang-found-guilty-in-manhattan-federal-court; Department

of Justice, "Sixteen Members of International Organized Crime Group Charged with Kidnapping, Narcotics, Robbery and Firearms Crimes," press release, June 8, 2010, http://www.fbi.gov/newyork/press-releases/2010/nyfo060810.htm.

[40] Department of Justice, "Ringleader of International Drug Trafficking Ring Pleads Guilty for Role in Drug Smuggling Case," press release, February 24, 2010, http://www.justice.gov/usao/pae/News/Pr/2010/feb/tran_guilty_plea_release.pdf; Troy Graham, "Woman at Center of Asian Drug-Trafficking Ring Gets Nearly Six Year Term," *Philadelphia Inquirer*, August 25, 2010, http://www.philly.com/inquirer/local/20100825_Woman_at_center_of_Asian_drug-trafficking_ring_gets_nearly_six-year_term.html.

[41] Brian Seymour, "Global Money Laundering," *Journal of Applied Security Research*, vol. 3, no. 3-4 (2008), pp. 374 375. (Hereafter, Seymour, "Global Money.")

[42] Dennis C. Blair, Director of National Intelligence, "Annual Threat Assessment of the US Intelligence Community for the Senate Select Committee on Intelligence," Office of the Director of National Intelligence, February 2, 2010, p. 31. (Hereafter, Blair, "Annual Threat Assessment.")

[43] William Booth and Nick Miroff, "Stepped-Up Efforts by U.S., Mexico Fail to Stem Flow of Drug Money South," *Washington Post,* August 25, 2010, http://www.washingtonpost.com /wp-dyn/content/article/2010/08/25/AR2010082506161.html.

[44] For a discussion of estimates, see Douglas Farah, *Money Laundering and Bulk Cash Smuggling: Challenges for the Mérida Initiative,* Woodrow Wilson International Center For Scholars, Mexico Institute and University of San Diego Trans-Border Institute, Working Paper Series on U.S.-Mexico Security Cooperation, Washington, DC, May 2010, p. 6, http://wilsoncenter.org/topics/pubs/Money%20Laundering%20and%20 Bulk%20Cash%20Smuggling.%20Farah.pdf. (Hereafter, Farah, *Money Laundering.*)

[45] A stored value card looks like a debit or credit card, but stores value directly on the card using magnetic strip technology.

[46] Legislation has been introduced in the 111th Congress (H.R. 5127) that would, among other things, classify stored value cards as monetary instruments in order to require individuals to declare to Customs over $10,000 that they are carrying on a stored value card.

[47] Farah, *Money Laundering*, 23.

[48] Seymour, "Global Money," pp. 375-376.

[49] U.S. Government Accountability Office (GAO), *Company Formations: Minimal Ownership Information Is Collected and Available*, GAO-06-376, April 2006, p. 1, http://www.gao.gov/new.items/d06376.pdf. Hereafter GAO, *Company Formations.*

[50] Jennifer Shasky Calvery, Senior Counsel to the Deputy Attorney General, Department of Justice, Statement Before the United States Senate Committee on Homeland Security and Governmental Affairs, Hearing, "Examining State Business Incorporation Practices: A Discussion of the Incorporation Transparency and Law Enforcement Assistance Act," June 18, 2009, pp 1-2, http://www.justice.gov/ola/testimony/111-1/2009-06-18-dag-shasky-incorporation.pdf. (Hereafter, Shasky, "Examining State Business.")

[51] GAO, *Company Formations,* p. 1.

[52] GAO, *Company Formations,* p. 13.

[53] Shasky, "Examining State Business," pp. 4-5; Seymour, "Global Money," p. 375.

[54] Jennifer Shasky, Senior Counsel to the Deputy Attorney General, Department of Justice, Statement Before the United States Senate Committee on Homeland Security and Governmental Affairs, Hearing, "Business Formation and Financial Crime: Finding a Legislative Solution," November 5, 2009, p. 1, http://hsgac.senate.gov/public/index.cfm? FuseAction=Hearings.Hearing&Hearing_ID=88d1a5fb-7312-4e9e-92b2-8558ccd44f22. Legislation has been introduced in the 111th Congress (S. 569, H.R. 6098) that would establish uniform requirements for states regarding beneficial ownership of public corporations and limited liability companies.

[55] Criminal Intelligence Service Canada (CISC), *2010 Report on Organized Crime,* May 2010, p. 12, http://www.cisc.gc.ca/annual_reports/annual_report_2010/document /report_oc_2010_ e.pdf. (Hereafter, CISC, *2010 Report.*)

[56] For information on unlawful Internet gambling, see CRS Report RS22749, *Unlawful Internet Gambling Enforcement Act (UIGEA) and Its Implementing Regulations*, by Brian T. Yeh and Charles Doyle.

[57] On the advent of Internet gambling, see David G. Schwartz, *Roll the Bones: The History of Gambling,* (New York: Gotham Books, Penguin Group (USA), 2006) pp. 488-494.

[58] George Anastasia, "Officials Charge Man Who Allegedly Ran Mob Gambling Website," *Philadelphia Inquirer,* May 29, 2010, http://www.philly.com/inquirer/local/nj/20100529_ Officials_charge_man_who_allegedly_ran_mob_gambling_website.html.

[59] International Mass-Marketing Fraud Working Group (IMMFWG), *Mass-Marketing Fraud: A Threat Assessment*, June 2010, p. 3. (Hereafter, IMMFWG, *Mass Marketing Fraud.*) The IMMFWG includes law enforcement, regulatory, and consumer protection agencies from Australia, Belgium, Canada, the Netherlands, Nigeria, the United Kingdom, and the United States. Europol is also involved.

[60] IMMFWG, *Mass Marketing Fraud*, p. 14.

[61] Ibid.

[62] Chad Bray, "FBI Raids Alleged Boiler Room," *Wall Street Journal,* June 10, 2010, http://online.wsj.com/article/SB10001424052748703890904575297220025441524.html.

[63] Federal Bureau of Investigation, "Common Fraud Schemes," http://www.fbi.gov/majcases /fraud/fraudschemes.htm.

[64] Federal Bureau of Investigation, Detroit Division, "Scam E-Mail/Letter Claiming To Be Associated with FBI Detroit SAC Arena," press release, May 25, 2010, http://detroit.fbi.gov/pressrel/pressrel10/de052510.htm.

[65] Harvey Glickman, "The Nigerian '419' Advance Fee Scams: Prank or Peril?," *Canadian Journal of African Studies*, vol. 39, no. 3 (2005), pp. 463-476.

[66] Edward Fokuoh Ampratwum, "Advance Fee Fraud, '419,' and Investor Confidence in the Economies of Sub-Saharan Africa (SSA) ," *Journal of Financial Crime*, vol. 16, no. 1 (2009), pp. 68-69.

[67] Matthew Zook, "Your Urgent Assistance Is Required: The Intersection of 419 Spam and New Networks of Imagination," *Ethics, Place, and Environment*, vol. 10, no. 1 (March 2007), pp. 66-70.

[68] Jeremy Kirk, "Advance Fee Fraud Scams Rise Dramatically in 2009," *Compuworld*, January 28, 2010, http://www.computerworld.com/s/article/9149890/Advance_fee_fraud_ scams_rise_dramatically_in_2009.

[69] Federal Bureau of Investigation, "Six Defendants Sentenced in Manhattan Federal Court for Their Involvement in a Multi-Million-Dollar Lottery Telemarketing Fraud Scheme," press release, July 1, 2011, http://www.fbi.gov/newyork/ press-releases/2011/six-defendants-sentenced-in-manhattan-federal-court-for-their-involvement-in-a-multi-milliondollar-lottery-telemarketing-fraud-scheme.

[70] Blaise J. Bergiel, Erich B. Bergiel, and Phillip W. Balsmeir, "Internet Cross Border Crime: A Growing Problem," *Journal of Website Promotion*, vol. 3, no. 3/4 (2008), p. 135.

[71] This parallels the first two elements in Kim-Kwang Raymond Choo's three-part typology of criminal activity in cyberspace. The typology includes "(1) traditional organized crime groups which make use of ICT [information and communications technologies] to enhance their terrestrial criminal activities; (2) organized cybercrime groups which operate exclusively online; and (3) organized groups of ideologically and politically motivated individuals who make use of ICT to facilitate their criminal conduct." See Kim-Kwang Raymond Choo, "Organized Crime Groups in Cyberspace: A Typology," *Trends in Organized Crime,* vol. 11, no. 3 (September 2008), pp. 271.

[72] Wade Baker et al., *2010 Data Breach Investigations Report: A Study Conducted by the Verizon RISK Team in Cooperation with the United States Secret Service,* Verizon, July 2010, pp. 2-15, http://www.verizonbusiness.com/ resources/reports/rp_2010-data-breach-report_en_xg. pdf.

[73] Department of Justice, "Foreign National Pleads Guilty for Role in International Money Laundering Scheme Involving More than $1.4 Million in Losses to Victims," press release, May 13, 2010, http://www.justice.gov/opa/pr/ 2010/May/10-crm-568.html.

[74] Angela Moscaritolo, "Romanian Police, FBI Break Up 70-Strong eBay Fraud Ring," *SC Magazine,* April 7, 2010, http://www.scmagazineus.com/romanian-police-fbi-break-up-70-strong-ebay-fraud-ring/article/167554/.

[75] Paul Teetor, "Russian or Armenian Mob Used 'Model Employee' Con at PCH Arco," *LA Weekly*, June 18, 2009.

[76] Lawrence Mower, "ID Theft Operation Outlined," *Las Vegas Review-Journal*, December 8, 2008.

[77] "Eurasian Organized Crime Task Force Members Arrest 12 Individuals Following Federal Credit Card Fraud and Identity Theft Charges," *States News Service*, December 9, 2008. See also: Department of Justice, "Men Sentenced for Credit Card Fraud Conspiracy," press release, June 10, 2011, http://www.justice.gov/usao/nv/press/june2011/ palikyan06102011. htm.

[78] "Three Arrested in Credit Card Forgery Ring," KTNV ABC, March 26, 2009.

[79] "18 Month Credit Card Fraud Ring Leads to Three Arrests," KTNV ABC, March 25, 2009. Additionally, in February 2011, DOJ announced an indictment charging 29 defendants tied to an organized crime group called "Armenian Power" or "AP." DOJ noted "Among the conspiracies charged in the racketeering indictment is a bank fraud and counterfeit credit card scheme that victimized hundreds of customers of 99 Cents Only Stores throughout Southern California. AP members allegedly caused more than $2 million in losses when they secretly installed sophisticated 'skimming' devices to steal customer account information at cash registers and then used the skimmed information to create counterfeit debit and credit cards." See Department of Justice, "Armenian Power Organized Crime Group Targeted in Federal Indictments That Allege Racketeering

Offenses, Including Bank Fraud Schemes, Kidnappings, and Drug Trafficking," press release, February 16, 2011, http://www.fbi.gov/losangeles/press-releases/2011/la021611.htm. For another case involving skimming, see Department of Justice, "Rancho Cordova Man Arrested for Identity Theft and Trafficking in Counterfeit Credit Card Information," press release, April 21, 2011, http://www.justice.gov/usao/cae/news/docs/2011/04-21-11Avagyan Indictment. html.

[80] Department of Justice, "Leader of Hacking Ring Sentenced for Massive Identity Thefts from Payment Processor and U.S. Retail Networks," press release, March 26, 2010, http://www.justice.gov/opa/pr/2010/March/10-crm-329.html.

[81] A "booster" is someone who steals merchandise and then sells it to a fence for a profit. A "fence" is someone who knowingly buys illegally obtained goods from a booster and then sells the goods for a profit. For more information on ORC, see CRS Report R41118, *Organized Retail Crime*, by Kristin M. Finklea.

[82] Ticket switching involves means by which criminals alter the UPC bar codes on merchandise so that the items ring up differently–significantly below the original price–at check-out.

[83] King Rogers, "Organized Retail Theft," in *Retail Crime, Security, and Loss Prevention: An Encyclopedic Reference*, ed. Charles A. Sennewald and John H. Christman (Elseiver Inc., 2008).

[84] National Retail Federation, *2009 Organized Retail Crime Survey*, 2009, p. 8.

[85] Department of Justice, "Pawn Shop Owner Pleads Guilty in Scheme to Launder $20 Million in Proceeds of Stolen Merchandise: Admitted Laundering Millions of Dollars in Proceeds of Stolen Over-the-Counter Medicines, Health and Beauty Aid Products, Gift Cards, DVDs, Tools, and Other Items," press release, September 3, 2010, http://baltimore.fbi. gov/dojpressrel/pressrel10/ba090310a.htm.

[86] Steven S. Dudley, *Drug Trafficking Organizations in Central America: Transportistas, Mexican Cartels, and Maras*, Woodrow Wilson International Center For Scholars, Mexico Institute and University of San Diego Trans-Border Institute, Working Paper Series on U.S.-Mexico Security Cooperation, Washington, DC, May 2010, p. 17, http://wilsoncenter.org/topics/pubs/ Drug%20Trafficking%20Organizations%20in%20Central%20America.%20Dudley.pdf.

[87] Rear Admiral Vincent Atkins, U.S. Coast Guard, Testimony before the House Subcommittee on Homeland Security, on Department of Homeland Security Air and Marine Operations and Investments, April 19, 2010, http://www.dhs.gov/ ynews/testimony/testimony_ 1271690315007.shtm.

[88] Jim Popkin, "Authorities in Awe of Drug Runners' Jungle-Built, Kevlar-Coated Supersubs," *Wired Magazine*, March 29, 2011, http://www.wired.com/magazine /2011/03/ff_drugsub/all/1; "DEA Intel Aids in Seizure of Fully-Operational Narco Submarine in Ecuador," press release, July 3, 2010; Chirs Kraul, "Ecuador Police Seize 100-foot NarcoSubmarine Being Built Secretly," *Los Angeles Times*, July 6, 2010, http://www.latimes.com/news/nationworld/world/ la-fg-ecuador-narco-sub-20100706, 0,162212.story; Douglas A. Kash and Eli White, "A New Law Counters the Semisubmersible Smuggling Threat," Federal Bureau of Investigation, March 2010, http://www.fbi.gov/publications/leb/2010/march2010 /smuggling_feature.htm; U.S. Southern Command, "The Self-Propelled Semi-Submersibles Threat," February 20, 2009, http://www.southcom.mil/appssc/factFiles.php?id=83.

[89] The Federal Aviation Administration (FAA) does not classify ultralights as "aircraft." For the FAA definition of an ultralight, see the Code of Federal Regulations (CFR) Title 14, Section 103, http://ecfr.gpoaccess.gov/cgi/t/text/textidx?c=ecfr&sid=77f64066b8e425c01339f918 e6e9f291&rgn=div5&view=text&node=14:2.0.1.3.16&idno=14. Legislation has been introduced in the 111th Congress (H.R. 5307) that would include ultralights in the definition of an aircraft in order to increase law enforcement's abilities to prosecute drug smuggling cases.

[90] Agence France-Presse, "Mexican Drug Traffickers Using Tiny Planes for US Market," *MSN News*, September 2, 2010, http://news.ph.msn.com/business/article.aspx?cp-documentid=4311772.

[91] U.S. Customs and Border Protection, "Ultralight Plane Crashes in Arizona, Smugglers Apprehended," press release, May 30, 2009, http://www.cbp.gov/xp/cgov/newsroom/news_ releases/archives/2009_news_releases /may_2009/ 05302009.xml.

[92] Ken Stier, "Underground Threat: Tunnels Pose Trouble from Mexico to Middle East," *Time*, May 2, 2009.

[93] U.S. Drug Enforcement Administration, "DEA/ICE Uncover 'Massive' Cross-Border Drug Tunnel, Cement lined passage thought to link warehouses in Tijuana and Otay Mesa," press release, January 26, 2006, http://www.justice.gov/dea/pubs/pressrel/pr012606.html.

[94] U.S. Drug Enforcement Administration, "Tunnel Task Force Discovers Cross Border Tunnel, 30 tons of Marijuana Seized in Investigation," press release, November 3, 2010, http://www.justice.gov/dea/pubs /states/newsrel/2010/ sd110310.html.

[95] Immigration and Customs Enforcement, "Highly Sophisticated Cross-Border Drug Tunnel Discovered Near San Diego," press release, November 15, 2011, http://www.ice.gov/news/releases/1111/111130sandiego.htm.

[96] Michael Thurston, "Record drugs haul seized from US-Mexico border tunnel," *AFP*, November 4, 2010, http://www.google.com/hostednews/afp/article/ALeqM 5jQ20K1Iy 7AaXLBGtqiAxnfkCMTGQ?docId= CNG.a14f67109bad6c916ff3ce51f338a2d8.3b1.

[97] For more information, see http://www.geophysical.com/militarysecurity.htm.

[98] Ken Stier, "Underground Threat: Tunnels Pose Trouble from Mexico to Middle East," *Time*, May 2, 2009.

[99] Klaus von Lampe, "Re-Conceptualizing Transnational Organized Crime: Offenders as Problem Solvers," *International Journal of Security and Terrorism*, vol. 2, no. 1 (2011), p. 9. (Hereafter: von Lampe, "Re-Conceptualizing.")

[100] Department of Justice, "Manhattan U.S. Attorney Charges 44 members and Associates of an Armenian-American Organized Crime Enterprise with $100 Million Medicare Fraud," press release, October 13, 2010, http://newyork.fbi.gov/dojpressrel/pressrel10/nyfo101310.htm. (Hereafter, DOJ press release, "Manhattan U.S. Attorney"; DOJ press release, "Seventy-Three Members.")

[101] DOJ press release, "Seventy-Three Members."

[102] Thomas Watkins, "Armenian Organized Crime Grows More Complex," *Associated Press*, October 16, 2010, http://news.yahoo.com/s/ap/20101016 /ap_on_re_us/us_armenian_ crime_2.

[103] In December 2011, one of the group's leaders, Robert Terdjanian, pled guilty to charges related to the case. See Bruce Golding, "Swan Song for Gangster," *New York Post,* December 20, 2011, http://www.nypost.com/p/news/local/ manhattan/swan_song_for_ gangster_T3KqaxeuQkAVNhHjioXmaJ.

[104] DOJ press release, "Manhattan U.S. Attorney."

[105] The indictment describes a thief-in-law as "a member of a select group of high-level criminal figures from Russia and the Former Soviet Union who receives tribute from other criminals, offers protection, and uses his recognized position of authority to resolve disputes among criminals, including through threats and instances of violence." See *United States vs. Armen Kazarian, Davit Mirzoyan, Robert Terdjanian, et al.*, Indictment in the U.S. District Court for the Southern District of New York, filed October 13, 2010, http://www.scribd.com/full/39274052?access_key=key7m8lpi9tq05hn86c111. (Hereafter, *United States vs. Armen Kazarian.*)

[106] Michael Wilson, William K. Rashbaum, "Real Patients, Real Doctors, Fake Everything Else," *New York Times*, October 13, 2010, http://www.nytimes.com/2010/10/14/nyregion /14fraud.html?_r=1&scp=1&sq= Real%20Patients,%20Real%20Doctors,%20Fake%20Everything%20Else&st=cse; *United States vs. Armen Kazarian.*

[107] Department of Justice, "Leader of Armenian Organized Crime Ring Pleads Guilty in Manhattan Federal Court to Racketeering," press release, July 8, 2011, http://www.justice.gov/usao/nys/pressreleases/July11/ kazarianarmenpleapr.pdf.

[108] *United States vs. Armen Kazarian.*

[109] Department of Justice, "Five Brothers Charged in Human Trafficking Scheme that Smuggled Young Ukrainian Migrants," press release, June 30, 2010, http://www.justice.gov/opa/pr/2010/June/10-crt-765.html; Nathan Gorenstein, "5 Brothers Charged with Human Trafficking," *Philadelphia Inquirer,* June 30, 2010, http://www.philly.com/philly/ news/breaking/97508149.html?cmpid=15585797; *United States v. Omelyan Botsvynyuk, et al,* Indictment in the U.S. District Court for the Eastern District of Pennsylvania, n.d. http://www.justice.gov/usao/pae/News/Pr/2010/Jun/ botsvynyuk_indictment.pdf. In October 2011, two of the brothers, Omelyan and Stepan Botsvynyuk, were convicted "of conspiracy to violate the Racketeer Influenced and Corrupt Organizations (RICO) Act in connection with a human trafficking scheme." At the time of the duo's trial, two other brothers were in Canada awaiting extradition and the remaining sibling was a fugitive. See Department of Justice, "Brothers Convicted in Human Trafficking Scheme," press release, October 12, 2011, http://www.fbi.gov/philadelphia/press-releases/2011/brothers-convicted-in-humantrafficking-scheme; Michael Matza, "Trial Set to Begin for Botsvynyuk Brothers in Human-Trafficking Case," *Philadelphia Inquirer,* September 13, 2011, http://articles.philly.com/2011-09-13/news/30149728_1_t-visa-programhuman-trafficking-immigrant-rights-groups.

[110] Federal Bureau of Investigation, "Leader of Asian Massage Parlor Scheme Sentenced for Coercing Prostitution, Money Laundering, Identity Theft," press release, October 14, 2009, http://kansascity.fbi.gov /dojpressrel/pressrel09/ kc101409.htm.

[111] IMMFWG, *Mass Marketing Fraud,* p. 15.

[112] Naím, *Illicit,* pp. 219-220. For a similar discussion that also cites Naím, see Juan Carlos Garzón, *Mafia & Co. The Criminal Networks in Mexico, Brazil, and Colombia*, (Washington, DC: Woodrow Wilson International

Center for Scholars, Latin American Program, English translation of 2008 Spanish ed., 2010) pp. 33-34. (Hereafter, Garzón, *Mafia & Co.*)

[113] Phil Williams, "Transnational Criminal Networks," in *Networks and Netwars*, ed. John Arquilla, David Ronfeldt (Santa Monica, CA: National Defenses Research Institute, RAND, 2002), pp. 77-78. (Hereafter: Williams, "Transnational Criminal Networks.")

[114] Scott H. Decker and Margaret Townsend Chapman, *Drug Smugglers on Drug Smuggling: Lessons from the Inside* (Philadelphia: Temple University Press, 2008), pp. 34-36.

[115] Stephen Aguilar-Millan et al., "The Globalization of Crime," *The Futurist*, November/December 2008, p. 42.

[116] Chatterjee, *The Changing Structure*. pp, 2, 7-8.

[117] Carlo Morselli, *Inside Criminal Networks* (New York: Springer, 2009), p. 71.

[118] Williams, "Transnational Criminal Networks," pp. 64-75.

[119] Mette Eilstrup-Sangiovanni and Calvert Jones, "Assessing the Dangers of Illicit Networks: Why al-Qaida May Be Less Threatening Than Many Think," *International Security*, Fall 2008, pp. 12-13.

[120] For networked structures among Colombian drug traffickers, see Michael Kenney, "The Architecture of Drug Trafficking," in *From Pablo to Osama: Trafficking and Terrorist Networks, Government Bureaucracies, and Competitive Adaptation* (University Park, PA: Pennsylvania State University Press, 2007), pp. 25-47. (Hereafter, Kenney, *From Pablo to Osama.*)

[121] National Gang Intelligence Center and National Drug Intelligence Center, *National Gang Threat Assessment, 2009*, January 2009, pp. 11-12, http://www.fbi.gov/publications /ngta2009.pdf.

[122] Ibid., p. 28. Barrio Azteca members are also involved in other crimes, such as extortion, kidnapping, and alien smuggling. For more information, see Tom Diaz, "Barrio Azteca—Border Boys Linked to Mexican Drug Trafficking Organizations—Part Three," April 17, 2009, http://tomdiaz.wordpress.com/2009/04/17/barrio-azteca%E2%80%93border-bad-boys-linked-to-mexican-drug-trafficking-organizations-%E2%80%94-part-three/. See also the Department of Justice website at http://www.usdoj.gov/criminal/gangunit /gangs /prison.html.

[123] Garzón, *Mafia & Co*. pp. 23-24.

[124] Intelligence Committee Futures Working Group, *Futures,* p. 2.

[125] Kenney, *From Pablo to Osama,* p. 132-133.

[126] Ibid.

[127] See the Omnibus Diplomatic Security and Antiterrorism Act of 1968, Title XII of P.L. 99-399. For more detailed information regarding the United States extraterritorial jurisdiction as well as the specific crimes included in this jurisdiction, see CRS Report 94-166, *Extraterritorial Application of American Criminal Law*, by Charles Doyle.

[128] Mette Eilstrup-Sangiovanni and Calvert Jones, "Assessing the Dangers of Illicit Networks: Why al-Qaida May Be Less Threatening Than Many Think," *International Security*, Fall 2008, pp. 16-33.

[129] von Lampe, "Re-Conceptualizing," p. 9.

[130] Ibid.

[131] CISC, *2010 Report,* p. 15, http://www.cisc.gc.ca/annual_reports/annual_report_ 2010/document/ report_oc_2010_e.pdf. See also Carlo Morselli and Cynthia Giguere, "Legitimate Strengths in Criminal Networks," *Crime, Law, and Social Change*, 2006, pp. 185-200.

[132] Tim McGlone, "Lawyer Sentenced for Part in Immigration Fraud Ring," *The Virginian-Pilot,* January 26, 2010; McGlone, "Belarus Man Gets 7 Years for Illegal Workers," *The Virginian-Pilot,* July 18, 2009, http://hamptonroads.com/2009/07/belarus-man-gets-7-years-illegal-workers; McGlone, "Prosecutors Tie Illegal Workers to International Crime Syndicate," *The Virginian-Pilot,* January 17, 2009; McGlone, "Illegal-Immigrant Network Supplied Region and Beyond," *The Virginian-Pilot,* January 14, 2009; Bureau of Immigration and Customs Enforcement, "22 Charged with Massive International Visa Scheme," press release, January 13, 2009. For similar examples involving Eurasian organized criminals, see Alexander Sukharenko, "The Use of Corruption by 'Russian' Organized Crime in the United States," *Trends in Organized Crime*, vol. 8, no. 2 (Winter 2004).

[133] Liz Benston, "As Baccarat Grows in Popularity, So Does Cheating," *Las Vegas Sun,* August 30, 2010, http://www.lasvegassun.com/news/2010/aug/30/baccarat-grows-popularity-so-does-cheating/.

[134] Department of Justice, "Former Mohegan Sun Card Dealer Sentenced to Prison for Involvement in Cheating Conspiracy," press release, April 7, 2010, http://newhaven.fbi.gov/dojpressrel/pressrel10/nh040710.htm; Department of Justice, "Leader of Casino-Cheating Criminal Enterprise Sentenced to 70 Months in Prison for Targeting Casinos Across the United States," press release, March 15, 2010, http://www.justice.gov/opa/pr/2010/March/10-crm-265.html.

[135] Department of Justice, "Eight More Individuals Charged in Casino-Cheating Conspiracy," press release, September 18, 2009, http://www.justice.gov/opa/pr/2009/September/09-crm-999.html.

[136] Department of Justice, "Tigard Man Pleads Guilty to Operating Illegal Money Transmitting Business," press release, March 1, 2011, http://www.justice.gov/usao/or /PressReleases/2011/20110301_Kaganov.html.

[137] Department of Justice, "Tigard Man Indicted in Connection with Illegal Money Transmitting Business Shell Corporations Created by Defendant to Move Millions of Dollars in and out of United States," press release, March 3, 2010, http://portland.fbi.gov/dojpressrel /pressrel10/pd030310.htm.

[138] Blair, "Annual Threat Assessment," p. 44.

[139] Gregory L. White and Diana Cimilluca, "Some Bankers Cool on Hot Rusal IPO," *Wall Street Journal*, November 9, 2009, http://online.wsj.com/article/NA_WSJ_PUB:SB1257 55269536534861.html. (Hereafter, White and Cimilluca, "Some Bankers.") Evan Perez, Gregory L. White, "FBI Lets Barred Tycoon Visit U.S.," October 30, 2009, http://online.wsj.com/article/NA_WSJ_PUB:SB125685578903317087.html. (Hereafter, Perez and White, "FBI Lets Barred Tycoon.")

[140] "The World's Billionaires: #9 Oleg Deripaska," *Forbes.com,* March 5, 2008, http://www.forbes.com/lists/2008 /10/ billionaires08_Oleg-Deripaska_UCP9.html.

[141] Perez and White, "FBI Lets Barred Tycoon."

[142] White and Cimilluca, "Some Bankers"; Perez and White, "FBI Lets Barred Tycoon."

[143] John Helmer, "Deripaska in 'Russian Mafia' Probe," *BusinessDay,* May 14, 2010, http://www.businessday.co.za/ articles/Content.aspx?id=108965; Misha Glenny, Robert Booth, and Tom Parfitt, "US Refused Oligarch Visa Over Alleged Criminal Associations," *The Guardian*, October 31, 2008, http://www.guardian.co.uk/world/2008/oct/31/olegderipaska-us-visa-rusal.

[144] White and Cimilluca, "Some Bankers."

[145] "Aluminum giant RusAl raises $2.24 bln with Hong Kong IPO," *RIA Novosti*, January 22, 2010, http://en.rian.ru/ business/20100122/157651607.html.

[146] Neil Gough, "Triads Thrive in Ho's Casinos, US Report Says," *South China Morning Post*, March 19, 2010. Alexandra Berzon and A.D. Pruitt, "MGM Mirage Knew Ally Was Unfit," *Wall Street Journal,* March 17, 2010, http://online.wsj.com/article/SB100014240527487047 43404575127673757750744.html.

[147] Formerly MGM Mirage.

[148] Tom Mitchell, "Spotlight on MGM Mirage's 'Wild Card," *Financial Times*, March 19, 2010.

[149] State of New Jersey Department of Law and Public Safety, *Special Report of the Division of Gaming Enforcement to the Casino Control Commission on Its Investigation of MGM Mirage's Joint Venture with Pansy Ho in Macau, Special Administrative Region, People's Republic of China,* Redacted, May 18, 2009, p. 1, http://www.state.nj.us/ casinos/home/info/docs/MGM/dge_%20report_redacted.pdf. (Hereafter, DGE, "Report.")

[150] DGE, "Report," pp. 70-71.

[151] DGE, "Report," p. 71.

[152] Wayne Parry, "NJ: Asian Casino Boss Has Mob Ties in China," *Associated Press*, March 17, 2010.

[153] Department of Justice, "Three More Sentenced as Part of Bureau of Motor Vehicle Fraud Ring," press release, August, 19, 2010, http://cleveland.fbi.gov/dojpressrel/pressrel10 /cl081910a.htm; Patrick O'Donnell, "Parma Clerk Issued Illegal Licenses, FBI Charges," *Cleveland Plain Dealer,* October 30, 2009.

[154] Ceci Connolly, "The Inside Woman," *Washington Post*, September 12, 2010, http://www.washingtonpost.com /wpdyn/content/article/2010/09/11/AR2010091105087.html. (Hereafter, Connolly, "The Inside Woman.")

[155] See testimony by Thomas M. Frost, Assistant Inspector General for Investigations, U.S. Department of Homeland Security before the U.S. Congress, Senate Committee on Homeland Security and Governmental Affairs, Ad Hoc Subcommittee on State, Local, and Private Sector Preparedness and Integration, *New Border War: Corruption of U.S. Officials by Drug Cartels*, 111th Cong., 1st sess., March 11, 2010.

[156] See testimony by James F. Tomsheck, Assistant Commissioner, Office of Internal Affairs, Customs and Border Protection before the U.S. Congress, Senate Committee on Homeland Security and Governmental Affairs, Ad Hoc Subcommittee on State, Local, and Private Sector Preparedness and Integration, *New Border War: Corruption of U.S. Officials by Drug Cartels*, 111th Cong., 1st sess., March 11, 2010.

[157] Immigration and Customs Enforcement, "Ex-CBP Employee Receives 20 Years in Drug, Alien Smuggling, Corruption Case," press release, August 26, 2010, http://www.ice.gov/pi/nr/1008/100826elpaso.htm.

[158] Connolly, "The Inside Woman."

[159] Department of Justice, "Former CBP Officer Sentenced to Prison for Bribery, Cocaine Trafficking, and Alien Smuggling," press release, March 31, 2010, http://sanantonio.fbi.gov/dojpressrel/pressrel10/sa033110.htm.

[160] Remarks by DOJ officials at the National Institute of Justice Conference 2010, panel on International Organized Crime: Recent Developments in Policy and Research, June 14, 2010. For this report, "public security threat" means threats to people, businesses, or property, and "national security threat" means threats to government, sovereignty, and economic stability. This differentiation is based on John Bailey, *Combating Organized Crime and Drug Trafficking in Mexico: What Are Mexican and U.S. Strategies? Are they Working?* Woodrow Wilson International Center For Scholars, Mexico Institute and University of San Diego Trans-Border Institute, Working Paper Series on U.S.-Mexico Security Cooperation, Washington, DC, May 2010, p. 3, fn. 2, http://wilsoncenter.org/topics/pubs/ Combating%20Organized%20Crime.%20Bailey.pdf.

[161] FBI, "Top Ten Fugitives: Global Con Artist and Ruthless Criminal," October 21, 2009, http://www.fbi.gov/page2/ oct09/mogilevich_102109.html. (Hereafter: FBI, "Global Con Artist.")

[162] FBI, "Philadelphia Fugitive Placed on the FBI's 'Ten Most Wanted Fugitives' List," press release, October 21, 2009, http://philadelphia.fbi.gov/pressrel/pressrel09/ph102109a.htm. Jeanne Meserve, "FBI: Mobster More Powerful than Gotti," *CNN*, October 24, 2009, http://articles.cnn.com/2009-10-21/justice/mogilevich.fbi.most. wanted_1_fbiwire-fraud-semion-mogilevich?_s=PM:CRIME.

[163] Williams, "Transnational Criminal Networks," p. 70.

[164] FBI, "Global Con Artist;" Attorney General Michael B. Mukasey, "Attorney General Michael B. Mukasey Delivers Remarks at the CSIS Forum on Combating International Organized Crime," April 23, 2008, *Political/Congressional Transcript Wire.*

[165] "Russian Court Releases Reputed Crime Boss," *The Associated Press,* July 27, 2009.

[166] This report focuses on U.S. agency and federal statutory definitions of organized crime. For a discussion of scholarly definitions, see CRS Report R40525, *Organized Crime in the United States: Trends and Issues for Congress*, by Kristin M. Finklea.

[167] *Strategy to Combat Transnational Organized Crime,* p. 5.

[168] *Strategy to Combat Transnational Organized Crime,* p. ii. This definition originally appeared in Department of Justice, *Overview of the Law Enforcement Strategy to Combat International Organized Crime*, April 2008, p. 2, http://www.justice.gov /ag/speeches/2008/ioc-strategy-public-overview.pdf.

[169] von Lampe, "Re-Conceptualizing," pp. 4-5, discusses the "nature of what crosses the border." This is subsumed by product provenance in this report. von Lampe also describes "directionality," which is part of supply chain complexity in this report.

[170] The product that a TOC group moves across borders should also likely factor in the threat it poses to national security. A group trafficking firearms may pose a higher threat to national security than an alien smuggling organization or vise versa. How the strategy ranks these threats is unclear.

[171] *Strategy to Combat Transnational Organized Crime,* p. 3.

[172] *Strategy to Combat Transnational Organized Crime,* pp. 5-8.

[173] Ibid. "Facilitators" are "semi-legitimate players such as accountants, attorneys, notaries, bankers, and real estate brokers, who cross both the licit and illicit worlds and provide services to legitimate customers, criminals, and terrorists alike." See Ibid., p. 8.

[174] Ibid., p. 1.

[175] Executive Order 13581, "Blocking Property of Transnational Criminal Organizations," 76 *Federal Register* 44757- 44759, July 24, 2011.

[176] *Strategy to Combat Transnational Organized Crime,* p. 1.

[177] The four TOC groups are the Brothers' Circle, Camorra, Yakuza, and Los Zetas.

[178] Omnibus Crime Control and Safe Streets Act of 1968, as amended (P.L. 90-351).

[179] 18 U.S.C. § 1961-1968. It was enacted as Title IX of the Organized Crime Control Act of 1970 (P.L. 91- 452).

[180] As defined in 18 U.S.C. § 1961, an "'enterprise' includes any individual, partnership, corporation, association, or other legal entity, and any union or group of individuals associated ... although not [necessarily] a legal entity," and a "'pattern of racketeering activity' requires at least two acts of racketeering activity" to occur within 10 years of one another for a criminal organization to be prosecuted for racketeering. Racketeering is defined as any number of violations, including an act or threat involving murder, kidnapping, gambling, arson, robbery, bribery, extortion, or dealing in a controlled substance. See 18 U.S.C. § 1961 for a comprehensive list of the predicate offenses for racketeering.

[181] Frank E. Hagan, "'Organized Crime' and 'organized crime' Indeterminate Problems of Definition," *Trends in Organized Crime,* vol. 9, no. 4 (Summer 2006), p. 127. See also James O. Finkenauer, "Problems of Definition: What Is Organized Crime?" *Trends in Organized Crime,* vol. 8, no. 3 (Spring 2005), pp. 63-83.

[182] 18 U.S.C. § 1961-1968. It was enacted as Title IX of the Organized Crime Control Act of 1970 (P.L. 91- 452).

[183] As defined in 18 U.S.C. § 1961, an "'enterprise' includes any individual, partnership, corporation, association, or other legal entity, and any union or group of individuals associated ... although not [necessarily] a legal entity," and a "'pattern of racketeering activity' requires at least two acts of racketeering activity" to occur within 10 years of one another for a criminal organization to be prosecuted for racketeering. Racketeering is defined as any number of violations, including an act or threat involving murder, kidnapping, gambling, arson, robbery, bribery, extortion, or dealing in a controlled substance. See 18 U.S.C. § 1961 for a comprehensive list of the predicate offenses for racketeering.

[184] Some may consider 18 U.S.C. § 1951-1968 (Chapters 95 and 96, Racketeering and RICO, respectively) to be a primary portion of the Code addressing organized crime.

[185] U.S. Department of Justice, "Statement of Assistant Attorney General Lanny A. Breuer Before the Senate Judiciary Subcommittee on Crime and Terrorism," press release, November 1, 2011, http://www.justice.gov/criminal/pr/ testimony/2011/crm-testimony-111101.html.

[186] International Peace Institute, *Transnational Organized Crime: Task Forces on Multilateral Security Capacity*, IPI Blue Papers No. 2, 2009, http://www.ipinst.org/media /pdf/publications/toc_final.pdf. (Hereafter, IPI, *Transnational Organized Crime.*)

[187] For more information on COPS, see CRS Report RL33308, *Community Oriented Policing Services (COPS): Background and Funding*, by Nathan James as well as CRS Report R40709, *Community Oriented Policing Services (COPS): Current Legislative Issues*, by Nathan James.

[188] For more information on JAG, see CRS Report RS22416, *Edward Byrne Memorial Justice Assistance Grant (JAG) Program*, by Nathan James.

[189] IPI, *Transnational Organized Crime.*

[190] Peer review systems are used in a variety of academic, professional, and government settings to evaluate an individual or organization's work or policies. The work or policies are open to examination by other experts and equivalent entities. For instance, the Office of Management and Budget (OMB) has promulgated guidelines for federal regulatory agencies to follow peer review requirements prior to disseminating influential scientific and statistical information. See Office of Management and Budget, "Guidelines for Ensuring and Maximizing the Quality, Objectivity, Utility, and Integrity of Information Disseminated by Federal Agencies; Republication," Vol. 67, No. 36, *Federal Register*, February 22, 2002.

[191] For a discussion of federal law enforcement efforts to combat organized crime, see CRS Report R40525, *Organized Crime in the United States: Trends and Issues for Congress*, by Kristin M. Finklea.

[192] In the FY2011 Budget Request, the Administration requests an additional $15.0 million for the Department of Justice to combat organized crime. $7.6 million of this is requested for funding DOJ staffing of the IOC-2. There were no specific funds requested for the other agencies contributing to the IOC-2.

[193] NCTC mission statement, available at http://www.nctc.gov/about_us/about_nctc.html.

[194] Ryan J. Reilly, "Gang Unit, Organized Crime Section to Merge," *Main Justice*, July 12, 2010.

[195] Department of Justice, Office of the Inspector General, *Review of the Drug Enforcement Administration's El Paso Intelligence Center*, I-2010-005, June 2010, pp. ii - iii, http://www.justice.gov/oig/reports /DEA/a1005.pdf.

[196] Department of Justice, Office of the Inspector General, *A Review of the Department's Anti-Gang Intelligence and Coordination Centers*, I-2010-001, November 2009, http://www.justice.gov/oig/reports/FBI/i2010001.pdf.

In: Organized Crime
Editors: F. B. Hall and F. C. Martin

ISBN: 978-1-62618-415-2

Chapter 2

ORGANIZED RETAIL CRIME*

Kristin M. Finklea

SUMMARY

Organized retail crime (ORC) involves the large-scale theft of everyday consumer items and potentially has much broader implications. Organized groups of professional shoplifters, or "boosters," steal or fraudulently obtain merchandise that is then sold, or "fenced," to individuals and retailers through a variety of venues. In an increasingly globalized society, more and more transactions take place online rather than face-to-face. As such, in addition to relying on physical resale markets, organized retail thieves have turned to online marketplaces as means to fence their ill-gotten goods.

ORC exposes the United States to costs and harms in the economic, public health, and domestic security arenas. The exact loss from ORC to the retail industry is unknown, but estimates have ranged from $15 billion to $37 billion annually. The economic impact, however, extends beyond the manufacturing and retail industry and includes costs incurred by consumers and taxes lost by the states. The theft and resale of stolen consumable or health and beauty products such as infant formula (that may have been repackaged, relabeled, and subjected to altered expiration dates) poses potential safety concerns for individuals purchasing such goods from ORC fences. In addition, some industry experts and policy makers have expressed concern about the possibility that proceeds from ORC may be used to fund terrorist activities.

Current efforts to combat ORC largely come from retailers, online marketplaces, and law enforcement alike. Retailers responding to the 2010 National Retail Security Survey spent an average of 0.46% of their annual sales on loss prevention measures. These loss prevention costs are ultimately borne by consumers in the form of higher prices on goods. Also, online marketplaces report taking various measures to combat the sale of stolen and fraudulently obtained goods on their websites, including educating sellers and consumers, monitoring suspicious activity, and partnering with retailers and law enforcement. Combating retail theft has traditionally been handled by state law enforcement under state criminal laws. Some, however, have begun to question whether state laws—which vary

---

* This is an edited, reformatted and augmented version of a Congressional Research Service publication, CRS Report for Congress R41118, prepared for Members and Committees of Congress, from www.crs.gov, dated December 11, 2012.

in the quantity of monetary losses that constitute major theft—are adequate to combat ORC.

While many agree that ORC is a national problem, there is debate over the federal government's role in deterring ORC and sanctioning various actors that may be involved in committing or aiding these crimes. One policy issue facing Congress is whether criminalizing organized retail crime in the *U.S. Code* would allow for more effective investigation and prosecution of these criminals. Congress may also wish to consider whether regulating resale marketplaces (online markets, in particular), to require such entities to increase information sharing with retailers and law enforcement, would strengthen investigations and prosecutions of ORC as well as decrease the prevalence of retail thieves relying on legitimate online marketplaces to fence stolen goods.

INTRODUCTION

Organized retail crime (ORC), often referred to as organized retail theft, typically refers to large-scale retail theft and fraud by organized groups of professional shoplifters, or "boosters."[1] It is an umbrella term encompassing a variety of retail crimes, including theft, gift card fraud, receipt fraud, ticket switching,[2] and cargo theft, just to name a few. Stolen and fraudulently obtained goods may be taken not only from retailers, but from manufacturers and distributors as well. The organized crime rings resell this illegally acquired merchandise via a variety of "fencing" operations such as flea markets, swap meets, pawn shops, and online marketplaces; these goods are sold to both individual buyers as well as retailers—potentially the very retailers from where the merchandise was originally stolen. ORC differs fundamentally from shoplifting in that amateur shoplifters tend to steal merchandise for personal consumption. Boosters, on the other hand, are professional thieves who make money by stealing merchandise from retail and other venues and reselling it to fences who in turn sell the goods—through legal or illegal economic outlets—for a fraction of the retail cost.

Organized retail crime exposes the United States to economic, public health, and domestic security dangers. It is a national problem, not only for retailers, but for manufacturers, consumers, taxpayers, and the states as well. According to one industry survey, about 96% of retailers surveyed in 2012 reported having been victimized by ORC in the previous 12 months. This is an increase from the about 90% that reported victimization in 2010 and the nearly 95% that reported victimization in 2011.[3] Estimates of retail losses to ORC range from as low as $15 billion to as high as $37 billion annually.[4] And this is the loss to retailers alone. The monetary loss, however, extends beyond the retail industry to the taxpayers and states. Consumers pay for these losses in the form of higher prices on goods, and states lose the tax revenue that would otherwise be generated from the sale of these goods by legitimate retailers.

In addition to the economic impact of ORC, the theft and resale of stolen consumable or health and beauty products, such as infant formula, may pose safety risks to individuals purchasing such goods from ORC fences. This is because such products may have been repackaged, relabeled, subjected to altered expiration dates, or stored improperly before being reentered into commerce. In addition, industry experts, law enforcement, and policy makers have expressed concern about the possibility that proceeds from ORC may be used to fund terrorist activities.[5] In particular, federal law enforcement has reputedly traced the illicit proceeds from the theft and resale of infant formula to terrorist organizations and insurgent groups, including Hamas and Hezbollah.[6]

Combating retail theft has traditionally been handled by state law enforcement under state criminal laws.[7] Some, however, have begun to question whether state laws—which vary in the quantity of monetary losses that constitute major theft—are adequate to combat ORC. While many agree that ORC is a national problem, there is debate over the federal government's role in deterring ORC and sanctioning various actors that may be involved in committing or aiding these crimes. One policy issue facing Congress is whether criminalizing organized retail crime in the *U.S. Code* would allow for more effective investigation and prosecution of these criminals. Another related issue that Congress may wish to consider is whether regulating resale marketplaces (online markets, in particular), to require such entities to increase information sharing with retailers and law enforcement, would strengthen investigations and prosecutions of ORC as well as decrease the prevalence of retail thieves relying on legitimate online marketplaces to fence stolen goods.

This report provides an overview of organized retail crime rings, their operations, and goods targeted. It then examines the domestic impact of ORC in the arenas of the economy, public health and safety, and domestic security. The report also outlines current efforts by retailers, resale markets, and the federal government to combat ORC. It then analyzes various policy issues that Congress may wish to consider, including whether current federal resources provided for the investigation of ORC are adequate, whether to amend the *U.S. Code* to criminalize ORC, and whether to regulate resale marketplaces that may be utilized as fences for criminals to sell stolen goods.

CHALLENGES IN DEFINING ORGANIZED RETAIL CRIME

The concept of organized retail crime tends to be discussed in terms of criminal networks engaged in large-scale theft. Descriptions of ORC also generally entail criminals fraudulently obtaining goods in quantities beyond what would normally be intended for personal consumption; reselling these ill-gotten goods; receiving, concealing, transporting, or disposing of these goods; or coordinating individuals to commit these retail crimes.[8] There is a lack of consensus, however, on the specific activities—particularly of boosters—that constitute ORC. On the one hand, most agree that ORC involves store theft or fraud schemes designed to obtain retail merchandise at a cost significantly below retail value or for free.

However, some also include specific activities, such as cargo theft,[9] in the definition of ORC,[10] while others either omit certain activities or do not specify the range of ORC activities.[11] For example, federal law enforcement agencies, such as the Federal Bureau of Investigation (FBI), tend to constrain discussions of ORC to situations in which boosters steal merchandise from retail establishments and resell it for profit. Similarly, retail organizations have generally focused on store theft when describing the problem of ORC. One possible explanation for this focus on store theft is that, although ORC may encompass multiple activities, including store theft and cargo theft, store theft has been cited as the most common.[12] Because retail organizations, scholars, industry experts, and law enforcement have provided varying definitions of ORC, this complicates analysts' abilities to evaluate the exact impact of ORC.[13]

Federal Definition

Currently, ORC is not a federal crime. Issues surrounding the debate over whether it should be included in the federal criminal code are analyzed later in this report. For data collection purposes, however, Congress has defined ORC as

- violating a state ban against shoplifting or retail merchandise theft—if the quantities of items stolen are of the amount that would not normally be purchased for personal use or consumption—and stealing for the purposes of reselling the items or reentering them into commerce;
- receiving, possessing, concealing, bartering, selling, transporting, or disposing of any property that is known to have been taken in the violation outlined above; or
- coordinating, organizing, or recruiting persons to undertake either of the two violations outlined above.[14]

Operation of Organized Retail Crime Groups

As mentioned, organized retail crime rings generally include individuals serving in one of two main capacities: boosters or fences. Generally, boosters act as professional shoplifters who steal or illegally obtain merchandise. Fences pay boosters for stolen goods and then resell them to witting or unwitting consumers and businesses.

Boosters work either alone or in groups to steal goods that they will later sell to fences for about 10% to 25% of the ticket value.[15] They often carry "fence sheets," or shopping lists provided to boosters by fences. These shopping lists itemize the goods fences desire, the amounts fences will pay for each item, and retail store locations where each item may be.[16] In some cases, boosters may travel across state lines to target specific establishments in multiple states. Consequently, many boosters will at some point transport stolen merchandise across state lines, either when shipping stolen goods to a fence or when physically delivering merchandise to a fence after stealing it in another state.

Fencing operations can be very straightforward or can involve multiple stages and a degree of operational sophistication. Most stolen merchandise is sold to a low-level fence, commonly called a "street fence." Street fences will either sell these goods directly to the public—through flea markets, swap meets, or the Internet—or will sell the merchandise to mid-level fences who run "cleaning operations." Cleaning operations remove security tags and store labels as well as repackage stolen goods so they appear as though they came directly from the manufacturer. A notable concern for public health and safety, this cleaning process may even involve changing the expiration date on perishable goods.[17] The "clean" goods may then be sold to the public or to higher-level fences, who often operate illegitimate wholesale businesses. Through these businesses, the fences can supply merchandise to retailers, often mixing stolen merchandise with legitimate goods. The illegal activities of fences may be of concern for policy makers and federal law enforcement because—like boosters—fences' activities may cross state lines. They may, for instance, purchase stolen goods from boosters in one state and send them to another state to be cleaned; they may then sell this "clean" merchandise to illegitimate wholesalers in another state. In addition, fences selling goods via online marketplaces may ship stolen goods across state or national lines.

Targeted Products

Investigations of organized retail crime rings have uncovered a wide variety of goods targeted to be stolen and resold on the black market. One researcher has noted that CRAVED items (meaning those goods that are Concealable, Removable, Available, Valuable, Enjoyable, and Disposable) are more often targeted because of the ease with which criminals can remove these items from stores and convert them into cash or other valuables.[18] On the one hand, some desirable—or "hot"[19]—products, such as cigarettes and alcohol, may always be popular products for thieves. The desirability of other products may be based on their current popularity (such as new movies, video games, and music titles) or on their use in drug manufacturing activities (such as ephedrine-based cold medications and lithium batteries). In addition, the popularity of products may also be brand-specific. For example, while certain brands of razor blades, printer cartridges, and designer clothing may be frequently targeted for theft, competing brands may be ignored.[20] Desirable products, in no specific order, include

- grocery items (cigarettes, energy drinks, high-end liquor, and infant formula);
- over-the-counter medicines (allergy medicine, diabetic testing strips, pain relievers, and weight loss pills);
- health and beauty items (electronic toothbrushes, lotions/creams, and pregnancy tests);
- clothing (designer brands, denim, and handbags);
- electronics (cell phones, digital cameras and recorders, GPS devices, laptops, televisions, and LCD monitors); and
- home goods (high-end vacuums and Kitchen Aid mixers).[21]

Methods Used by Boosters

Boosters working in groups rather than alone often have at least one member of the group act as a lookout who scouts for employees, plain clothes security officers, or cameras. These lookouts may create diversions or distract employees to facilitate the work of the boosters actually stealing the merchandise.[22]

To help prevent thieves from stealing these goods, many retailers place electronic detection tags on merchandise. Boosters often circumvent detection systems by cutting off or melting the tags, covering the tags in foil or concealing the merchandise in foil-lined bags (often referred to as "magic" bags), or lifting goods over the antennas of the electronic detection systems.[23] In some instances, boosters take shopping bags directly from the store, fill them with merchandise, and walk out of the store, appearing as though they are carrying purchased goods. Store employees may be less likely to stop and question boosters carrying shopping bags from the store because they incorrectly assume that the merchandise has indeed been paid for.[24]

In addition, boosters do not always steal merchandise from retailers during business hours. Some may hide in stores and wait for all employees to leave before removing large amounts of goods through emergency exits. Others conduct "smash-and-grab" burglaries, in which they steal trucks and vans to ram through store walls and windows, load the vehicles with merchandise, and drive away.[25]

Employee Collusion

At times, boosters also conspire with current or former store employees. Employees may take goods from storage rooms or receiving areas in stores and provide them directly to boosters. They may also help thieves by disabling store alarms, leaving doors unlocked, or providing information about computer passwords, alarm codes, keys, and management and security schedules.[26] Industry studies estimated the proportion of inventory loss due to employee theft.[27] However, it is currently unknown how often employee theft or fraud is directly implicated in cases of organized retail crime. For example the 2010 National Retail Security Survey reports that retailers estimate about 45% of retail losses are due to employee theft. They further estimate that slightly over 18% of these internal losses involve employees colluding with individuals outside of the given retail store. Of this 18% of internal loss cases, an unknown proportion may be attributed to employees working with organized retail criminals.[28]

Fraud Schemes

Not all organized retail crime involves traditional theft from retail stores. ORC groups have employed numerous tactics to defraud retailers and obtain merchandise. In receipt fraud, for example, thieves steal merchandise, create counterfeit receipts for the stolen goods, return these stolen goods to the retailers using the counterfeit receipts, and collect money off of the fraudulent returns.[29] This cuts out the fence altogether, potentially netting a higher return.

Another method by which ORC groups defraud retailers is through gift card fraud, of which there are several forms. For one, thieves may purchase legitimate gift cards using stolen credit cards and then sell the gift cards to the highest bidder using an online auction website. In other instances, thieves may purchase low-value gift cards, electronically reprogram the cards to contain a higher value, and resell these reprogrammed cards.[30]

Similarly, ORC thieves may use ticket-switching scams to fraudulently obtain high-value items at a relatively low cost. Thieves use devices that create fake barcodes that they adhere to packages, covering the original barcodes; when scanned, these new barcodes ring up the items at lower costs. If, at check-out, a retail employee scanning the barcodes is not paying close attention or does not have a strong knowledge of items' values, the thief may get away with paying the price indicated by the counterfeit barcode. Criminals can then resell, or fence, the goods at prices higher than those which they paid, but still lower than their retail values.[31]

Cargo Theft

As mentioned, some scholars and experts include cargo theft as an element of organized retail crime while others do not. It is nonetheless of value to note how retail goods are vulnerable to criminals at various points throughout the supply chain. Further, goods that are stolen from either cargo trucks or from retail stores may be fenced by criminals for a profit, and both affect society's economy, public health, and domestic security.

Because trains and trucks of cargo often travel with large quantities of desirable products, some have suggested that this presents a low-risk, high-reward situation appealing to criminals.[32] Thieves use a variety of methods to obtain merchandise from cargo, from hijacking entire trucks to colluding with current or former employees. These criminals may break or compromise security locks on trucks (possibly with the aid of security codes provided by dishonest employees) to remove entire boxes of desired goods. Other times, they may pilfer cargo boxes of their goods and then reseal them so the boxes appear as though they have not been tampered with.[33]

Researchers have begun studying how cargo theft—under the broader context of ORC—impacts retailers. According to the National Retail Federation's 2012 survey on ORC, over half of the survey respondents (52.1%) reported being a victim of cargo theft within the past year. Most of these thefts occurred en route from the distribution center to the store (68.1%)."[34] Other cargo thefts, however, occurred en route from the manufacturer to the distribution center, at the distribution center, at the store, and en route from one store to another.

Methods Used by Fences

Fences use various methods to sell stolen goods that they purchase from boosters. As mentioned, some fences may sell stolen merchandise back to retailers through illegitimate wholesale operations. They may also operate legitimate businesses, such as pawn shops, convenience stores, repair shops, second-hand stores, and salvage yards, that serve as fronts for their illegal fencing operations.[35] In addition, fences may sell their goods at a variety of resale marketplaces, including flea markets. At flea markets, illegitimate wholesalers are able to sell stolen goods that have been damaged and cannot be resold to retailers. Also, flea markets have been known to serve as recruiting grounds for fences looking for boosters, and vice-versa.[36]

Impact of Globalization and Technology

In an increasingly globalized society, more and more transactions take place online rather than face-to-face. As such, in addition to relying on physical resale markets, organized retail thieves have turned to the Internet and online marketplaces as means to fence their ill-gotten goods.[37] This practice of fencing via the Internet is commonly referred to as "e-fencing." According to the most recent National Retail Federation survey of retailers, 73.4% of surveyed retailers indicated that they had identified or recovered stolen merchandise (including gift cards) that was being fenced online.[38]

E-fencing has affected organized retail crime in several arenas, including criminal anonymity, global reach, and profitability. Whereas criminals fencing goods at physical locations (such as flea markets) must have face-to-face interactions, those who rely on e-fencing are better able to remain anonymous to customers, victimized retailers, and law enforcement alike. Further, the use of online markets has allowed criminals to more easily distribute stolen goods not only within the metropolitan areas where they were originally obtained, but throughout the United States and across the globe. E-fencing has also proven to be more profitable to criminals than has fencing at physical locations; while criminals may profit about 30 cents on the dollar (30% of the retail price) by selling goods at physical fencing locations, they can make about 70 cents on the dollar via e-fencing.[39]

It has been suggested that the face-to-face nature of physical marketplaces allows consumers to recognize the questionable legality of goods, and thus consumers are willing to pay less for goods in these physical markets than online.[40]

Domestic Impact of Organized Retail Crime

At first glance, the impact of organized retail crime may appear to be limited to monetary losses to retailers. The economic impact, however, extends beyond the manufacturing and retail industry and affects costs incurred by consumers and taxes lost by the states. Beyond the economic impact, the theft of stolen consumable or health and beauty products may pose safety risks to individuals purchasing such goods from ORC fences. In addition, some industry experts and policy makers have expressed concern about the possibility that proceeds from ORC may be used to fund terrorist activities.

Economic Impact: A Lack of Consensus

The exact loss from organized retail crime to the retail industry is unknown.[41] An often-cited estimate of this loss is $15 billion to $30 billion annually.[42] The original source of this figure, however, has not been identified; while the FBI cites this figure as coming from retail industry estimates,[43] industry experts cite the FBI.[44] As of 2007, the FBI revised the estimated annual loss from ORC and placed it between $30 billion and $37 billion.[45] Of note, these ranges are broad estimates, and it is not precisely evident what the estimated loss includes. On one hand, it may include only the retail value of the merchandise stolen. Alternatively, it may include collateral costs, such as replacement costs or costs for implementing and maintaining various loss prevention measures.

Another unanswered question is whether estimates of losses from ORC include or overlap with estimates of losses from cargo theft. The FBI estimates that cargo theft costs $15 billion to $30 billion annually in the United States[46] and notes that it is a growing crime.[47] It is not specified, however, what proportion—if any—of cargo theft losses may be attributed to ORC groups. Other estimates have placed the losses from cargo theft at $30 billion to $50 billion annually, with about half of these losses (roughly $15 billion to $25 billion annually) attributed to ORC.[48] If these data are correct, it suggests that the FBI's estimate of cargo theft losses may be largely attributed to either the proportion of cargo theft committed by ORC groups or the proportion of cargo theft not committed by ORC groups. Another explanation may be that industry estimates of losses may differ from law enforcement estimates based on differing criteria for counting an incident as a loss.

The National Retail Security Survey (NRSS) collects data on the levels and causes of inventory "shrinkage"—the reduction in physical inventory caused by shoplifting, employee and vendor theft, and administrative error—as well as data on loss prevention budgets, personnel, and strategies, and responses to shoplifting and employee theft.[49] For the retail sectors surveyed by the NRSS, total sales for 2010 were estimated at over $2.374 trillion[50]—54% of the more than $4.4 trillion annual sales estimated for the entire retail industry.[51]

As outlined in the NRSS, not all retailers are equally susceptible to "shrinkage," and therefore, the NRSS surveys only those sectors that are able to generate "shrinkage" data.[52] Therefore, any conclusions drawn from the NRSS are only generalizable to those retail sectors included in the survey—comprising about 54% of total retail sales.

As illustrated in *Figure 1*, data from the 2010 NRSS indicate that total inventory shrinkage costs amounted to about $35.3 billion in 2010.[53] Of this shrinkage, theft (both internal/employee theft and shoplifting) cost retailers about $26.8 billion. In other words, theft accounted for about 76% of overall 2010 shrinkage.[54] Within the broad category of theft, internal/employee theft accounted for about $15.9 billion in losses to retailers, and shoplifting led to about $10.9 billion in losses. As mentioned, although retailers estimate that over 18% of internal theft cases involve collusion with outsiders, it is unknown what proportion (if any) of these involve collusion with organized retail crime groups.

Costs to retailers participating in the 2010 National Retail Security Survey

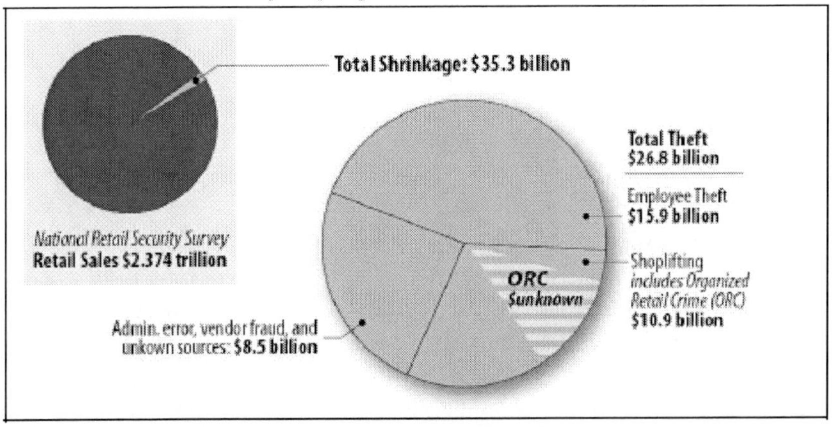

Source: CRS presentation of data from the 2010 National Retail Security Survey Final Report. Graphic prepared by CRS Graphics.

Note: This does not include losses to ORC as a result of cargo theft.

Figure 1. 2010 Retail Shrinkage Costs.

As a direct result of retailers' losses to ORC, retailers may take various measures to strengthen retail security and mitigate any financial deficit from the lost revenue. In order to increase merchandise security, prevent future losses, and recoup the lost profits from the retail crime, retailers take measures such as hiring additional loss prevention personnel or increasing the price of goods. These costs are then borne by consumers. The price increase may result in some consumers declining to purchase a given product, which may then have a circular effect and result in a loss in sales (and revenue) for the retailers. Retailers may also lock up "hot" products, which, in addition to making the products harder to steal, makes it more difficult for consumers to find and purchase the merchandise. In other cases, the products are simply not available for the customer to purchase because the entire inventory of the product has been stolen.[55]

In addition to the cost of organized retail crime to retailers and consumers, ORC can negatively affect state tax revenue. When goods are stolen rather than purchased, the state does not collect sales tax on the merchandise. The Food Marketing Institute (on behalf of the Coalition Against Organized Retail Crime) estimated that for 2007, the loss of sales tax revenue across the United States totaled about $1.6 billion.[56]

Public Health and Safety Risks

Several of the goods targeted by organized retail crime groups are consumable items or health and beauty products—infant formula, diabetic test strips, and over-the-counter and prescription medications, to name a few. There are public health and safety issues associated with the theft and resale of this merchandise by ORC rings. For instance, after boosters steal perishable goods, these goods may be sold to fencing operations that "clean" the products; as mentioned, this cleaning process may involve repackaging goods (sometimes incorrectly relabeling them) and altering expiration dates before selling the merchandise back to retailers or to the general public. Further, these goods may be stored for indefinite periods of time in trucks or warehouses that are not climate-controlled. These factors may pose risks to the health of people who consume perishable goods that they believe to be safe, but have actually been tampered with or expired.

Potential Links to Terrorism

In addition to the economic and potential public health risks associated with ORC, law enforcement and policy makers have expressed concern that proceeds from organized retail crime may be used to finance terrorist activities.[57] In fact, federal concern over the link between ORC and terrorism was present even before the terrorist attacks of September 11, 2001.[58] Federal law enforcement has traced the illicit proceeds from retail crime, specifically from the theft and resale of infant formula, to terrorist organizations and insurgent groups, including Hamas and Hezbollah.[59] For instance, following the terrorist attacks of 2001, the former U.S. Customs Service established Operation Green Quest—a now-defunct, multi-agency terrorist financing task force—to combat the various sources of terrorist financing; one such source was identified as the "theft, adulteration, and resale of infant formula."[60]

While there may be suspicions that profits from ORC rings have been sent to certain countries to support terrorist activities, it is important to note that no members of ORC rings discussed in the organized retail crime literature have been convicted of providing material support to terrorist organizations. Nevertheless, there are instances in which profits—often from the sale of stolen infant formula—have been transferred to certain countries known to support terrorists, though it has not been determined whether these profits have ultimately been transferred to terrorist organizations.

Three notable investigations of large organized retail crime rings uncovered evidence that the ORC ringleaders had transferred profits from their fencing operations to several countries known to support terrorists. In one case, an investigation into the Jamal Trading Company in Phoenix, AZ, uncovered a money-laundering operation that allegedly funneled the illicit proceeds to countries where several members of the crime ring had ties, such as Iraq, Jordan, and Lebanon. The ringleader, Samih Fadl Jamal, and 15 co-conspirators had been profiting on the sale of stolen infant formula worth $22 million.[61] Another case involved the Ghali organized retail crime ring, led by Mohammed Khalil Ghali, which was involved in the sale of stolen infant formula and other "hot" products, as well as the laundering of the proceeds. An investigation into the Ghali organization found that some of the profits were wired to financial institutions in Jordan, Egypt, and Palestine, and some were smuggled out of the United States on international flights. Further, the Immigration and Customs Enforcement (ICE) has indicated that several members of the Ghali organization allegedly had direct ties to terrorist acts and/or organizations.[62] In a third case, an investigation by the FBI's Joint Terrorism Task Force (JTTF) revealed that the Hamed Organization was a criminal enterprise involved in purchasing and selling stolen and contraband goods, including infant formula, computers, Global Positioning System devices, and cigarettes.[63] Members of the Hamed Organization used convenience stores in which they worked or managed to fence stolen goods and then illegally transferred the proceeds to the Palestinian territories. None of these investigations, however, resulted in defendants being charged with providing material support to terrorists.

There have also been reports of Hamas receiving material support from non-government organizations (NGOs) in the United States, some of which may have received funds from criminal activities such as the sale of stolen infant formula.[64] For instance, it has been suggested that one Muslim charity organization previously operating in the United States, the Holy Land Foundation of Relief and Development (HLF), may have been supported in part by proceeds generated by ORC rings.[65] In 2001, the federal government seized HLF's assets and ordered the organization closed. Five members of HLF were convicted of providing funding, over a period of six years, to Hamas—a specially designated terrorist organization.[66]

As policy makers continue to consider the potential nexus between organized retail crime and terrorism, one important note is that, similar to other organized crime groups, ORC rings are motivated by money. Although this differs from the ideological motivation of terrorist organizations, both organized criminals and terrorists require money.[67] As a means of bringing in this needed income, terrorist groups may model their money-generating criminal activities after those of organized crime groups—including ORC rings. Indeed, federal law enforcement continues to be concerned that organized crime groups may form short-term business partnerships with terrorist organizations if offered enough money.[68]

DOMESTIC EFFORTS TO COMBAT ORC

Retailers

There is a growing awareness among retailers about the consequences of organized retail crime. In its 2012 survey of organized retail crime, the National Retail Federation (NRF) reported that 96% of the retailers surveyed indicated that their companies had been victimized by ORC, an increase from the 90% that reported victimization in 2010 and 94.5% that reported victimization in 2011. In addition to the percentage of retailers reporting victimization increasing in 2012, 66.1% of all retailers surveyed also reported an increase in ORC activity over the previous year.[69] Further, of the retailers responding to the NRF's 2011 survey, nearly half (46.5%) indicated that they were allocating additional resources to combating ORC.[70] It is unknown, however, whether these trends in *reported* victimization and in *reported* ORC activity levels are clear reflections of *actual* ORC activity or whether these reports are a reflection of the level of attention that retailers pay to ORC.

Despite this knowledge about ORC activity, special ORC task forces had been established only in about 23% of loss prevention departments as of 2009.[71] And, the proportion of annual sales spent on loss prevention measures has generally declined over the last decade. Prior to 2004, the proportion of annual sales allocated to loss prevention had generally remained above 0.50%.[72] In 2010, however, retailers reported spending an average of 0.46% of annual sales on loss prevention.[73]

Retailers' loss prevention strategies can take various different forms, including pre-employment integrity screening measures, employee awareness programs, asset control policies, and loss prevention systems. Data from the 2010 NRSS indicate that over half of retailers use the following loss prevention systems or personnel:

- burglar alarms;
- digital video recording systems;
- live, visible closed circuit TV (CCTV);
- point of sale (POS) data mining software;
- armored car deposit pickups;
- check approval database screening systems;
- acousto-magnetic, electronic security tags;
- live, hidden CCTV;
- uniformed guards;
- cables, locks, and chains;
- web-based case management and reporting;
- drop safes; and
- remote CCTV video and audio.[74]

In addition to their in-house loss prevention measures, some retailers and retail organizations also partner with law enforcement to share information about potential cases of organized retail crime (for more information on these partnerships, see the "Federal Law Enforcement" section). Retailers indicated that almost 58% of ORC investigations were coordinated with local, state, or federal law enforcement in 2009. As a result, almost 49% of those ORC cases were prosecuted.[75]

Online Marketplaces

With an increase in the e-fencing of stolen merchandise, attention has recently turned to the role of Internet marketplaces such as eBay and Overstock in combating ORC. These marketplaces take various measures to combat the sale of stolen and fraudulently obtained goods—not solely by organized retail criminals—on their websites, including educating sellers and consumers, monitoring suspicious activity, and partnering with retailers and law enforcement. For instance, these marketplaces may provide guidelines for website use and require users to acknowledge policies regarding goods that may or may not be sold through the website. In addition, online markets may create filters to search for prohibited items up for auction. They may then take actions such as removing the prohibited items, sanctioning the policy violator, or referring the case to law enforcement. For example, eBay has created such filters based on input from regulatory agencies, law enforcement agencies, the retail industry, and member reports.[76]

Another means by which Internet auction sites may combat the sale of stolen goods is to collaborate with retailers and law enforcement. This could occur through the establishment of investigative task forces or information sharing programs. Of the e-commerce websites most commonly used by criminals to fence stolen goods, eBay claims to be the leader in working with retailers and law enforcement to combat the online sale of stolen goods. For instance, in April 2008, eBay created PROACT (Partnering with Retailers Offensively to Attack Crime and Theft), a program designed to combat the sale of stolen goods on eBay. In this program, retailers voluntarily submit and can receive information about potentially stolen or fraudulently obtained goods being sold on eBay. Between the start of the program and January 2011, eBay received 2,340 requests for information through the PROACT program.[77] It is unknown, however, how many of the cases brought forth by retailers may be directly related to organized retail crime. In addition to creating its own programs to combat ORC, eBay partnered with the NRF in March 2010 to fight this growing crime. The NRF/eBay partnership utilizes PROACT and Law Enforcement Retail Partnership Network (LERPnet) technologies to help track ORC rings, collaborate with the FBI to identify retail crime enterprises, and promote legislation to provide law enforcement with adequate tools to combat ORC thieves.[78]

Federal Law Enforcement

As mentioned, state and local law enforcement have held the primary responsibility for investigating and prosecuting organized retail crime. However, as the scope of the crime has increased, so too has the involvement of federal law enforcement. Retail criminals are no longer selling goods simply at local flea markets; rather, they are using interstate transportation routes to move stolen goods, as well as the Internet to ship this merchandise across the country and around the world.

Much like other forms of organized crime,[79] organized retail crime is becoming increasingly transnational. For law enforcement to effectively combat ORC, it must rely on multilateral coordination, via both domestic and international task forces and partnerships. In addition to expanding multilateral law enforcement partnerships, federal law enforcement has partnered with the retail industry and online markets to combat the theft and illicit resale of stolen goods. Law enforcement has also indicated that it has built cooperative relationships with retailers and online markets and has generally not had trouble obtaining the needed information to investigate potential cases of ORC.[80]

The following section provides a discussion of various federal law enforcement agencies' current efforts to combat organized retail crime.

Federal Bureau of Investigation (FBI)

In December 2003, the FBI established an Organized Retail Theft (ORT) Initiative aimed at identifying and dismantling multi-jurisdictional retail crime rings.[81] The Initiative focuses on information sharing between law enforcement and the private sector in order to investigate

ORC and develop a greater understanding of the nature and extent of ORC around the country. The Initiative relies on federal statutes such as the Money Laundering,[82] Interstate Transportation of Stolen Property,[83] and Racketeer Influenced and Corrupt Organizations (RICO)[84] to investigate and prosecute ORC rings. In addition to the Initiative, the FBI leads seven Major Theft Task Forces around the country that are responsible for investigating a host of major theft areas, including ORC. These task forces are composed of local, state, and federal law enforcement agencies, as well as retail industry loss prevention experts.[85]

In the Violence Against Women and Department of Justice Reauthorization Act of 2005, Congress directed the Attorney General and FBI to establish a clearinghouse within the private sector for information sharing between retailers and law enforcement.[86] The result was LERPnet.[87] LERPnet began as a partnership between the FBI, ICE, various local police departments, individual retailers, and retail organizations including the Food Marketing Institute (FMI), National Retail Federation (NRF), and Retail Industry Leaders Association (RILA). As of January 2010, LERPnet has been linked with the FBI's Law Enforcement Online (LEO) system, providing federal and local law enforcement a direct link to retail industry crime reports.

Despite the establishment of the ORT Initiative, the use of the Major Theft Task Forces to investigate ORC rings, and the creation of LERPnet, the FBI continues to focus most of its resources on counterterrorism efforts. The FBI has indicated that the primary barrier to increasing its involvement in ORC investigations is the lack of resources dedicated directly to combating retail crime. Although the FBI has reportedly requested this directed funding, it has yet to be realized.[88]

U.S. Immigration and Customs Enforcement (ICE)

Because ORC often involves interstate and international transportation of stolen goods and the movement of illicit proceeds associated with the sale of these goods, ICE has become increasingly involved in investigating ORC. Further, ICE may become ever more involved in ORC investigations if reports indicating that ORC rings rely on unauthorized (illegal) aliens[89] (particularly from Mexico) to act as boosters are true.[90] Employing these aliens as low-level boosters allows them to earn an income while protecting the higher-ups in the organization from being apprehended while stealing; if apprehended, unauthorized aliens may be jailed and then deported, saving higher-ups from the fines or jail time that they could otherwise face if arrested.

In July 2009, ICE launched an ORC Pilot Program. This program, originally slated to last for six months in Houston, Los Angeles, Miami, and New York, focused on developing (1) an ORC threat assessment, (2) a tracking system for ORC cases, (3) a database of retail industry contacts to complement the LERPnet database, and (4) an investigation of how ORC groups exploit vulnerabilities in the nation's banking systems to launder illicit proceeds.[91] In February 2011, this program was expanded into a national initiative—the Seizing Earnings and Assets from Retail Crime Heists (SEARCH) Initiative.[92] As of November 2011, over 129 cases had been initiated through SEARCH, resulting in 84 criminal arrests, 56 indictments, and 23 convictions. Through these cases, about $8.2 million in cash, property, and monetary instruments was seized. [93]

U.S. Secret Service (USSS)

The USSS is most well known for protecting the President and Vice President of the United States, as well as visiting heads of state and government.[94] However, it was originally established as a law enforcement agency charged with investigating and preventing the counterfeiting of U.S. currency. The USSS's authorities have expanded, and the agency now investigates crimes ranging from counterfeiting and financial institution fraud to identity crimes, computer crimes, and money laundering.[95] Through investigations into crimes such as credit card fraud,[96] access device fraud,[97] and computer fraud,[98] the USSS has occasionally become involved in investigating organized retail crime groups who steal or fraudulently purchase merchandise from retailers (both traditional and online) and then resell these goods for a profit online.[99] The USSS receives ORC case referrals from state and local law enforcement, retail industry investigators, and online marketplaces fighting the sale of stolen goods.

The USSS has 31 Electronic Fraud Task Forces and 38 Financial Crimes Task Forces that investigate various financial crimes, including ORC.[100] In addition to state and local law enforcement agencies, these task forces consist of investigators from retail stores, online auction houses, and the banking and finance industries. There are an estimated 100 or more retail investigators participating in the USSS task forces.[101]

U.S. Postal Inspection Service (USPIS)

The USPIS works to prevent mail fraud as well as illegal substances, contraband, and dangerous products from entering the mail system. When investigating cases of ORC, the USPIS investigates individuals using the mail to ship stolen products or to transmit payment to a seller. These ORC schemes tend to fall into the categories of Internet auction fraud and re-shipper fraud.[102] In cases of Internet auction fraud, the criminals sell stolen goods and ship them domestically and internationally. In cases of re-shipper fraud, criminals may recruit individuals (often unwitting accomplices[103]) to receive the stolen goods and then ship them (often internationally) to other members of the criminal organization or to the buyer of the goods.[104]

ISSUES FOR CONSIDERATION

When debating the federal government's role in combating organized retail crime, including sanctioning various actors that may be involved in committing or aiding these crimes, there are several issues that policy makers may consider. One is whether retailers are taking sufficient preventive measures to prevent retail theft. Another issue is whether criminalizing organized retail crime at the federal level would allow for more effective investigation and prosecution of these criminals. Yet another issue is whether regulating online marketplaces to require that such entities increase information sharing with retailers and law enforcement would improve investigations and prosecutions of ORC as well as decrease the prevalence of retail thieves fencing stolen goods via legitimate online marketplaces.

Are Retailers Doing Enough?

The first line of defense against organized retail crime is preventing the crimes from ever occurring. This involves security at the manufacturing sites, distribution centers, retail stores, and in the transportation throughout this supply chain.[105] The NRSS presents trends in retail industry loss prevention measures since 1991. The 2010 NRSS reports that retailers spent 0.46% of annual sales on loss prevention measures such as contract services, security equipment, and loss prevention personnel.[106] This includes about 33 loss prevention employees for every $100 million in annual sales—nearly half of the 70 employees reported in the 2009 survey and less than one-quarter of the 170 employees reported in the 2008 survey.[107] As mentioned, prior to 2004, the percent of annual sales spent on loss prevention was consistently above 0.50%, but that amount then decreased through 2008 before rising to 0.46% in 2010. Some experts explained this trend in loss prevention spending as a reaction to changes in overall inventory shrinkage.[108] Also trending along with the increase in loss prevention budgets, more than 66% of retailers surveyed in 2012 reported an increase in ORC activity—an increase over the 64% who reported an increase in 2011.[109] It is unknown, however, whether retailers are making changes to their loss prevention budgets and funding allocation based on overall inventory shrinkage or based on specific threats such as ORC.

For multiple reasons, it is difficult to empirically determine whether retailers are doing "enough" to combat ORC. For one, retailers typically try to strike a balance between protecting their merchandise from thieves and creating an environment where honest consumers can easily find and purchase the desired products. If retailers take every precaution to lock up "hot" products and install security measures that make it difficult for consumers to get the desired product in a hassle-free and timely fashion, they may risk losing customers to competitors who provide a more relaxed shopping environment. If, on the other hand, retailers err on the side of being "customer friendly" by keeping products out in the open, they may open themselves up to thieves. There are several policy options that may enhance retailers' abilities to combat ORC that policy makers may consider. In the literature, there appears to be a lack of research on the effectiveness of various loss prevention strategies on combating retail theft in general and ORC in particular. Understanding the strategies that have proven to reduce retail theft related to ORC may enhance retailers' abilities to secure their merchandise. Consequently, one option may be for Congress to commission a national study to examine promising loss prevention strategies. A second option may be for Congress to consider establishing a grant program that would provide funding to retailers to install or upgrade security systems and loss prevention measures in their stores. Congress could require that retailers comply with various benchmarks in order to receive grant funding; for instance, a grant program may require that retailers work with law enforcement to identify and apprehend members of ORC rings. Another potential requirement could be that retailers join LERPnet in order to be eligible for grant funding. Yet another eligibility requirement could be that retailers provide matching loss prevention funds.

Federally Criminalizing ORC

Combating retail theft has primarily been handled by state law enforcement under state criminal laws. In particular, major theft laws are the statutes that states have relied upon most to investigate and prosecute ORC. These major theft laws, however, vary from state to state with respect to the monetary threshold that constitutes major theft. While some states, such as New Jersey and Massachusetts, have relatively low thresholds, other states, such as Wisconsin and Pennsylvania, have relatively higher thresholds. Over one-third of states have felony theft thresholds that meet or exceed $1,000, and a number of states have already passed legislation criminalizing ORC.[110]

There is currently no federal law specifically prohibiting organized retail crime as such. There are, however, provisions in the *U.S. Code* that federal law enforcement uses to bring forth cases against ORC rings. Examples of such provisions include

- 18 U.S.C. Section 1956, "Laundering of monetary instruments";
- 18 U.S.C. Section 1957, "Engaging in monetary transactions in property derived from specified unlawful activity";
- 18 U.S.C., Chapter 96, the Racketeer Influenced and Corrupt Organizations (RICO) provisions;
- 18 U.S.C. Section 2314, "Transportation of stolen goods, securities, moneys, fraudulent State tax stamps, or articles used in counterfeiting"; and
- 18 U.S.C. Section 2315, "Sale or receipt of stolen goods, securities, moneys, or fraudulent State tax stamps."

Current federal law addressing theft does not criminalize the theft itself, but rather prohibits the transportation of stolen goods across state lines[111] as well as the sale or receipt of these goods.[112] For these activities to be considered federal crimes, the monetary value of the stolen goods must meet or exceed $5,000.

When debating the federal government's role in combating organized retail crime, Congress may consider whether current law should be amended to create new provisions that would provide penalties for ORC. Proponents of such legislation argue that criminalizing ORC may benefit law enforcement in several ways, including (1) illuminating the growing problem of ORC and (2) providing a statutory framework for tracking ORC case data rather than lumping these cases into other categories for statistical purposes. Opponents of legislation criminalizing ORC argue that already existing statutes allow for effective investigation and prosecution of ORC (as outlined above) and that creating a separate provision for ORC would be redundant. Representatives from federal law enforcement agencies have provided congressional testimony indicating that they indeed have sufficient laws and procedural tools to investigate ORC.[113] As mentioned, impediments to investigating and prosecuting these cases may come more from a lack of resources than from a need for better investigative and prosecutorial tools.

Another policy option that Congress may consider could be enacting provisions that would lower the monetary threshold from $5,000 for the sale, receipt, or transportation of stolen goods across state lines (18 U.S.C. §2314 and 18 U.S.C. §2315). Savvy criminals know each state's felony theft level and steal merchandise valuing just under this level so as to avoid state felony charges if caught. Federal investigators and prosecutors may rely upon the sum total of merchandise stolen in various states and moved across state lines in order to prosecute these thieves. The average value of goods transported, sold, or received by members of ORC rings is currently unknown. If this value were under the current federal threshold of $5,000, the data may support legislation decreasing the threshold. One issue that Congress may face if it amends the $5,000 limit for the sale, receipt, or transportation of stolen goods across state lines may be whether such a policy shift would also open the doors for the federal government to prosecute individuals not involved in ORC rings.

If Congress determines that there are sufficient investigative and prosecutorial tools available for law enforcement to combat ORC, one issue that policy makers may face is whether to provide dedicated funding to law enforcement to enhance their ability to take on more ORC cases. Law enforcement has suggested that although the investigative tools are available, it may prioritize and utilize resources in higher-priority areas[114]—such as counterterrorism and fraud investigations.[115] Therefore, another policy option may be to provide directed resources to federal law enforcement to investigate and prosecute ORC cases.

Regulation of Online and Physical Marketplaces

As mentioned, organized retail criminals use both physical and online marketplaces as fences to sell stolen goods. With an increasingly globalized society, these criminals take advantage of the Internet for their illegal activities. In an effort to curb sales of stolen goods online, one policy option that Congress may consider is increased regulation of certain actions on the Internet. In the past, Congress has regulated actions on the Internet that involve interstate commerce. For example, Congress enacted legislation that prohibited unlawful Internet gambling. [116] Among other things, this legislation also included provisions holding certain computer services, Internet websites, telecommunications services, and financial transaction providers liable for illegal gambling if they aid or have knowledge of the Internet gambling.[117] Along the same lines, Congress may consider whether to regulate online auction websites to require them to document, retain, and disclose—to designated law enforcement—information about specified sellers, including those suspected of fencing stolen goods. Proponents of such regulation argue that this could better enable law enforcement to track suspected fences and that it may act as a deterrent, discouraging potential thieves from fencing stolen goods. Opponents of this type of regulation argue that online marketplaces already share such information because it is in their best interests to prevent the sale of stolen goods, promote the business of legitimate sellers, and ensure that customers receive genuine and safe products.

Another policy option that policy makers may consider is the regulation of physical marketplaces, such as flea markets. One the one hand, some may argue that flea markets should be regulated by state laws because the face-to-face transactions at these markets do not directly involve interstate commerce. Others, however, may contend that the federal government could regulate the goods sold at flea markets because they were likely involved in interstate commerce before being sold at the market. Further, it could be argued that the federal government could direct this regulation toward the sale of certain, already-regulated products such as goods regulated by the Food and Drug Administration (FDA) under the Federal Food, Drug, and Cosmetic Act.[118]

End Notes

[1] A "booster" is someone who steals merchandise and then sells it to a fence for a profit. A "fence" is someone who knowingly buys illegally obtained goods from a "booster" and then sells the goods for a profit.

[2] Ticket switching involves thieves utilizing devices that create fake barcodes that they adhere to packages, covering the original barcodes. When scanned, these new barcodes ring up items at lower prices than their retail values.

[3] See the National Retail Federation, 2011 Organized Retail Crime Survey, 2011, p. 4; National Retail Federation, 2012 Organized Retail Crime Survey, 2011, p. 7. The percentage of surveyed retailers who reported victimization generally increased between 2005 and 2009 and then decreased slightly in 2010 before increasing again in 2011 and 2012.

[4] Issues involved in determining the exact losses are discussed later in the report. The National Retail Federation (NRF) has estimated that losses amass to between $15 billion and $30 billion annually. The Federal Bureau of Investigation (FBI) has provided varying estimates. In 2005, the FBI cited losses as between $15 billion and $30 billion annually. See testimony of Chris Swecker, Assistant Director, Criminal Investigative Division, Federal Bureau of Investigation before the U.S. Congress, House Committee on the Judiciary, Subcommittee on Crime, Terrorism, and Homeland Security, Responding to Organized Crimes Against Manufacturers and Retailers, 109th Cong., 1st sess., March 17, 2005. As of 2007, the FBI estimated losses as between $30 billion and $37 billion annually. See the Federal Bureau of Investigation, Organized Retail Theft: New Initiative to Tackle the Problem, April 6, 2007, http://www.fbi.gov/page2/ april07/retail040607.htm.

[5] See testimony of Chris Swecker, Assistant Director, Criminal Investigative Division, Federal Bureau of Investigation before the U.S. Congress, House Committee on the Judiciary, Subcommittee on Crime, Terrorism, and Homeland Security, Responding to Organized Crimes Against Manufacturers and Retailers, 109th Cong., 1st sess., March 17, 2005. See also Federal Bureau of Investigation, Organized Retail Theft: A $30 Billion-a-Year Industry, January 3, 2011, http://www.fbi.gov/news/stories/2011/january/retail_010311.

[6] Charles I. Miller, Organized Retail Theft: Raising Awareness, Offering Solutions, National Retail Federation Foundation, 2005, p. 4. See also Food Marketing Institute, Media Reports—Middle East Connection: Organized Retail Crime, http://www.fmi.org/ docs/loss/ORCMiddleEast.pdf. See also testimony by David Johnson, Section Chief, Criminal Investigative Division, Federal Bureau of Investigation, before the U.S. Congress, House Committee on the Judiciary, Subcommittee on Crime, Terrorism, and Homeland Security, Combating Organized Retail Crime: The Role of Federal Law Enforcement, 111th Cong., 1st sess., November 5, 2009.

[7] From a statement by Representative Robert C. "Bobby" Scott before the U.S. Congress, House Committee on the Judiciary, Subcommittee on Crime, Terrorism, and Homeland Security, E-Fencing Enforcement Act of 2008, The Organized Retail Crime Act of 2008, and The Combating Organized Retail Crime Act of 2008, 110th Cong., 2nd sess., September 22, 2008.

[8] Walter E. Palmer and Chris Richardson, Organized Retail Crime: Assessing the Risk and Developing Effective Strategies, ASIS Foundation Research Council, 2009, p. 4.

[9] For statistical purposes, the FBI defines cargo theft as "the criminal taking of any cargo including, but not limited to, goods, chattels, money, or baggage that constitutes, in whole or in part, a commercial shipment of freight moving in commerce, from any pipeline system, railroad car, motortruck, or other vehicle, or from any tank or storage facility, station house, platform, or depot, or from any vessel or wharf, or from any aircraft, air terminal, airport, aircraft terminal or air navigation facility, or from any intermodal container, intermodal chassis, trailer, container freight station, warehouse, freight distribution facility, or freight consolidation facility. For purposes of this definition, cargo shall be deemed as moving in commerce at all points between the point of origin and the final destination, regardless of any temporary stop while awaiting transshipment or otherwise." U.S. Department of Justice, Federal Bureau of Investigation, Criminal Justice Information Services Division, Uniform Crime Reporting Program, National Incident-Based Reporting System Addendum for Submitting Cargo Theft Data, January 2010, p. iii, http://www.fbi.gov/ucr/ nibrs/downloadables /nibrs_cargo_theft_downloadable.pdf.

[10] See, for example, Read Hayes, Organized Retail Crime Annual Report 2008: Describing a Major Problem, Loss Prevention Research Council, 2008, hereafter Organized Retail Crime Annual Report 2008: Describing a Major Problem. The issue of cargo theft will be discussed in more detail in the section, "Methods Used by Boosters."

[11] See, for example, Walter E. Palmer and Chris Richardson, Organized Retail Crime: Assessing the Risk and Developing Effective Strategies, ASIS Foundation Research Council, 2009.

[12] Organized Retail Crime Annual Report 2008: Describing a Major Problem.

[13] This issue is discussed further in the section "Domestic Impact of Organized Retail Crime."

[14] P.L. 109-162, §1105, codified at 28 U.S.C. §509 note. In the Violence Against Women and Department of Justice Reauthorization Act of 2005, Congress defined organized retail theft and directed the Attorney General and FBI to establish a task force to combat organized retail theft as well as a clearinghouse within the private sector for information sharing between retailers and law enforcement.

[15] Charles I. Miller, Organized Retail Theft: Raising Awareness, Offering Solutions, National Retail Federation Foundation, 2005, p. 17.

[16] Ibid.

[17] Ibid., pp. 17-20. The public health and safety risks and possible repercussions of these cleaning operations are discussed elsewhere in this report.

[18] Ronald V. Clarke, "Hot Products: Understanding, Anticipating, and Reducing Demand for Stolen Goods," Police Research Series, Paper 112 (1999), p. 23.

[19] Ibid., p. 1.

[20] Organized Retail Crime Annual Report 2008: Describing a Major Problem, p. 20. Benadryl, for instance, has been identified as one of the over-the-counter medications targeted by ORC groups, where competing brands of antihistamines have not.

[21] National Retail Federation, 2012 Organized Retail Crime Survey, 2011, p. 12.

[22] Read Hayes and King Rogers, "Catch Them if You Can: This Study of Organized Retail Crime Looks at How These Criminal Groups Operate and What Measures Might Help Stores Fight Back," Security Management, vol. 47, no. 10 (2003), hereafter "Catch Them if You Can."

[23] Ibid.

[24] From information provided to CRS during an organized retail crime briefing by members of the Retail Leaders Industry Association and the Coalition Against Organized Retail Crime, June 4, 2009.

[25] "Catch Them if You Can."

[26] Ibid.

[27] Richard C. Hollinger and Amanda Adams, 2010 National Retail Security Survey Final Report, Security Research Project, Department of Sociology and Criminology & Law, University of Florida, 2011, hereafter 2010 National Retail Security Survey Final Report.

[28] Ibid. In addition to employees colluding with ORC thieves, they may also conspire with individuals to steal merchandise for personal use—either for the employees' own use or for the co-conspirators' use.

[29] From information provided to CRS during an organized retail crime briefing by members of the Retail Leaders Industry Association and the Coalition Against Organized Retail Crime, June 4, 2009.

[30] Ibid.

[31] Ibid.

[32] Organized Retail Crime Annual Report 2008: Describing a Major Problem, pp. 17-18.

[33] Ibid., Walter E. Palmer and Chris Richardson, Organized Retail Crime: Assessing the Risk and Developing Effective Strategies, ASIS Foundation Research Council, 2009, p. 14.

[34] National Retail Federation, 2012 Organized Retail Crime Survey, 2012, p. 9.

[35] Tracy Johnson and Read Hayes, "Behind the Fence: Buying and Selling Stolen Merchandise," Security Journal, vol. 16, no. 4 (2003).

[36] Organized Retail Crime Annual Report 2008: Describing a Major Problem.

[37] King Rogers, "Organized Retail Theft," in Retail Crime, Security, and Loss Prevention: An Encyclopedic Reference, ed. Charles A. Sennewald and John H. Christman (Elseiver Inc., 2008).

[38] National Retail Federation, 2012 Organized Retail Crime Survey, 2012, p. 11.

[39] National Retail Federation, 2012 Organized Retail Crime Survey, 2012, p. 6; National Retail Federation, 2009 Organized Retail Crime Survey, 2009, p. 8.

[40] See, for example, testimony of Brad Brekke, Vice President of Assets Protection, Target Corporation, before the U.S. Congress, House Committee on the Judiciary, Subcommittee on Crime, Terrorism, and Homeland Security, Organized Retail Theft Prevention: Fostering a Comprehensive Public-Private Response, 110th Cong., 1st sess., October 25, 2007, H.Hrg. 110-122.

[41] Walter E. Palmer and Chris Richardson, Organized Retail Crime: Assessing the Risk and Developing Effective Strategies, ASIS Foundation Research Council, 2009, p. 5.

[42] See, for example, testimony of Chris Swecker, Assistant Director, Criminal Investigative Division, Federal Bureau of Investigation before the U.S. Congress, House Committee on the Judiciary, Subcommittee on Crime, Terrorism, and Homeland Security, Responding to Organized Crimes Against Manufacturers and Retailers, 109th Cong., 1st sess., March 17, 2005.

[43] Ibid.

[44] Testimony of Karl Langhorst, Director of Loss Prevention, Randall's/Tom Thumb, a Safeway Company before the U.S. Congress, House Committee on the Judiciary, Subcommittee on Crime, Terrorism, and Homeland Security, Organized Retail Theft: Fostering a Comprehensive Public-Private Response, 111th Cong., 2nd sess., October 25, 2007.

[45] Federal Bureau of Investigation, Organized Retail Theft: New Initiative to Tackle the Problem, April 6, 2007, http://www.fbi.gov/page2/april07/retail040607.htm.

[46] Federal Bureau of Investigation, Cargo Theft's High Cost: Thieves Stealing Billions Annually, July 21, 2006, http://www.fbi.gov/page2/july06/cargo_theft072106.htm.

[47] Federal Bureau of Investigation, Inside Cargo Theft: A Growing, Multi-Billion-Dollar Problem, November 12, 2010, http://www.fbi.gov/news/stories/2010/ november/cargo_ 111210/cargo_111210.

[48] As cited by Claire Mayhew, "The Detection and Prevention of Cargo Theft," Trends & Issues in Crime and Criminal Justice, no. 214 (September 2001), p. 1.

[49] 2010 National Retail Security Survey Final Report.

[50] Ibid., p. 7.

[51] National Retail Federation, Retail Sales Growth 2009 – 2010, http://www.nrf.com/ modules.php?name=Pages& sp_id=1237.

[52] The NRSS surveyed retailers from the following sectors: optical; children's apparel; strip center; women's apparel; discount store; crafts and hobbies; men's and women's apparel; entertainment, media, games, video, and music; sporting goods and recreational products; shoes; department store; accessories; supermarket and grocery; household furnishings and housewares; cards, gifts, floral, and novelties; office supplies; stationery; books, magazines, and music; drug store; homecenter, hardware, lumber, and garden; electronics, computers, and appliances; and furniture. Of note, the NRSS does not include data from retailers such as restaurants, bars, motor vehicle dealers, auto service stations, direct catalog sale outlets, and Internet "e-tailers" because these sectors do not produce comparable "shrinkage" data to the other retailers that are included in the survey.

[53] 2010 National Retail Security Survey Final Report, p. 7.

[54] The other known sources of shrinkage were administrative errors and vendor fraud.

[55] From information provided to CRS during an organized retail crime briefing by members of the Retail Leaders Industry Association and the Coalition Against Organized Retail Crime, June 4, 2009.

[56] Food Marketing Institute, on behalf of the Coalition Against Organized Retail Crime, Organized Retail Crime: Estimated Lost Sales Tax Revenue by State (2007), September 2009. The most recent data available come from 2007.

[57] Federal Bureau of Investigation, Organized Retail Theft: A $30 Billion-a-Year Industry, January 3, 2011, http://www.fbi.gov/news/stories/2011/january/retail_010311. See also testimony of Chris Swecker, Assistant Director, Criminal Investigative Division, Federal Bureau of Investigation before the U.S. Congress, House Committee on the Judiciary, Subcommittee on Crime, Terrorism, and Homeland Security, Responding to Organized Crimes Against Manufacturers and Retailers, 109th Cong., 1st sess., March 17, 2005.

[58] Karen E. Thuermer, "Retailers Organize Against Crime," Security Management, July 2007.

[59] Charles I. Miller, Organized Retail Theft: Raising Awareness, Offering Solutions, National Retail Federation Foundation, 2005, p. 4. See also Food Marketing Institute, Media Reports—Middle East Connection: Organized Retail Crime, http://www.fmi.org/ docs/loss/ORCMiddleEast.pdf. See also testimony by David Johnson, Section Chief, Criminal Investigative Division, Federal Bureau of Investigation, before the U.S. Congress, House Committee on the Judiciary, Subcommittee on Crime, Terrorism, and Homeland Security, Combating Organized Retail Crime: The Role of Federal Law Enforcement, 111th Cong., 1st sess., November 5, 2009.

[60] U.S. Department of the Treasury, U.S. Customs Service, Office of Investigations, Green Quest, Customs Publication No. 0000-0171, October 2002, p. 2, http://www.portal.state. pa.us/portal/server.pt/document /437021/ green_quest_brochure_pdf.

[61] Charles I. Miller, Organized Retail Theft: Raising Awareness, Offering Solutions, National Retail Federation Foundation, 2005, pp. 25 - 27.

[62] Testimony by Janice Ayala, Assistant Director for Investigative Programs, Office of Investigations, U.S. Immigration and Customs Enforcement, Department of Homeland Security, before the U.S. Congress, House Committee on the Judiciary, Subcommittee on Crime, Terrorism, and Homeland Security, Combating Organized Retail Crime: The Role of Federal Law Enforcement, 111th Cong., 1st sess., November 5, 2009.

[63] United States Attorney's Office Eastern District of Missouri, "Eight Area Men Plead Guilty to Federal Racketeering Charges Involving Conspiracy to Transfer Cash and Checks to the Palestinian Territories," press release, November 24, 2009, http://stlouis.fbi.gov/ dojpressrel/pressrel09/sl112409a.htm.

[64] From testimony by John S. Pistole, Assistant Director, Counterterrorism Division, Federal Bureau of Investigation, before the U.S. Congress, House Committee on Financial Services, Subcommittee on Oversight and Investigations, Hamas Asset Freeze and Other Government Efforts To Stop Terrorist Funding, 108th Cong., 1st sess., September 24, 2003.

[65] Charles I. Miller, Organized Retail Theft: Raising Awareness, Offering Solutions, National Retail Federation Foundation, 2005, pp. 12 – 13.

[66] In November, 2008, a federal jury returned convictions for five members of the HLF accused of providing about $12.4 million in material support to Hamas. For more information, see http://www.fbi.gov/page2/nov08/ hlf_112508.html and http://www.justice.gov/opa/pr/ 2008/November/08-nsd-1046.html.

[67] For more information on the potential links between organized crime in the United States and terrorist organizations, see CRS Report R40525, Organized Crime in the United States: Trends and Issues for Congress, by Kristin M. Finklea.

[68] Pat Milton, "FBI Worries About an Osama-Sopranos Link," Associated Press, October 1, 2006, http://www.redorbit.com/news/general/676652/fbi_worries_about_an_ osamas opranos_link/index.html. See also Mapping the Global Structure, National Intelligence Council, Report of the National Intelligence Council's 2020 Project, Based on consultations with nongovernmental experts around the world, Washington, D.C., December 2004, p. 96.

[69] National Retail Federation, 2011 Organized Retail Crime Survey, 2011, p. 8; National Retail Federation, 2012 Organized Retail Crime Survey, 2012, p. 7.

[70] Ibid., p. 16.

[71] Richard C. Hollinger and Amanda Adams, 2009 National Retail Security Survey Final Report, Security Research Project, Department of Sociology and Criminology & Law, University of Florida, 2010, p. 30, hereafter 2009 National Retail Security Survey Final Report.

[72] 2010 National Retail Security Survey Final Report, p. 16.

[73] Ibid.

[74] Ibid., pp. 23-26.

[75] 2009 National Retail Security Survey Final Report, p. 30.

[76] From information provided to CRS during ORC briefing by representatives from eBay on July 27, 2009.

[77] U.S. Government Accountability Office, Organized Retail Crime: Private Sector and Law Enforcement Collaborate to Deter and Investigate Theft, GAO-11-675, June 14, 2011, http://www.gao.gov/assets/320 /319548.pdf.

[78] National Retail Federation, "National Retail Federation, eBay Announce Partnership to Fight Organized Retail Crime," press release, March 22, 2010, http://www.nrf.com/modules.php? name=News&op=viewlive&sp_ id=906.

[79] For further information on organized crime, see CRS Report R40525, Organized Crime in the United States: Trends and Issues for Congress, by Kristin M. Finklea; as well as CRS Report R41547, Organized Crime: An Evolving Challenge for U.S. Law Enforcement, by Jerome P. Bjelopera and Kristin M. Finklea.

[80] Testimony by law enforcement representatives from the FBI, ICE, USSS, and USPIS before the U.S. Congress, House Committee on the Judiciary, Subcommittee on Crime, Terrorism, and Homeland Security, Combating Organized Retail Crime: The Role of Federal Law Enforcement, 111th Cong., 1st sess., November 5, 2009. Also from an ICE briefing for CRS, October 14, 2009 and a USSS briefing for CRS, November 13, 2009.

[81] The FBI utilizes the term ORT rather than ORC so as not to create a confusion between organized retail crime and what the FBI considers traditional organized crime.

[82] 18 U.S.C. §1956.

[83] 18 U.S.C. §2314.

[84] 18 U.S.C., Chapter 96.

[85] Testimony by David Johnson, Section Chief, Criminal Investigative Division, Federal Bureau of Investigation, before the U.S. Congress, House Committee on the Judiciary, Subcommittee on Crime, Terrorism, and Homeland Security, Combating Organized Retail Crime: The Role of Federal Law Enforcement, 111th Cong., 1st sess., November 5, 2009.

[86] P.L. 109-162, §1105, codified at 28 U.S.C. §509 note.

[87] For more information on LERPnet, see http://www.lerpnet2.com/.

[88] Testimony by David Johnson, Section Chief, Criminal Investigative Division, Federal Bureau of Investigation, before the U.S. Congress, House Committee on the Judiciary, Subcommittee on Crime, Terrorism, and Homeland Security, Combating Organized Retail Crime: The Role of Federal Law Enforcement, 111th Cong., 1st sess., November 5, 2009.

[89] An alien is anyone who is not a citizen or national of the United States and is synonymous with non-citizen.

[90] See, for example, Charles I. Miller, Organized Retail Theft: Raising Awareness, Offering Solutions, National Retail Federation Foundation, 2005, p. 1. Some have suggested that unauthorized aliens may be particularly vulnerable to being recruited by ORC groups because they are looking to earn money while in the United States and may be seen as expendable by higher-ups in the organization.

[91] Testimony by Janice Ayala, Assistant Director for Investigative Programs, Office of Investigations, U.S. Immigration and Customs Enforcement, Department of Homeland Security, before the U.S. Congress, House Committee on the Judiciary, Subcommittee on Crime, Terrorism, and Homeland Security, Combating Organized Retail Crime: The Role of Federal Law Enforcement, 111th Cong., 1st sess., November 5, 2009.

[92] For more information on this Initiative, see http://www.ice.gov/search/.

[93] Questions for the Record, Kumar C. Kibble, U.S. Immigration and Customs Enforcement, for the hearing, Combating International Organized Crime: Evaluating Current Authorities, Tools, and Resources, November 1, 2011, http://www.judiciary.senate.gov/resources/ transcripts/upload/110111QFRs-Kibble.pdf.

[94] See http://www.secretservice.gov/investigations.shtml.

[95] According to the USSS, "investigations include counterfeiting of U.S. currency (to include coins); counterfeiting of foreign currency (occurring domestically); identity crimes such as access device fraud, identity theft, false identification fraud, bank fraud and check fraud; telemarketing fraud; telecommunications fraud (cellular and hard wire); computer fraud; fraud targeting automated payment systems and teller machines; direct deposit fraud; investigations of forgery, uttering, alterations, false impersonations or false claims involving U.S. Treasury Checks, U.S. Saving Bonds, U.S. Treasury Notes, Bonds and Bills; electronic funds transfer (EFT) including Treasury disbursements and fraud within the Treasury payment systems; Federal Deposit Insurance Corporation investigations; Farm Credit Administration violations; and fictitious or fraudulent commercial instruments and foreign securities." For more information, see http://www.secretservice.gov/criminal.shtml.

[96] 18 U.S.C. §1029(a)(10).

[97] 18 U.S.C. §1029.

[98] 18 U.S.C. §1030.

[99] USSS briefing for CRS, November 13, 2009.

[100] Information provided to CRS by USSS Congressional Affairs, November 22, 2011.

[101] Ibid., See also testimony by John R. Large, Special Agent in Charge, Criminal Investigative Division, Office of Investigations, U.S. Secret Service before the U.S. Congress, House Committee on the Judiciary, Subcommittee on Crime, Terrorism, and Homeland Security, Combating Organized Retail Crime: The Role of Federal Law Enforcement, 111th Cong., 1st sess., November 5, 2009.

[102] Testimony of Zane M. Hill, Deputy Chief Postal Inspector, U.S. Postal Inspection Service before the U.S. Congress, House Committee on the Judiciary, Subcommittee on Crime, Terrorism, and Homeland Security, Combating Organized Retail Crime: The Role of Federal Law Enforcement, 111th Cong., 1st sess., November 5, 2009.

[103] One common method of recruiting these unwitting accomplices is through employment websites where the criminals advertise work-from-home jobs as shippers.

[104] For more information on re-shipping scams, see https://postalinspectors.uspis.gov/ radDocs/consumer/ ReshippingScam.html.

[105] Detailed information on retailers' efforts to combat ORC is provided in the "Retailers" section of this report.

[106] 2010 National Retail Security Survey Final Report, p. 16.

[107] Ibid., p. 17.

[108] 2009 National Retail Security Survey Final Report, pp. 12-15.

[109] National Retail Federation, 2012 Organized Retail Crime Survey, 2012, p. 7.

[110] From an organized retail crime and felony theft level database maintained and provided to CRS by Frank Muscato, ORC Investigations Supervisor, Organized Retail Crime Division, Walgreens, November 9, 2009.

[111] 18 U.S.C. §2314.

[112] 18 U.S.C. §2315.

[113] Testimony by law enforcement representatives from the FBI, ICE, USSS, and USPIS before the U.S. Congress, House Committee on the Judiciary, Subcommittee on Crime, Terrorism, and Homeland Security, Combating Organized Retail Crime: The Role of Federal Law Enforcement, 111th Cong., 1st sess., November 5, 2009.

[114] Testimony by David Johnson, Section Chief, Criminal Investigative Division, Federal Bureau of Investigation, before the U.S. Congress, House Committee on the Judiciary, Subcommittee on Crime, Terrorism, and Homeland Security, Combating Organized Retail Crime: The Role of Federal Law Enforcement, 111th Cong., 1st sess., November 5, 2009.

[115] Testimony by Robert S. Mueller, III, Director, Federal Bureau of Investigation, before the U.S. Congress, Senate Committee on the Judiciary, Oversight of the Federal Bureau of Investigation, 111th Cong., 1st sess., September 16, 2009.

[116] See 18 U.S.C. §1084 and Title VIII of P.L. 109-347, Unlawful Internet Gambling Enforcement, codified at 31 U.S.C. §5361 et seq.

[117] See 31 U.S.C. §5365 - 5366.

[118] 21 U.S.C. §301.

In: Organized Crime
Editors: F. B. Hall and F. C. Martin
ISBN: 978-1-62618-415-2

Chapter 3

MEXICO'S DRUG TRAFFICKING ORGANIZATIONS: SOURCE AND SCOPE OF THE RISING VIOLENCE*

June S. Beittel

SUMMARY

Violence has been an inherent feature of the trade in illicit drugs, but the violence generated by Mexico's drug trafficking organizations (DTOs) in recent years has been unprecedented and remarkably brutal. The tactics—including mass killings, the use of torture and dismemberment, and the phenomena of car bombs—have led some analysts to speculate whether the violence has been transformed into something new, perhaps requiring a different set of policy responses. According to government and other data, the best estimates are that there were slightly more than 50,000 homicides related to organized crime from December 2006 through December 2011. Some analysts see in this year's data about Mexico's organized crime-related homicides the possibility that the violence may have peaked or reached a plateau, if it has not begun to decline. Many observers maintain that the steep increase in organized crime-related homicides in recent years is likely to trend down far more slowly.

In December 2006, Mexico's newly inaugurated President Felipe Calderón launched an aggressive campaign against the DTOs—an initiative that has defined his administration—that has been met with a violent response from the DTOs. Of the seven most significant DTOs operating during the first five years of the Calderón Administration, the government successfully removed key leaders from each of them, through arrests or by death in arrest efforts. However, these efforts add to the dynamic of change—consolidation or fragmentation, succession struggles, and new competition—that generates more conflict and violence among competing criminal groups. In the last six years, fragments of some of the DTOs have formed new criminal organizations, while two DTOs have become dominant and polarized rivals: the Sinaloa DTO in the western part of the country and Los Zetas in the east. In addition, the DTOs have increasingly diversified into other criminal activities, now posing a multi-faceted organized criminal challenge to governance in Mexico.

* This is an edited, reformatted and augmented version of Congressional Research Service, Publication No. R41576, dated August 3, 2012.

U.S. citizens have also been victims of the security crisis in Mexico. In March 2010, three individuals connected to the U.S. consulate in Ciudad Juárez, two of them U.S. citizens, were killed by a gang working for one of the major DTOs operating in that city. In February 2011, two U.S. Immigration and Customs Enforcement (ICE) agents were shot, one fatally, allegedly by Los Zetas, one of Mexico's most violent DTOs. In the U.S. Congress, these events have raised concerns about the stability of a strategic partner and neighbor. Congress is also concerned about the possibility of "spillover" violence along the U.S. border and further inland. The 112th Congress has held several hearings on DTO violence, the efforts by the Calderón government to address the situation, and implications of the violence for the United States. Members have maintained close oversight of U.S.-Mexico security cooperation and related bilateral issues.

This report provides background on drug trafficking in Mexico: it identifies the major DTOs; examines how the organized crime "landscape" has been altered by fragmentation; and analyzes the context, scope, and scale of the violence. It examines current trends of the violence, analyzes prospects for curbing violence in the future, and compares it with violence in Colombia.

INTRODUCTION

The brutal drug trafficking-related violence in Mexico has been dramatized graphically by beheadings, public hanging of corpses, killing of innocent bystanders, car bombs, torture, and assassination of numerous journalists and government officials. Beyond the litany of these brazen crimes, the violence has also spread deeper into Mexico's interior over the course of 2011. Organized crime groups have fragmented and diversified their crime activities, turning to extortion, kidnapping, auto theft, human smuggling, resource theft, and other illicit enterprises. In March 2012, head of the U.S. Northern Command General Charles Jacoby testified to the Senate Armed Services Committee that Mexico had succeeded in capturing or killing 22 out of 37 of Mexico's most wanted drug traffickers identified by the Mexican government. Despite these operations, General Jacoby noted that the removal of these crime leaders had not had "any appreciable positive effect" in reducing the violence, which continued to climb in 2011.[1]

According to the estimates of the University of San Diego's Trans-Border Institute (TBI), the actual number of organized crime-related murders exceeded 16,000 last year. When President Calderón's six-year term draws to a close late in 2012, an average of 10,000 organized crime-related murders per year will have taken place in each year of his term if current projections hold. According to the Mexican government, there was an 11% increase of organized crime-related murders in the first nine months of 2011, over the same period in 2010. However, the *rate* of increase is much lower than the nearly 60% increase between 2009 and 2010, leading some analysts to forecast that the number of killings is beginning to decline. Because casualty estimates are reported differently by the Mexican government from the media outlets that track the violence, there is some debate on exactly how many have perished. This report favors government data, but they have not always been reported promptly or completely. (See "Casualty Estimates in Context and for Special Populations.")

Violence is an intrinsic feature of the trade in illicit drugs. As in other criminal endeavors, violence is used by traffickers to settle disputes, and a credible threat of violence maintains employee discipline and a semblance of order with suppliers, creditors, and buyers.[2] This type of drug trafficking-related violence has occurred routinely and intermittently in U.S. cities since the early 1980s. The violence now associated with drug trafficking organizations in Mexico is of an entirely different scale. In Mexico, the bloodletting is not only associated with resolving disputes or maintaining discipline, but it is directed toward the government and the news media, and is not bounded by traditional objectives of such violence.

With national elections in both the United States and Mexico in 2012,[3] the bilateral efforts to confront organized crime and reduce the violence are at an important crossroads. Despite some fears that violence or threats might disrupt Mexico's presidential and congressional elections held on July 1, 2012, the elections were peaceful with a record turnout. In contrast, in 2010 several local office holders and candidates were killed, allegedly by traffickers. For example, on June 28, 2010, Tamaulipas gubernatorial candidate Rodolfo Torre Cantú of the Institutional Revolutionary Party (PRI) was killed, the highest level political assassination in 15 years, allegedly by the drug trafficking organizations (DTOs).[4] In addition, 15 mayors, most from small towns, were killed during 2010 (see Figure 4). The 2010 uptick in political assassinations occurred during an important election year. But threats and assassinations have also taken place in less prominent elections. In elections held in Michoácan state in late 2011, organized crime groups reportedly intimidated National Action Party (PAN) sympathizers (President Calderón's party) and killed a PAN mayor in early November. (A total of six mayors were slain in 2011.) In the 2012 campaign period, there was an upsurge of extreme violence during several weeks in April and May, when at least 111 severely brutalized corpses were discovered in different locations in the country.[5] The government and most analysts, however, did not view these atrocities as campaign-related and suggested instead that they represented a "heating up" of criminal rivalries.

As predicted, Enrique Peña Nieto of the PRI won the July presidential vote. His margin of victory was narrower than forecast and the outcome of the election has been challenged by the other two major parties based on allegations of vote buying and other irregularities in the Peña Nieto campaign. As the presumed winner, Peña Nieto has begun to outline how he might manage the security crisis in Mexico in more detail than he did as a candidate. He has clearly asserted that there will be a continuation of close collaboration with the United States and that a reduction of violence will be his priority while pledging not to negotiate a truce with the DTOs.[6] He announced during his campaign that General Oscar Naranjo, Colombia's former police chief, will be his key security advisor. General Naranjo has reportedly embraced a four point plan that describes a national policy on security (not limited to the current administration), a plan to support victims of organized crime, a reliance on law enforcement free from corruption, and a regional approach, not one limited to state or municipal boundaries. Based on his experience in Colombia, Naranjo wants to focus resources on areas with the highest levels of violent crime and perhaps reduce the presence of the armed forces more rapidly than envisaged by Peña Nieto in earlier campaign statements. Finally, General Naranjo proposes measuring success by how rapidly the violence declines and setting specific targets.[7]

During the current six-year term of President Calderón, DTOs have conducted widely reported attacks on drug rehabilitation centers; decimated private parties (often with teenagers killed); firebombed a Monterrey casino in August 2011, killing 52 patrons and employees; and relentlessly targeted Mexico's journalists. In September 2010, the leading newspaper in Ciudad Juárez published an editorial to seek a truce with the DTOs it identified as the "de facto authorities" in the city.[8] According to the Organization of American States' Special

Rapporteur on Freedom of Expression, 10 communications workers were killed in Mexico during 2011, including 8 professional journalists.[9]

In late August 2010, 72 Central and South American migrants passing through Mexico were found massacred in Tamaulipas. According to a survivor, Los Zetas attempted to recruit the migrants to assist in moving drugs and killed them when they refused. The Zetas are reported to be significantly involved in human smuggling.[10] In 2011, the DTOs' recruitment of children became another prominent concern, with reports that over 1,000 children have been killed in the fighting since Calderón came to office. From March through May 2011, mass graves were discovered in Durango and Tamaulipas, adding to the death toll linked to the DTOs in those states.

Mexico's Strategy

Since coming to office in December 2006, after winning the presidency with a very slim margin, President Calderón made an aggressive campaign against the DTOs the centerpiece of his administration's policy. He called the increased drug trafficking violence a threat to the Mexican state and sent thousands of military troops and federal police to combat the DTOs in drug trafficking "hot spots" throughout the country. The federal crackdown on the DTOs led by the well-regarded Mexican military was met with violent resistance by the trafficking organizations. At the same time, there have been some dramatic successes in capturing and arresting drug leaders. According to the U.S. Drug Enforcement Administration (DEA), more than 35 "high value targets"—DTO leaders identified mutually by the U.S. and Mexican governments—were arrested or killed in operations to detain them between January 2010 and July 2011. The pace of removing mid- and high-level DTO leaders has increased sharply during the Calderón Administration.[11]

However, the so-called kingpin strategy, of taking down top DTO leaders, which worked to fragment and help destroy the Cali and Medellin organizations in Colombia in the 1990s, has not been replicated as successfully in Mexico to date. Many analysts maintain that the implementation of the kingpin strategy in Mexico has created more instability and, at least in the near term, more violence.[12] These analysts suggest that intense but unfocused enforcement efforts against the DTOs have increased fragmentation and upset whatever equilibrium the organizations are trying to establish by their displays of violent power.[13] As a result, the violence in Mexico is more extensive, more volatile, and less predictable. Communities that have experienced increases in drug trafficking-related violence, such as Monterrey, have successfully called for troops of the Mexican army and marines to be sent to protect them. Despite government efforts, President Calderón's strategy has been criticized for not reducing the violence, which continued to increase through 2011, while sharply increasing human rights violations by the military, which is largely untrained in domestic policing.[14] President Calderón has indicated that he does not foresee turning the drug war over to the Mexican police, and that he expects to stay the course with a large military presence through the end of his term in 2012. As violence continues to escalate and reach more of Mexico's territory, some observers and policy analysts are raising concerns about the Mexican state's stability. The U.S. government and the administration of Mexican President Felipe Calderón strongly deny the so-called "failed state" thesis that was put forward by some analysts in 2008 and 2009, which suggested that the Mexican government was no longer exercising sovereignty in all areas of the country.[15] However, in early August 2010, when President Calderón initiated a series of meetings to open up public dialogue about his counterdrug strategy, he described the violence perpetrated by the DTOs as "a challenge to the state, an attempt to replace the state."[16] While some observers consider parts of Mexico lost to DTO control, this is definitely not the case for most of the country.[17] In September 2010, U.S. Secretary of State Hillary Clinton, in remarks to the Council on Foreign Relations, said that the violence by the DTOs in Mexico may be "morphing into or making common cause with what we would call an insurgency."[18] This characterization was quickly rejected by the Mexican government and revised by then-Assistant Secretary of State for Western Hemisphere Affairs Arturo Valenzuela, the Director of the White House's Office of National Drug Control Policy Gil Kerlikowske, and later reportedly by President Barack Obama.[19] It became clear that the Obama Administration generally rejects the term "insurgency" to describe the violence of drug traffickers in Mexico and their objectives. However, many U.S. government officials have concerns about the Mexican government's capacity to lower the violence in Mexico and control insurgent-like or terrorist tactics being employed by the DTOs. Mexico's stability is of critical importance to the United States and the nature and the intensity of the violence has been of particular concern to the U.S. Congress. This immense neighbor shares a nearly 2,000-mile border with the United States and has close trade and demographic ties. In addition to U.S. concern about this strategic partner and close neighbor, policy makers are concerned that the violence in Mexico could "spill over" into U.S. border states or further inland despite beefed up security measures. According to the 2011 *National Drug Threat Assessment*, the potential harm of Mexico's organizations is formidable. Mexican DTOs and their affiliates "dominate the supply and wholesale distribution of most illicit drugs in the United States" and are present in more than 1,000 U.S. cities.[20]

Congressional Concerns

The 111th Congress held more than 20 hearings dealing with the violence in Mexico, U.S. foreign assistance, and border security issues. Related hearings have continued during the 112th Congress. Congressional concern heightened after the March 2010 killing of three individuals connected to the U.S. consulate in Ciudad Juárez, Mexico, and the murder of Jaime Zapata, a U.S. ICE agent, on February 15, 2011. Following the explosion of a car bomb in July 2010 that was allegedly planted by a drug trafficking organization in Ciudad Juárez (killing four), additional car bombs have been exploded in border states and elsewhere. These acts and occasional use of grenades and rocket launchers have raised widespread concern that some Mexican drug traffickers may be adopting insurgent or terrorist techniques. Congress has expressed its concern over the escalating violence by enacting resolutions and considering legislation.

BACKGROUND ON DRUG TRAFFICKING IN MEXICO

Drug trafficking organizations have operated in Mexico for more than a century. The DTOs can be described as global businesses with forward and backward linkages for managing supply and distribution in many countries. As businesses, they are concerned with bringing their product to market in the most efficient way in order to maximize their profits. The Mexican DTOs are the major wholesalers of illegal drugs in the United States and are increasingly gaining control of U.S. retail level distribution through alliances with U.S. gangs. Their operations, however, are markedly less violent in the United States than in Mexico despite their reported presence in more than 1,000 U.S. cities.[21] The DTOs use the tools of bribery and violence, which are complementary. Violence is used to discipline employees, enforce transactions, limit the entry of competitors, and coerce. Bribery and corruption help neutralize government action against the DTOs, ensure impunity, and facilitate smooth operations.

The proceeds of drug sales (either laundered or as cash smuggled back to Mexico) are used in part to corrupt U.S. and Mexican border officials[22] and Mexican law enforcement, security forces, and public officials to either ignore DTO activities or to actively support and protect them. Mexican DTOs advance their operations through widespread corruption; when corruption fails to achieve cooperation and acquiescence, violence is the ready alternative. Police corruption has been so extensive that law enforcement officials working for the DTOs sometimes carry out their violent assignments. Purges of municipal, state, and federal police have not contained the problem. The continuing challenge of police corruption was illustrated in the August 2010 firing of 3,200 officers, about 10% of the 34,500-person federal force, by Mexico's Federal Police Commissioner after they failed basic integrity tests.[23]

Arrests of public officials accused of cooperating with the DTOs have not been followed by convictions. For example, in May 2009, federal authorities arrested 10 Mexican mayors and 18 other state and local officials in the president's home state of Michoacán for alleged ties to drug trafficking organizations. All but one individual were subsequently released because their cases did not hold up in court.[24] In 2011, the former mayor of the resort city Cancun, Gregorio "Greg" Sanchez, was released 14 months after his arrest on drug trafficking and money laundering charges when his case collapsed in federal court.[25] Similarly, the former mayor of Tijuana, Jorge Hank Rhon, was released less than two weeks after his arrest in June 2011 on weapons and murder charges due to mistakes made in the arrest procedures.[26] The corruption has taken place in states and localities governed by each of the three major political parties in Mexico, indicating that no party is immune.[27]

The relationship of Mexico's drug traffickers to the government and to one another is now a rapidly evolving picture and any current snapshot (such as the one provided in this report) must be continually adjusted. In the early 20th century, Mexico was a source of marijuana and heroin to the United States, and by the 1940s, Mexican drug smugglers were notorious in the United States.[28] The growth and entrenchment of Mexico's drug trafficking networks occurred during a period of one-party rule in Mexico by the PRI, which governed for 71 years.[29] During that period, the government was centralized and hierarchical, and, to a large degree, it tolerated and protected some drug production and trafficking in certain regions of the country, even though the PRI government did not generally tolerate crime.[30] According to numerous accounts, for many years the Mexican government pursued an overall policy of accommodation. Under this system, arrests and eradication of drug crops took place, but due to the effects of widespread corruption the system was "characterized by a working relationship between Mexican authorities and drug lords" through the 1990s.[31]

The stability of the system began to fray in the 1990s as Mexican political power decentralized and the push toward democratic pluralism began first at the local level and then nationally with the election of the National Action Party (PAN) candidate Vicente Fox as president in 2000.[32] The process of democratization upended the equilibrium that had developed between state actors (such as the Federal Security Directorate that oversaw domestic security from 1947 to 1985) and organized crime. No longer were certain officials able to ensure the impunity of drug traffickers to the same degree and to regulate competition among Mexican DTOs for drug trafficking routes, or *plazas*. To a large extent, DTO violence directed at the government appears to be an attempt to re-establish impunity while the inter-cartel violence seems to be attempts to re-establish dominance over specific drug trafficking plazas. The intra-DTO violence (or violence inside the organizations) reflects reaction to suspected betrayals and the competition to succeed killed or arrested leaders.

Before this political development, an important transition in the role of Mexico in the international drug trade took place during the 1980s and early 1990s. As Colombian DTOs were forcibly broken up, the highly profitable traffic in cocaine to the United States was gradually taken over by Mexican traffickers. The traditional trafficking route used by the Colombians through the Caribbean was shut down by intense enforcement efforts of the U.S. government. As Colombian DTOs lost this route, they increasingly subcontracted the trafficking of cocaine produced in the Andean region to the Mexican DTOs, who they paid in cocaine rather than cash. These already strong organizations gradually took over the cocaine trafficking business, evolving from being mere couriers for the Colombians to being the wholesalers they are today. As Mexico's drug trafficking organizations rose to dominate the U.S. drug markets in the 1990s, the business became even more lucrative. This "raised the stakes," which encouraged the use of violence in Mexico to protect and promote market share. The violent struggle between DTOs over strategic routes and warehouses where drugs are consolidated before entering the United States reflects these higher stakes.

Today the major Mexican DTOs are polydrug, handling more than one type of drug although they may specialize in the production or trafficking of specific products. Mexico is a major producer and supplier to the U.S. market of heroin, methamphetamine, and marijuana and the principal transit country for cocaine sold in the United States.[33] The west coast state of Sinaloa (see map in Figure 1), which has a long coastline and difficult-to-access areas favorable for drug cultivation, is the heartland of Mexico's drug trade. Marijuana and poppy cultivation has flourished in this state for decades.[34] It has been the source of Mexico's most notorious and successful drug traffickers. In April 2012, violence began to spike in Sinaloa, including a lengthy engagement with Mexican military and police, thought to be caused by resident drug traffickers protecting their drug growing turf or an important leader.[35]

According to the U.S State Department's *2012 International Narcotics Control Strategy Report,* about 95% of the cocaine that is seized in the United States has transited the Central America/Mexico corridor. In the United States, the availability of cocaine began to decline in 2009, which some authorities have attributed in part to an increase in law enforcement efforts in both Mexico and the United States. Coca production in Colombia has also declined, and there has been an increasing flow of Colombian cocaine to other regions such as West Africa and Europe. At the same time, cultivation of opium poppy (from which heroin is derived) and marijuana doubled in Mexico between 2006 and 2011.[36] The U.S. government estimated that Mexico produced 19,500 hectares of poppy in 2009, surpassing Burma as the second-largest cultivator of poppy in the world.[37] Domestic consumption of heroin inside Mexico is increasing. Production of methamphetamine is also believed to be climbing, suggested by the number of laboratories that were destroyed by the Mexican authorities in 2009 (three times greater than the year before).[38]

MEXICO'S MAJOR DRUG TRAFFICKING ORGANIZATIONS

The DTOs have been in constant flux. By some accounts, when President Calderón came to office in December 2006, there were four dominant DTOs: the Tijuana/Arellano Felix organization (AFO), the Sinaloa cartel, the Juárez/Vicente Carillo Fuentes organization (CFO), and the Gulf cartel.

Since then, the more stable organizations that existed in the earlier years of the Calderón Administration have fractured into many more groups. For a time, according to the U.S. DEA, seven organizations were dominant. These included Sinaloa, Los Zetas, Tijuana/AFO, Juárez/CFO, Beltrán Leyva, Gulf, and La Familia Michoacana. However, many analysts suggest that these seven now seem to have fragmented to between 12 and as many as 20 organizations. Today, two large "national" DTOs—Sinaloa and Los Zetas—appear to be preeminent. But the diversification into other crime, the ephemeral prominence of new gangs and DTOs, and shifting alliances make a static DTO landscape difficult to portray.

For instance, the Gulf cartel, based in northeastern Mexico, had a long history of dominance in terms of power and profits with the zenith of its power in the early 2000s. However, the Gulf cartel's enforcers—Los Zetas, who were organized around Mexican military deserters—split to form a separate DTO and turned against their former employers. The well-established Sinaloa DTO, with roots in western Mexico, has fought brutally for increased control of routes through Chihuahua and Baja California with the goal of becoming the dominant DTO in the country. Sinaloa has a more decentralized structure of loosely linked smaller organizations, which has been susceptible to conflict when units break away. Nevertheless, the decentralized structure has enabled it to be quite adaptable in the highly competitive and unstable environment that now prevails.[39] Finally, La Familia Michoacana—a DTO based in the Pacific southwestern state of Michoácan and influential in surrounding states—split apart in early 2011 and has fought a bitter turf battle with its violent successor, the Knights Templar, that is expected to continue.

From open source research, there is more available information about the seven "traditional" DTOs (and their successors). Current information about the array of new regional and local crime groups is more difficult to assess. The seven organizations and their successors are still operating, both in conflict with one another and at times working in collaboration. A brief sketch of each of these groups, portrayed in Figure 1 (the U.S. DEA map from January 2012), follows:

Tijuana/Arellano Felix Organization (AFO). One of the founders of modern Mexican DTOs, Miguel Angel Felix Gallardo, a former police officer from Sinaloa, created a network that included the Arellano Felix family, and numerous other DTO leaders such as Rafael Caro Quintero, Amado Carrillo Fuentes, and current fugitive Joaquín "El Chapo" Guzmán. The seven "Arellano Felix" brothers and four sisters inherited the drug fiefdom (AFO) from their uncle, Miguel Angel Felix Gallardo, after his arrest in 1989 for the murder of DEA Special Agent Enrique "Kiki" Camarena.[40]

By the late 1990s and the early 2000s, this DTO, based in Tijuana, was one of the two dominant organizations, and competed against the more powerful Juárez organization. The AFO structure began to dissolve after several of its leaders were arrested. Of the Arellano Felix brothers, in 2002 Ramón was killed and Benjamin was later arrested. In October 2008, Eduardo Arellano, the last of the five brothers involved in the drug business, was apprehended in Tijuana.

A bloody battle for control broke out in 2008 when the AFO organization split into two factions. In the vacuum left by the arrests of the AFO's key players, other DTOs in the region attempted to assert control over the profitable Tijuana/Baja California-San Diego/California border plaza. The AFO suffered another blow when Eduardo Teodoro "El Teo" Garcia Simental, a former AFO lieutenant, aligned himself with the Sinaloa cartel, which led to a surge of violence in Tijuana.[41] Since the January 2010 arrest of Garcia Simental, violence in Tijuana has markedly decreased.[42]

Some observers have claimed the decrease in violence is an important law enforcement success, while others suggest competing DTOs may have come to an agreement on the use of the drug trafficking route.[43]

Fernando Sanchez Arellano (alias "El Ingeniero") is a nephew of the founding Arellano Felix brothers. According to several sources, he maintains leadership of the diminished AFO (also known as the Tijuana DTO). *STRATFOR* reports that he has worked out a deal with the dominant Sinaloa organization to pay a fee for the right to use the lucrative plaza once under the AFO's control.[44] Other analysts suggest the Tijuana leader is purposefully maintaining a low profile to reduce attention from the media and Mexican government while maintaining a steady business moving drugs North into California.[45]

Sinaloa DTO. This organization retains the Sinaloa core that has descended from the Felix Gallardo network. Headed by the fugitive prison escapee and billionaire Joaquín "El Chapo" Guzmán, the Sinaloa DTO emerged as an effective leader in moving cocaine from South America to the United States. Early in 2008, a federation dominated by the Sinaloa cartel (which included the Beltrán Leyva organization and the Juárez cartel) broke apart. Sinaloa, still composed of a network of smaller organizations, has grown to be the dominant DTO operating in Mexico today, controlling by one estimate 45% of the drug trade in Mexico.[46] In addition to Guzmán, top leadership of the DTO includes Ismael "El Mayo" Zambada García.[47] Examining arrest data of the Calderón antidrug effort, some analysts believe they have detected a pattern of arrests demonstrating favor toward the Sinaloa DTO, whose members have not been arrested at the same rates as competing DTOs. President Calderón has strongly denied any accusation of favoritism.[48] The Mexican military's July 2010 killing of Ignacio Coronel Villarreal (alias "El Nacho"), reportedly the third-highest leader overseeing Sinaloa operations in central Mexico, has given credence to the argument that Sinaloa has taken serious hits like the others.

Sinaloa reportedly has a substantial presence in some 50 countries, including throughout the Americas, Europe, West Africa, and Southeast Asia.[49] Often described as the most powerful mafia organization in the Western Hemisphere, Sinaloa is also reported to be the most cohesive. In 2011, it expanded operations into Mexico City, and into Durango, Guerrero, and Michoacán states while continuing its push into territories in both Baja California and Chihuahua once controlled by the Tijuana and Juárez DTOs.

There has been increasing focus on the capture of Sinaloa leader Joaquín "El Chapo" Guzmán in recent months, a priority for both the U.S. government and the Calderón

Administration in its last months in office. The Sinaloa leader ranks number one on the Mexican authorities' list of 37 top narco-traffickers (of whom 23 were captured or killed by mid-2012). Nevertheless, Mexican security forces have had near misses in capturing Guzmán, as allegedly happened in the resort area of Los Cabos in the Baja California peninsula in March 2012. Efforts to tighten the noose around members of his family have also been unsuccessful. In early June 2012, U.S. authorities sanctioned Guzmán's ex-wife and his son, Jesus Alfredo Guzmán Salazar, under the Foreign Narcotics Kingpin Designation Act for their material support and involvement with the operations of the Sinaloa DTO. However, in an embarrassing case of mistaken identity, on June 23, 2012, Mexican authorities announced they had arrested El Chapo's son, a rising leader within the cartel, only to have it later revealed that their captive was not the son but another person entirely. The lawyers for the person being held in custody, Felix Beltrán León, claimed he was innocent and had no ties to the Sinaloa DTO.[50]

Juárez/Vicente Carrillo Fuentes Organization. This DTO is led by Vicente Carrillo Fuentes, who took over from his brother Amado, founder of the DTO, who died in 1997. Vicente oversaw the operations when the Juárez DTO was part of the Sinaloa federation, from which it split in 2008.[51] The Juárez DTO and its enforcement arm, La Línea, have ferociously fought their former Sinaloa ally to maintain their core territory, the Ciudad Juárez corridor abutting El Paso, TX. Since 2008, this inter-DTO battle has raged, resulting in thousands of deaths in Ciudad Juárez, making the surrounding Mexican state of Chihuahua the deadliest in the country.[52] The Juárez DTO has reportedly been worn down by the conflict and resorted to other lucrative activities to finance its battle, including domestic drug sales in Ciudad Juárez (where rates of abuse are among the highest in Mexico). The Juárez DTO has battled for control of local drug markets with proxy street gangs. Los Aztecas, one of the larger gangs, is fighting for the Juárez organization against two gangs, the Artistas Asesinos and the Mexicales, representing the Sinaloa DTO.[53]

The degree of decline this organization has suffered is contested. Some analysts believe it is a "spent force," while others have identified a tenacity to hold on to parts of Ciudad Juárez and other cities in Chihuahua.[54] The DTO's enforcement arm, the La Linea gang, suffered a major loss when leader José Antonio Acosta Hernández (alias "El Diego") was arrested in late July 2011. He confessed to ordering more than 1,500 murders and was convicted of the March 2010 murder of the three people connected to the U.S. consulate in Juárez. After his extradition to the United States, he was convicted in U.S. federal court on charges of murder and drug trafficking and sentenced to four consecutive life sentences in April 2012. The case represents increasingly close cooperation between Mexican and U.S. authorities on bringing hyper-violent offenders to justice.[55]

Gulf DTO. The Gulf DTO is based in the border city of Matamoros in the northeastern Mexican state of Tamaulipas. It arose in the bootlegging era of the 1920s. In the 1980s, its leader, Juan García Abrego, developed ties to Colombia's Cali cartel as well as to the Mexican Federal Police. His violent successor, Osiel Cárdenas Guillén, successfully corrupted elite Mexican military forces sent to capture him. Those corrupted military personnel became known as Los Zetas and fused with the Gulf cartel. At the beginning of the 21st century, Gulf was considered one of the most powerful Mexican DTOs. Cárdenas was arrested by Mexican authorities in 2003, but he successfully ran his drug enterprise from prison.[56] The violent struggle to succeed him did not begin until his extradition to the United States in early 2007. (In February 2010, Cárdenas was sentenced to serve 25 years in a U.S.

prison.) Despite a difficult internal succession battle and successful law enforcement operations against it, the Gulf organization continues to successfully move drugs. On November 5, 2010, Osiel's brother, Antonio Ezequiél Cárdenas Guillén (alias Tony Tormenta), was killed in Matamoros in a gun battle with Mexican marines. He had risen to a top position in the Gulf DTO following his brother's extradition. His death set off renewed violence as the weakened Gulf DTO attempted to fight off the continued assault by its former allies, Los Zetas.[57] In 2011, Gulf continued its battle with the Zetas for control over its former strongholds in Tamaulipas, Nuevo León, and Veracruz.[58] Although identified by some observers as a "national" cartel, its area of influence has become quite diminished (see Figure 1).

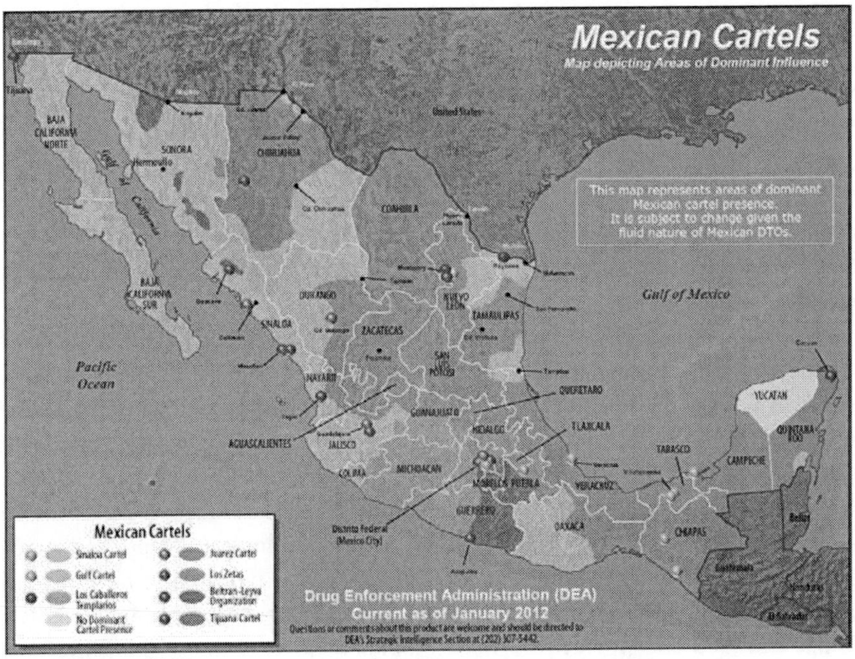

Source: DEA, January 2012

Notes: The DEA uses the term "cartel" in place of DTO. Also, the DTO identified as the Knights Templar in the report text is labeled in the map key by its Spanish name, "Los Caballeros Templarios."

Figure 1. Map of DTO Areas of Dominant Influence in Mexico by DEA.

Los Zetas. This group was originally composed of former elite airborne special force members of the Mexican Army who defected to the Gulf cartel and became their hired assassins.[59] In 2008, Los Zetas began to contract their services to other DTOs operating throughout the country, notably the Beltrán Leyva organization and the Juárez DTO.[60] Los Zetas split with the Gulf cartel in the period of late 2008 to 2010 (analysts disagree on the exact timing) to become an independent DTO. Since February 2010, Los Zetas and the Gulf cartel have been battling in Tamaulipas, Nuevo León, and other Gulf territory for control of drug smuggling corridors. What is especially significant is that in order to fight Los Zetas, the Gulf cartel has allied itself with two former enemies—La Familia Michoacana (LFM) and the Sinaloa cartel—creating an environment of urban warfare with commando-style raids on state prisons, abduction of journalists, murder of police, and attacks on military posts. They have organized elaborate road blockades during their violent operations to prevent legitimate police from responding.[61] In 2010, the battle for territory between the Zetas and the Gulf-Sinaloa-La Familia alliance (a temporary alliance of convenience) increased casualties among the government's security forces.[62] Some observers argue that this killing does not suggest a tactic by the DTOs to target government officials, but rather an increase in inter-cartel rivalry.[63]

Los Zetas gained power under the leadership of Heriberto Lazcano Lazcano.[64] The Zetas have expanded their operations to Central America to collaborate with their Guatemalan equivalent, Los Kaibiles, and with Central American gangs in an effort to take control of cocaine shipments from Guatemala to Mexico.[65]

Currently, Los Zetas appear to have the largest area of geographic influence in Mexico and to be growing stronger in Guatemala. The Zetas are also believed to have achieved the most diversification in other criminal activities. (See section "DTO Fragmentation, Competition, and Diversification.") While they have been aggressively expansionist, some analysts question if this DTO is responsible for the largest portion of the violent conflict in Mexico. The Zetas were targeted by both the Mexican and U.S. governments for increased enforcement in 2011. While this additional government pressure does not appear to have diminished their areas of influence, the Sinaloa DTO is still considered by many observers to be the most dominant.[66]

Beltrán Leyva Organization (BLO). Until 2008, this syndicate was a part of the Sinaloa federation and controlled access to the U.S. border in Sonora state. The January 2008 arrest of Alfredo Beltrán Leyva, brother of the syndicate's leader, Arturo, and a leading lieutenant in the organization, is believed to have been abetted by "El Chapo" Guzmán, the top leader of the Sinaloa DTO. The loss of Alfredo cemented the animosity between the two organizations. Despite resistance from the Sinaloa federation, the BLO successfully secured drug transport routes in the states of Sinaloa, Durango, Sonora, Jalisco, Michoacán, Guerrero, and Morelos. In addition, the BLO, like other dominant Mexican DTOs, is believed to have infiltrated the upper levels of the Mexican government to help maintain its strong presence and control.[67] The BLO has executed uncooperative officials, and is believed to be responsible for the May 2008 assassination of acting federal police director Edgar Millan Gomez.[68] The organization has shown a high level of sophistication in its operations, forming a strategic alliance with Los Zetas to fight for important drug territory against the Gulf, Sinaloa, and La Familia DTOs. The BLO had long-standing links to Colombian sources, and control over multiple and varied routes into Mexico. Along with the Sinaloa DTO, it had also enjoyed a significant presence in southern Mexico.

The organization suffered a series of setbacks at the hands of the Mexican security forces beginning with the December 2009 killing of Arturo Beltrán Leyva during a raid conducted by Mexican marines, and the arrest of Carlos Beltrán Leyva in January 2010. Some experts believe that the remaining Beltrán Leyva brother, Hector, is the acting head of the organization now that the three others have been arrested or killed. Gerardo Alvarez-Vazquez, who was arrested in April 2010, had been fighting Hector Beltrán Leyva for control of the DTO along with Edgar Valdez Villarreal (alias "La Barbie"), who was arrested in August 2010.[69]

Valdez's arrest was a major victory for the Mexican authorities and for President Calderón's drug strategy.[70] He reportedly was one of the rare Mexican-Americans who was a top leader of a Mexican DTO.[71] The power vacuum left by the death of Arturo Beltrán Leyva had led to major fighting among members of the BLO and contributed significantly to violence in the central region of the country such as the state of Morelos in early and mid-2010.[72] Following the killing of Arturo Beltrán Leyva, two new organizations have emerged: the South Pacific Cartel, reportedly led by Arturo's brother Hector, and the Independent Cartel of Acapulco, which contains remnants of the old BLO that were loyal to Valdez ("La Barbie"). The capture of Valdez (who had a $2 million reward for his arrest in both the United States and Mexico) may decrease the BLO's importance, continue the internal power struggle, or tempt other DTOs to take control of the BLO routes.

La Familia Michoacana (LFM)/Knights Templar. This DTO, first known as LFM, acquired notoriety for its hyper-violent crimes in 2006, although it traces its roots back to the 1980s. Ironically, it started as a vigilante group to eradicate drug use in Mexico and particularly in Michoacán, where it is based. But as a DTO it has specialized in methamphetamine production and smuggling (reportedly for sale in the United States only) and is also a vigorous trafficker of marijuana, cocaine, and heroin.[73] LFM was known for its use of extreme, symbolic violence and a pseudo-ideological or religious justification for its existence. According to one study, the LFM represented "a hybrid fusion of criminal drug enterprise entity and Christian evangelical beliefs" combining social, criminal, and religious elements in one movement.[74] LFM was known for leaving signs ("narcomantas") on corpses and at crime scenes, describing their actions as "divine justice."[75] LFM members have reportedly made donations of food, medical care, and schools to benefit the poor in order to project a "Robin Hood" image.[76] Once affiliated with Los Zetas (when the Gulf and Zetas DTOs were merged), the LFM turned to oppose Los Zetas. Declared Mexico's most violent DTO in 2009 by Mexico's then-attorney general, LFM used some of the ruthless techniques learned from the paramilitary Zetas.[77]

In 2010, however, LFM played a less prominent role, and in November 2010, the LFM reportedly called for a truce with the Mexican government and announced it would disband.[78] In a December 10, 2010, gun battle with the Mexican federal police, the LFM's spiritual leader Nazario Moreno González (alias "El Más Loco") was killed, according to Mexican authorities.[79] In June 2011, LFM leader José de Jesús Méndez Vargas was arrested. A new organization that emerged in early 2011 calling itself the Knights Templar claims to be a successor or offshoot of LFM, and is led by charismatic former lieutenant Servando Gomez (alias "La Tuta"). The Knights Templar may replace the older organization with which it is now locked in competition. Like LFM, it claims to have a code of conduct and has published a 22-page booklet laying out its ethics.[80] The Knights Templar have emulated LFM's supposed commitment to "social justice" and reportedly LFM's penchant for diversification into crime such as extortion. According to some analysts, the Knights Templar have been engaging in combat with the remnants of the LFM throughout 2011, including clashes in the states of Michoacán, Mexico, Morelos, and Guerrero, and have been used as a proxy by the Sinaloa DTO in its battles with Los Zetas and affiliated gangs.[81]

DTO Fragmentation, Competition, and Diversification

As stated earlier, the DTOs today are more fragmented, more violent, and more competitive than the larger and more stable organizations that President Calderón faced at the beginning of his administration.[82] Analysts disagree about the extent of this fragmentation and its importance, and whether the group of smaller organizations will be easier to dismantle. There is more agreement that the environment is growing more violent and that the "violent free for all" is a relatively new development in Mexico.[83]

Fragmentation that began in 2010 and accelerated in 2011 has redefined the "battlefield" and brought new actors, such as Los Zetas and the Knights Templar, to the fore. An array of smaller organizations are now active, including the Resistance and the Jalisco Cartel–New Generation, who are reportedly competing for territory in the coastal states of Nayarit, Colima, and Jalisco.[84]

Contrary to the experience in Colombia with the sequential dismantling of the enormous Medellin and Cali cartels,[85] fragmentation in Mexico has been associated with escalating violence.[86] A "kingpin strategy" implemented by the Mexican government has successfully "taken down" numerous top- and mid-level leaders in all the major DTOs, either through arrests or deaths in operations to detain them. However, this strategy with political decentralization has contributed to violent succession struggles, shifting alliances among the DTOs, a proliferation of new gangs and small DTOs, and the replacement of existing leaders and criminal groups by ones who are even more violent.[87] Analysts disagree about the extent of this fragmentation and its importance. Several analysts have observed that as the Mexican DTOs have fragmented and multiplied, violence has escalated to an all-time high.[88] Others analysts caution not to overstate the level of fragmentation. Many of these organizations and smaller gangs are new and it is premature to predict how they will fare or whether the resulting highly competitive group of smaller organizations will be easier to dismantle. The Mexican government, on the other hand, has asserted that the removal of DTO leadership through government enforcement operations has not caused violence to spike.[89]

Another emerging factor has been the criminal diversification of the DTOs. In addition to selling illegal drugs, they have branched into other profitable crimes such as kidnapping, assassination for hire, auto theft, controlling prostitution, extortion, money-laundering, software piracy, resource theft, and human smuggling. The surge in violence due to inter- and intra-cartel conflict over lucrative drug smuggling routes has been accompanied by an increase in kidnapping for ransom and other crimes. According to recent estimates, kidnappings in Mexico have increased by 188% since 2007, armed robbery by 47%, and extortion by 101%.[90] Some believe diversification may be evidence of organizational vitality and growth. Others contend that diversification signals that U.S. and Mexican drug enforcement measures are cutting into profits from drug trafficking, or constitutes a response to shifting U.S. drug consumption patterns.[91]

The growing public condemnation of the DTOs may also be stimulated by their diversification into street crime, which causes more harm to average Mexican civilians than intra- and inter-DTO violence related to conflicts over drug trafficking.

Because the DTOs have diversified, many analysts now refer to them as transnational criminal organizations (TCOs), as organized crime groups, or as mafias.[92] Others maintain that much of their non-drug criminal activity is in service of the central drug trafficking business.[93] Whatever the label, no one has an accurate way to assess how much of the DTOs' income is earned from their non-drug activities.

Los Zetas are one of the most diversified DTOs. Their satellite businesses include the theft of petroleum from the state-owned oil company PEMEX, product piracy, and human smuggling, as well as extortion, money laundering, and robbery.[94]

In July 2011, the Obama Administration released a new *Strategy to Combat Transnational Organized Crime*, citing the Mexican DTOs as some of its target subjects.[95] On July 25, the White House issued an executive order that named four groups around the world that presented transnational organized crime threats to U.S. national security. Not surprisingly, Los Zetas were identified for their diverse criminal activities and their propensity to commit mass murder. Some analysts have questioned why Los Zetas were singled out, when Sinaloa and other Mexican DTOs are also known to be significantly involved in other forms of crime.[96]

The current crime organization landscape is exceptionally fluid, yet several analysts are attempting to define it. For example, in Southern Pulse's publication *Beyond 2012*, Sam Logan and James Bosworth describe the increasing multiplication of groups:

> The tendency for criminal groups in Mexico is toward small and local ... as the number of well-armed criminal groups jumps from the six significant groups we counted in 2006 ... to over 10 in 2012 with a steady growth of new groups to bring the total to possibly over 20 by the end of 2014.[97]

Analyst Eric Olson of the Woodrow Wilson Center for International Scholars believes the DTOs are more accurately described as "organized crime groups" and notes that these groups are extremely local in character while engaged in diverse criminal activity. (Many of the actors have diversified beyond the transnational drug trade, as noted above.) Mexican political scientist Eduardo Guerrero-Gutiérrez also describes fragmentation and has provided a very useful typology of different DTOs (see Table 1). He defines four types: National Cartels, Toll-taker Cartels, Regional Cartels, and Local Mafias.

Guerrero identifies as many as 64 organizations across the country in the final category. Some of these groups do not participate in drug trafficking-related violence, but are only engaged in what he terms "mafia-ridden" violence. Guerrero attributes the proliferation of new criminal groups to a "non-selective arrest policy" by the Mexican government that has taken out kingpins and leaders and produced violent competition to replace those who have been arrested or killed.[98]

A couple of generalizations can be made about the current DTO landscape. First, there is more competition and more violence. Second, few large actors remain except for the two dominant ones, Sinaloa and Los Zetas, which have become polarized in their battle for supremacy.

Sinaloa, based in the western part of the country, was present in some 17 states as of August 2011 according to one analysis. Los Zetas, which cover the eastern portion of the country, had operations in 21 states as of August 2011, giving them greater geographic presence.[99]

The Zetas had the reputation for being the most violent, but the Sinaloa cartel, trying to deliver a devastating blow to their rivals, has emulated the newer DTO's most violent tactics.

Both Sinaloa and Los Zetas have made grisly incursions into the home turf of their opponent, either directly or through proxies (smaller organizations which have affiliated with one side or the other at least temporarily), leaving behind headless torsos and bodies hanging from bridges among other atrocities.[100]

Table 1. Drug Trafficking Organizations Typology

CATEGORY	DESCRIPTION	ORGANIZATIONS
National Cartels	Cartels control or maintain presence along routes of several drugs. They also operate important international routes to and from Mexico. These DTOs keep control of drug points of entry and exit in the country. However, they are interested in expanding their control of new points of exit along the northern border, and this is why they currently sustain disputes with other cartels to control these border localities. These DTOs are present in broad areas of the country and have sought to build upon the profits they receive from drug trafficking through diversifying their illegal activities towards human smuggling and oil and fuel theft.	Sinaloa, Los Zetas, and Gulf cartels (although Gulf has a significantly less important role than the other two).
"Toll Collector" Cartels	These are the cartels whose main income comes from toll fees received from the cartels and regional cartels that send drug shipments through their controlled municipalities along the northern border. Given that these cartels are largely confined to some border municipalities, they cannot diversify their illegal activities as actively as the national cartels. If these cartels eventually lose control of their respective border areas they will either intensify their diversification efforts to other business (such as extortion or kidnapping) or they will disappear.	Tijuana and Juárez cartels
Regional Cartels	These DTOs keep limited control over segments of drug trafficking routes that pass through their territory. Like the toll collector cartels, the regional cartels play a secondary role in the drug trading business and receive small profits from it and have limited capabilities to diversify to other criminal businesses like human smuggling or oil and fuel theft.	The Knights Templar and South Pacific cartels
Local Mafias	The mafias are disbanded cells from fragmented national or regional cartels. These are locally based and their range can extend from a few contiguous localities to several states. Their business activities are mainly focused in drug distribution and dealing within their controlled municipalities, and they have extended their illegal business towards extortion, kidnapping and vehicle theft.	The Resistance; Jalisco Cartel–New Generation; Cártel del Charro; The Hands with Eyes; Los Incorriegibles; La Empresa; Independent Cartel of Acapulco; and others.

Source: Eduardo Guerrero-Gutiérrez, *Security, Drugs, and Violence in Mexico: A Survey*, 7th North American Forum, Washington, DC, 2011.
Notes: Text modified in consultation with the author on May 21, 2012.

CHARACTERISTICS OF THE INCREASED VIOLENCE

As the DTOs have fractured and more organizations vie for control of trafficking routes, the level of inter- and intra-cartel violence has spiked. Inter-DTO violence is used when the cartels fight one another to dominate trafficking routes. Besides inter-DTO violence (between the different organizations), there has been widespread violence within the organizations, as factions battle in succession struggles to replace fallen or arrested leaders. The succession battles are hastened by the drug war victories by the Mexican government. In describing the violence resulting from the elimination of a leader, one observer refers to "internal vacancy chains" that result when an organization is squeezed by the government and there is great uncertainty about how the leader will be replaced (either through internal succession or external replacement). In some cases, a weakened DTO will be attacked by other DTOs in a "feeding frenzy" until the uncertainty of succession is resolved.[101] Thus highly charged violence may result from asymmetric weakening of competitive organizations.[102] Intra-DTO violence is used to assert leadership inside the cartel or to impose organizational discipline and loyalty. The violent response of the DTOs to the government's aggressive security strategy is a third key element leading to escalation. Gun battles between government forces and the DTOs are regular occurrences. And with the expansion of democratic pluralism, DTOs are fighting the state to reassert their impunity from the justice system.

Drug trafficking-related violence in Mexico has been brutal, and, in an apparent contradiction, both widespread and relatively concentrated. However, since 2010 the violence has dispersed considerably to new areas and involved more municipalities. The violence, while still concentrated along drug trafficking routes and in a small percentage of Mexican municipalities, has spread to every state and flared in the northern border states. In 2011, the violence moved towards Mexico's interior, exploding in such states as Veracruz (a Gulf state) and in Guerrero on Mexico's southern Pacific coast. According to analysis by University of San Diego's Trans-Border Institute (TBI), 84% of Mexico's municipalities have been affected in some way by organized crime violence (with only 16% violence free) and over time violence has spread to a larger number of municipalities.[103] There remains a debate about exactly how many have perished in the violence.

The Mexican government has released data on homicides in Mexico linked to organized crime during the Calderón Administration in January 2011 and January 2012.[104] In these two releases, the government reported that between December 2006 and September 2011 more than 47,500 killings were organized crime-related homicides. These official figures are about 15% to 25% higher than the tallies provided in some media reporting, such as that of the Mexican media outlet *Grupo Reforma*, which have been used by TBI to track violence in Mexico because the data has been released more consistently. The *Reforma* data are reported weekly and collected by a national network of newspaper correspondents spread across the country.[105]

While casualty estimates from the government and media sources have not been identical, they have reflected similar trends. All reports have shown the violence rising sharply since early 2007 and spreading to new parts of Mexico. This report gives preference to officially reported data. According to government data, in 2007 (the first full year of the Calderón government), there were more than 2,800 organized crime-related homicides, which more than doubled in 2008. Between 2008 and 2009, the rate of increase was about 40%. Between 2009 and 2010, organized crime-related homicides grew by almost 60%. Finally the rate of increase started to come down between 2010 and 2011 (see Figure 2). The government's second data release in January 2012, only included data for the first three quarters of 2011 (January–September 2011), reporting a total of 12,903 homicides. Consequently, when measured against the same nine-month period in 2010, the number of organized crime killings grew by only 11% in 2011. There is some disagreement if the killings have plateaued and even begun to decline in 2012.[106] (Characterizations of the "trend" depend on comparing the first quarter of 2012 with either the first or last quarter of 2011, for example). At this point it is premature to make an estimate, although some commentators have suggested that a decline is likely to proceed more slowly than the rapid rise in killings.

Casualty Estimates in Context and for Special Populations

The Mexican authorities maintained in July 2010 that more than 90% of the casualties (those who have died since President Calderón's crackdown in December 2006) were individuals involved with or linked in some way to the criminal activities of the DTOs. Critics, however, have questioned this assertion and noted it does little to mitigate the Mexican public's growing alarm about public safety. Mexican government information has neither been easy to access nor reported regularly. To track the violence, TBI and others have turned to Mexican media reporting. Newspapers and other media organizations keep daily tallies of the killings that are considered a close approximation of the overall situation. TBI's Justice in Mexico project has used the data collected by the national Mexican newspaper *Reforma* to tabulate Mexico's drug trafficking violence over the past decade.

TBI has found that *Reforma* is generally more conservative and cautious about classifying a death as drug trafficking-related than are official sources and other media outlets.[107] *Reforma's* classification of a homicide attributed to the drug trafficking organizations is based on criminal justice protocols and the presence at the crime scene of characteristics traditionally used by DTOs, such as high-caliber weapons, decapitations, or "narco" messages.[108] The possibility that other criminals could carry out murders in a manner to make them appear to be those of the DTOs is one cause to question the accuracy of the figures. Further concerns are that authorities often fail to identify and fully investigate drug trafficking-related homicides, some DTOs will attempt to eliminate all evidence of murders, and some leave confusing messages either accepting blame or trying to shift it to a rival. According to the *Reforma* data, there were 11,583 drug trafficking-related homicides in 2010, and according to the government database the total murders attributed to organized crime exceeded 15,270. The higher government figure may be due to a definition of organized crime which is broader than drug trafficking. But the trends in the data produced by *Reforma* closely correlate with those trends in the data released by the government.[109]

Mexican government data are compiled by a collaborative task force coordinated by the Technical Secretary for the National Security Council (CNS) and that involves multiple intelligence and law enforcement agencies.[110] The two releases of aggregate data by the Mexican government task force in January 2011 and January 2012 had slightly different definitions. For the first release of data (January 2007–December 2010), the Mexican government labeled the information as "homicides allegedly linked to organized crime." The second release of data (January 2011– September 2011) was defined as "homicides allegedly caused by criminal rivalry."[111] Like the *Reforma* data, there are a number of characteristics utilized by the government to identify such homicides. These homicides generally have not been fully investigated, so accuracy is always an issue. TBI has found that the government count was consistently about 25% greater than the *Reforma* count and that the media company consistently underestimates organized crime homicides, but this has the advantage of reducing the frequency of "false positives."

Because the Mexican government released data for only three quarters of 2011, there is no "official tally" for 2011. As shown in Figure 2, the government reported nearly 13,000 organized-crime related homicides for the first three quarters of the year. TBI has calculated the killings in the last three months of 2011, basing its projections on *Reforma*'s data for the last quarter of the year expanded by 24%. This estimate incorporates a decline in the level of homicides in the last quarter observed in the *Reforma* data trends and therefore "provides what is probably a more precise estimate of the government's final tally for 2011."[112]

As shown in Figure 3, the TBI estimate for the entire year is slightly more than 16,400 organized crime-related homicides. The TBI data have been mapped and a geographic explanation of the violence will be addressed in the next section. With that number of organized crime homicides in 2011 (16,414), the total number of organized crime homicides for the December 2006–December 2011 period is slightly more than 50,900. As TBI notes, this calculation is consistent with the estimates of various non-governmental organizations and other observers.[113] As discussed above, violence did continue to rise in 2011, but far less sharply. Many observers have noted that the level of organized crime killings in 2011 was several times higher than 2007 and TBI's annual report on the violence summarized it vividly:

> On average, for every day of 2011, 47 people were killed, three of whom were tortured, one of whom was decapitated, two of whom were women, and ten of whom were young people whose lives ended in organized-crime-related violence.[114]

The Trans-Border Institute has tracked violent crimes against journalists, mayors, and other special groups who were victims of violent crime (see Figure 4). Violent crimes targeting journalists, and high levels of impunity for perpetrators of those crimes, have caused Mexico to be ranked among the most dangerous places in the world to work as a journalist. In the first half of 2012, at least six journalists were slain in Mexico, several in the troubled state of Veracruz. Crime against journalists runs from harassment to murder, and often causes journalists to self-censor their work and news outlets to stop publishing or broadcasting stories on violent crime.

In response to the spike in journalist murders and criticism that the Mexican judiciary was not resolving such cases, the Calderón government took some steps in 2011 to improve security measures for journalists at risk of being victimized (frequently those include reporters who cover crime or government corruption beats). In April 2012, a law to enhance protection for journalists and human rights defenders passed both houses of the Mexican Congress. Nevertheless, in May 2012, a newspaper in Nuevo Laredo, the Mexican city contiguous to Laredo, TX, announced it would no longer report on violent rivalries between crime groups *anywhere* in the country after being subject to threats and attacks. According to the Committee to Protect Journalists, this announcement of such broad self-censorship may be the first of its kind.[115] In July, three offices of the newspaper *El Norte* (located in different parts of Nuevo León state) were separately attacked. One attack involved setting a fire and armed gunmen storming the media outlet's offices, and in the other instances attackers used grenades and heavy artillery.

Media groups and other observers have expressed support for beleaguered Mexican media that are being pressured by the DTOs to not cover the violence and have criticized the Mexican government for not extending adequate protection. Organized crime is also reported to be targeting citizens who use social media to report on the violence. In some cities, social media such as Twitter have become an important news source because traditional news outlets have been silenced by threats from reporting on violent crime.[116]

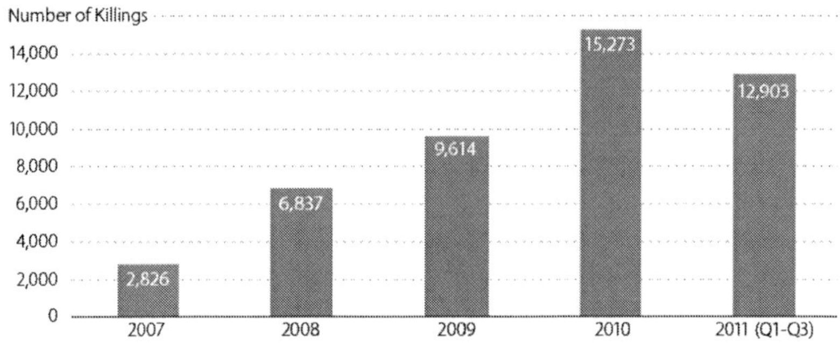

Source: Mexican government data for 2007-2010 is available at http://www.presidencia.gob.mx/base- and data for January through September 2011 is available at http://www.pgr.gob.mx/temas%20relevantes/estadistica/estadisticas.asp.

Note: The Mexican government's Attorney General's office (PGR) released data only for the first three quarters of 2011 (January–September).

Figure 2. Organized Crime-Related Killings (2007-2011); (Reported by the Mexican Government).

Pressure from organized crime is often greatest at the local level. Fifteen mayors were killed in 2010 and six in 2011, according to TBI (see Figure 4). Another population hard hit by the violence is young people between 15 and 29 years of age. The Mexican newspaper *El Universal* reported that drug trafficking-related violence had become the leading cause of death for young people in recent years, growing 10-fold between 2007 and 2010.[117] Not all victims are known. According to Mexico's National Human Rights Commission, more than 5,300 people have disappeared since December 2006, when Calderón came to office, and another 9,000 bodies have not been identified, some because of mutilation. The number of disappearances is probably greater because many disappearances, like so many other violent crimes, go unreported to Mexican authorities.[118]

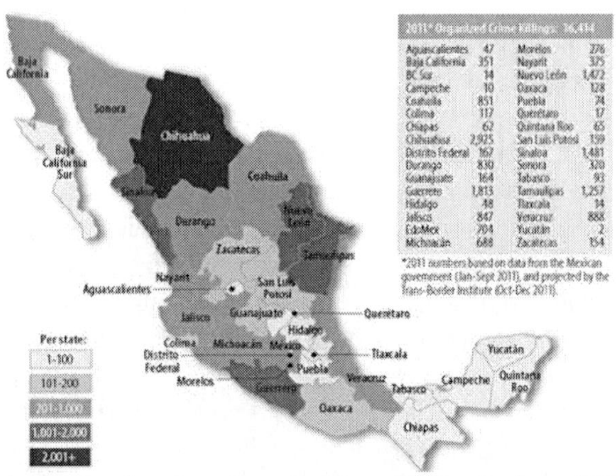

Source: Map created by CRS using data from the Trans-Border Institute (TBI), University of San Diego.

Notes: Mexican government and TBI data drawn from presentation in Cory Molzahn, Viridiana Ríos, and David A. Shirk, *Drug Violence in Mexico: Data and Analysis Through 2011*, Trans-Border Institute, March 2012.

Figure 3. Organized Crime-Related Killings in Mexico in 2011 by State.

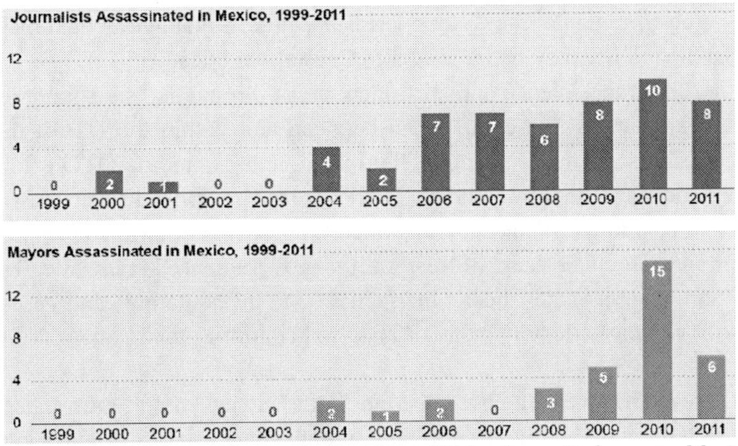

Source: Cory Molzahn, Viridiana Ríos, and David A. Shirk, *Drug Violence in Mexico: Data and Analysis Through 2011*, Trans-Border Institute, March 2012.

Notes: Data provided in report adapted by CRS.

Figure 4. Journalists and Mayors Assassinated in Mexico, 1999-2011.

Locations of the Violence and Its Impact on Tourism and Business

As the violence in Mexico has sharply increased over the past several years, it has also shifted locations. Drug trafficking-related violence has noticeably increased in the northern border states, including Tamaulipas and Nuevo León, and remained high in Chihuahua although it amounted to a smaller percentage of the total in 2011. As it has spread to new locations, the fear of violence has closed businesses and had an impact on tourism. American investors in Mexico have grown concerned about the violence and businesses have sent home dependents or closed operations altogether in some cities. Small and medium-sized businesses have been particularly hard hit, without the resources to hire private security firms and provide for employee safety as have the larger businesses and multinational corporations.[119] The Mexican government recently published a report indicating that foreign direct investment (FDI) has continued to pour into some of the most violent states at levels exceeding the investment prior to 2006, but others argue that job creating investment has been moving into safer cities in central Mexico where drug trafficking-related violence is lower.[120]

In 2008, drug trafficking-related violence was concentrated in a few cities and states. About 60% of the killings took place in three cities: Tijuana (Baja California), Culiacán (Sinaloa), and highly contested Ciudad Juárez (Chihuahua). By far, the largest number of drug trafficking-related deaths took place in Ciudad Juárez, a city of approximately 1.3 million inhabitants across the border from El Paso, TX. The Mexican border city is where the conflict between the Sinaloa and Juárez DTOs is most focused. (Mexico's National Public Security Council estimates that 36% of the drug trafficking-related deaths in Mexico's drug war from December 2006 through July 2010 could be attributed to the conflict centered in Ciudad Juárez.)[121] According to the U.S. State Department and media reports, some 3,100 people were killed in Ciudad Juárez in 2010 alone, making it one of the most violent cities in the world.[122] However, in 2011 total homicides in Ciudad Juárez declined to 1,933, still the most violent city in Mexico, but behind San Pedro Sula, Honduras, now estimated to be the city with the highest homicide rate in the world.[123] (This shift suggests the epicenter of drug trafficking-related violence may be moving into Central America.

Starting in 2009, the violence spread to new areas throughout the country for the usual reasons: changing alliances and competition between and within the DTOs, the succession struggles when leaders are taken down or eliminated, and expanding DTO efforts to corrupt and intimidate officials to permit the trade.[124] The intense government crackdown using army and navy forces and the Mexican Federal Police has provoked a violent response from the DTOs to communicate their lack of fear of the government. Meanwhile, Mexico's law enforcement and courts have been ineffective in investigating and prosecuting the perpetrators of violence, leaving the DTOs to continue their attacks free of legal consequences.

Violence spread from near the border in northern Mexico south to the states of Durango and Guerrero in 2009, with homicides doubling in both states.[125] As in 2009, violence in 2010 continued along the U.S./Mexico border, including the states of Chihuahua, Nuevo León, and Tamaulipas (the latter two states being the locus of the 2010 conflict between the Zetas and the Gulf DTOs), and with notable increases in Sinaloa, Guerrero, Durango, and the state of Mexico.[126] In 2010, some of the Central Pacific states experienced a large increase in violent activity, including Jalisco and Nayarit. Violence in the Central Pacific states (including the state of Mexico, Guerrero, Morelos, Jalisco, and Nayarit) has been attributed to the conflict between factions of the Beltrán Leyva organization, La Familia Michoacana, and the Sinaloa DTO.[127]

The violence is highly concentrated along key drug routes and within a relatively few cities and towns. In August 2010, a Mexican government report on 28,000 homicides linked to organized crime (from December 2006 through July 2010), revealed that 80% of drug trafficking-related homicides occurred in 162 of Mexico's 2,456 municipalities (less than 7%).[128] Through additional analysis of municipal-level data, analyst Eduardo Guerrero identified six clusters of the most violent municipalities in late 2010.[129] The 36 municipalities he classified as the most violent are located in five states (there are two high-violence zones in the border state of Chihuahua). Guerrero argues that if an effective anti-violence strategy targeted these zones, the drug trafficking-related violence could be reduced.[130]

In 2011, the violence continued to grow and spread. While violence in Baja California and Chihuahua declined somewhat, it spiked in Tamaulipas, Coahuila, and Nuevo León (see Figure 3). The Gulf DTO's struggle to dislodge the Zetas from Monterrey, Nuevo León, the major industrial and financial hub 140 miles from the Texas border, is a near-paralyzing conflict that has frightened business owners and destroyed the city's reputation as one of Mexico's safest cities.[131] The six border states with the United States continued to experience a majority of the violence. According to government data, Mexico's northern border states accounted for 44% of the homicides in 2011, down from 50% in 2010. Reductions in Tijuana and Juárez were offset by increases in Monterrey and elsewhere,[132] and violence dispersed south toward Mexico's interior. In other words, violence remained high in crucial transit regions near the border and along the coasts, but it dispersed to a greater number of cities and states. In 2011, violence in the coastal state of Sinaloa declined in comparison with the prior year, but increased in Guerrero and Michoácan further south. Jalisco, home to Mexico's second-largest city, Guadalajara, saw violence flare, and, in the latter half of 2011, Veracruz became a hot spot with incursions against Los Zetas in territory they had dominated. The discoveries of mass graves in Durango and Tamaulipas in the middle of the year added to the drug trafficking death tolls in those states.[133]

While drug trafficking-related killings remain concentrated in a relatively few cities, the violence is spreading to more populated and economically important urban centers. Killings, kidnappings, and other violence have dramatically increased in Monterrey, Mexico's third-largest city. The resort city of Acapulco, a seaport in Guerrero state, has also seen a sharp increase in violence and was the second-most violent city in Mexico in 2011. Guadalajara, Mexico's second-largest city, saw increasing violence in 2011 and has continued to experience incidents in 2012.[134] Finally, Nuevo Laredo in Tamaulipas state has again been immersed in conflict as Los Zetas defend their important stronghold in one of the busiest land ports handling U.S.-Mexico trade.[135]

According to some estimates, the violence costs the country roughly one percentage point of annual economic growth.[136] However, Mexico's economy grew an estimated 4% in 2011 and the government has argued that overall growth and foreign investment have not been harmed. In April 2012, the government vigorously denied the claim of an important national employers' federation (Coparmex) that violence and threats of violence caused 160,000 businesses to leave Mexico in 2011.[137] Similarly, with regard to tourism the record is mixed. While the U.S. government has issued increasingly foreboding travel warnings and tourism has declined in the border region, more than 22 million tourists visited Mexico in 2011, breaking records set in 2008.[138] Some of this increase can be attributed to policies adopted by the Calderón government to make tourism more attractive to foreign visitors.

The government has touted the decline in violence in Ciudad Juárez in 2011 as evidence their law enforcement efforts and social reforms are working. But another possible cause is that the rival Sinaloa DTO and Carillo Fuentes/Juárez DTOs have come to some accommodation on use of the drug corridor. According to many assessments, the Sinaloa DTO is the most powerful DTO in Mexico.[139] It has successfully pushed into Baja California and Chihuahua, which were once controlled by the Tijuana and Juárez DTOs. Some analysts have speculated that Sinaloa's dominance may be the reason for a decline in violence in both border cities.[140]

Recently, some analysts have identified Tijuana as an example of a qualified success in its reduction of violence. They maintain that Tijuana's significantly lower number of homicides resulted from an effective government strategy of building trust and communication between civil society and enforcement authorities, which was aided by a respected policing role for the military. Furthermore, the DTOs operating in Tijuana were broken up but retained sufficient organizational coherence to order a reduction in violence in response to a well-executed and targeted "hot spot" policing effort.[141]

Major tourist destinations, such as Acapulco, Cancún, Mazatlan, Taxco, and Cuernavaca, have been hit by violence, and the economically vital tourist industry has been affected. As noted above, tourism along the U.S.-Mexico border has also suffered a dramatic decline because of fears of violence. According to the U.S. State Department, foreign tourists have not been a DTO target. But there have been several incidents of Mexican tourists becoming victims. The State Department's travel warning updated in February 2012 reported that the number of Americans murdered in Mexico rose from 35 in 2007 to 120 in 2011.[142]

One consequence of the intense violence in many municipalities is the displacement of residents fleeing for safety. The Internal Displacement Monitoring Centre estimated in December 2010 that 230,000 persons were displaced, roughly half of whom fled to the United

States. The other estimated 115,000 were internally displaced persons inside Mexico.[143] According to the Monitoring Centre's annual report covering 2011, about 140,000 people have been displaced by drug-cartel violence since 2007. The report criticizes the Mexican government for not initiating a program to recognize or assist this population.[144] However, in contrast to this finding, the United Nations has identified only 1,570 people as a "population of concern" inside Mexico as of January 2011.[145] In addition, many Mexican nationals fearing that they could be victims of the violence (including journalists and law enforcement officers) have sought asylum in the United States.[146] According to the U.S. Department of Justice, there were 6,133 requests for asylum from Mexico in FY2011, about double the number of requests made in 2010, and only 104 requests (1.7%) were granted.[147]

MEXICO'S ANTIDRUG STRATEGY AND REACTION[148]

President Calderón's military-led crackdown on the drug trafficking organizations has been at the center of his domestic policy, and he launched his aggressive approach almost immediately after his inauguration in December 2006. He has since deployed more than 50,000 Mexican military and thousands of federal police around the country to combat the DTOs.[149] A leading element of the strategy has been to confront and dismantle the drug trafficking organizations by going after the high-value targets: the leadership of the major DTOs.

The DTOs have fought back strongly, refusing to allow law enforcement actions from taking place and making an all-out effort to neutralize repressive measures. The DTOs have also demonstrated an unanticipated resilience as their leadership is arrested or killed. Mexico's Secretary of Public Security Genaro Garcia Luna and others have acknowledged that removing the high-value targets at the top of the organizations has not paralyzed the DTOs because in most cases the organizations have transferred power to new and sometimes more violent leaders.[150] An additional complexity is that the drug organizations are adapting and transforming themselves from hierarchical and vertical organizations to become more multi-nodal and horizontal in their structure. Some of the DTOs have adopted a more decentralized and networked model with independent cell-like structures that make it harder for law enforcement to dismantle.[151] As the Mexican military has shifted resources to pursue leaders of the DTOs, it appears to have fewer resources to devote to older missions such as eradication efforts. This may be contributing to the increases in the cultivation of opium and marijuana, and production of heroin and methamphetamine, which, unfortunately, are generating more income for the DTOs.

In carrying out his antidrug strategy, President Calderón has demonstrated an unprecedented willingness to collaborate with the United States, and the United States has shown a new trust and respect for its Mexican partners. U.S.-Mexican security cooperation has been structured upon the Mérida Initiative, a bilateral counterdrug and security effort first funded in 2008.[152] The initiative, as it was originally conceived by Presidents George W. Bush and Felipe Calderón, was to end with the FY2010 budget cycle. Its focus has evolved from providing hardware to Mexican security forces to modernizing and strengthening institutions of law enforcement and the judiciary in Mexico. A successor to the Mérida Initiative—called "Beyond Mérida"—was introduced by the Obama Administration in the

FY2011 budget request. The "four pillars" of the current strategy are (1) disrupting organized crime groups; (2) institutionalizing the rule of law; (3) building a 21st-century border; and (4) building strong and resilient communities. The Obama Administration's funding priorities have shifted from providing expensive equipment to Mexican security forces to supporting institutional reform programs in the Mexican federal government and more recently to assisting certain key states.

A parallel shift is evident in Mexico's domestic strategy. Following a brutal massacre of 15 youth at a party in Ciudad Juárez in January 2010, President Calderón made a series of visits to the border city and announced that police and military action alone were insufficient to address Juárez's problems. Within weeks, the Calderón Administration released a plan, "Todos Somos Juárez," to address social causes that sustain the drug trade such as unemployment and a weak education system, which parallels Pillar 4 of the Beyond Mérida strategy.[153] In addition, the Calderón government has taken advantage of improved sharing of U.S. intelligence, and vigorously responded to extradition requests of suspects wanted by the United States.[154] The Calderón administration is also implementing a major restructuring of the judicial system and has successfully expanded and restructured the Mexican Federal Police (which went from 6,000 to 35,000 officers), improved their pay, and implemented procedures to vet and train officers to combat corruption. Efforts to reform the Attorney General's Ministerial Police have lagged and steep challenges remain in cleaning up and reforming Mexico's municipal and state forces that number over 300,000.

President Calderón convened for the first time a "dialogue on security," bringing together government officials with business leaders, civic leaders, and academics in August 2010 to publicly discuss the country's antidrug strategy. These discussions were partly a response to the Mexican government's inconsistent and incomplete releases of public information on drug trafficking-related homicides.[155] President Calderón notably said at one forum he would be willing to discuss the option of drug legalization, although he quickly announced that he was not a proponent.[156] He reaffirmed his government's commitment to the antidrug fight observing that the violence threatened the media and democratic governance.[157] In April 2012, in the lead up to the Summit of the Americas in Colombia, when the subject of alternative drug strategies was being discussed, President Calderón expressed the view that the United States might consider "market alternatives" in its efforts to reduce drug demand.[158]

The Mexican military had initially been in the forefront of the government's counterdrug campaign as an interim solution until enough police could be vetted, trained, and equipped to be given back the lead in the public security function. By late 2010, the Calderón Administration had apparently assessed that current programs of police and justice reform would be insufficient to rid the system of corruption before Calderón's six-year term expired in December 2012, and that the military would retain its lead role until the end of his term.[159] Persistent police corruption was highlighted in the August 2010 purge of the federal police in which more than 3,000 officers were fired. On the other hand, four high-ranking army officers (three of them generals) were arrested for suspicion of drug trafficking and corruption in May 2012.[160] On July 31, 2012, a Mexican federal judge charged them (now three former officers and one active duty general) with criminal links to the Beltrán Leyva Organization (BLO). Among the officers charged is retired army general Tomas Angeles Dauahare, who served as Deputy Secretary of Defense under Calderón from 2006 to 2008.[161] Some analysts maintain that the outcome of this sensitive case could affect the legacy of Calderón's security strategy.[162] The military is highly esteemed in Mexico, but since it took on a major role in the

Calderón antidrug campaign it has been dogged by allegations of corruption and violations of human rights (charges most frequently directed toward the Mexican Army). However, supporters of the Calderón strategy maintain that for the state to confront well-armed DTOs equipped with military-style weapons the only viable option was to use the well-armed military.

Another challenge for the Calderón strategy has been a rise in drug abuse in border cities such as Ciudad Juárez and Tijuana, and the gang warfare that has broken out to control that local drug trade.[163] Local drug dealing increased because drugs headed for the U.S. market are being stopped from going over the border. Gangs that are hired by the DTOs for protection and other "outsourced" services are paid in product (illegal drugs) and need to convert the drugs to cash. Fighting to control street corner sales, DTO-supplied gangs are killing each other in both border cities. Unemployment, caused by the economic downturn and businesses fleeing the violence, has also provided ready recruits for the gangs, who are frequently hired by the DTOs to fight as their proxies.

In order to improve intelligence sharing and increase U.S. support for Mexico's struggle against organized crime, binational cooperation in 2011 included the deployment of U.S. unmanned aerial vehicles to gather intelligence on DTO activities[164] and the opening of a compound to gather intelligence in northern Mexico.[165] The compound, reportedly staffed by DEA, Central Intelligence Agency (CIA), and civilian personnel from the Pentagon's Northern Command, is to be modeled on "fusion intelligence centers" operated by the United States in Afghanistan and Iraq.[166] Responding to concerns about the fusion center, William J. Burns, U.S. Deputy Secretary of State, in a roundtable with Mexican news media, stressed that this intelligence analysis program is not a basis for U.S. personnel to conduct operations or engage in law enforcement activities in Mexico.[167] In remarks made in August 2011, he stated that the United States would always respect Mexican sovereignty and provide cooperation based upon the request of Mexican authorities.[168]

TRENDS AND OUTLOOK

Notwithstanding how the violence is characterized, a few trends are clear. First, the drug-trafficking related violence continued to rise from December 2006 through December 2011. While the rate of increase may be leveling off, it is premature to predict if 2012 will see an increase or a decrease over the prior year. If current trends hold, it is likely that there will have been more than 60,000 organized crime-related homicides during President Calderón's term.

Second, the violence is concentrated in a few cities and towns, with 80% of the deaths concentrated in slightly under 7% of Mexico's municipalities, according to Mexican government data released in August 2010.[169] According to the newer Mexican government data, violence in 2010 continued to be concentrated in relatively few cities, with over 70% of the violence in just 80 municipalities.[170] In 2011, violence dispersed to a greater number of cities. While the five most violent cities accounted for roughly 32% of the violence in 2010, they accounted for about 24% of the violence in 2011.[171]

Third, the violence is largely targeted at people with ties to the drug trafficking organizations because much of the violence is open warfare between and within the organizations. The number of Mexican security forces (military and police) killed is believed to be approximately 7% of the total, although estimates vary.[172] Some of the deaths of Mexican officials may involve individuals who at some time colluded with one DTO or another. Until recently, the Mexican government maintained that most of the victims are tied to the DTOs and suggested the extensive violence should be seen as a sign of success.

Fourth, the power of the DTOs is fluid and the boundaries of their operations change. Even the seven organizations that formerly dominated the picture a year ago were only loosely geographically based. The conflict evolves as fighting between DTOs over drug plazas and corridors is exacerbated or resolved. Some DTOs have fragmented and this has generated more violence. But there is a debate if fragmentation represents a long-run weakening of the DTOs' influence and makes them more susceptible to state penetration.[173]

While forecasting changes in the violence is speculative, many observers see continued high levels of violence for the near term.[174] The inputs from the United States that fuel the violence—high-powered guns and illicit profits—have not been significantly disrupted.[175] According to the U.S. government, nearly 100,000 guns have been turned over to the U.S. Department of Justice's Bureau of Alcohol, Tobacco, Firearms, and Explosives (ATF) for tracing by the Mexican government which were seized by authorities between 2007 through 2011. Of those, some 68,161 (68% of the total) were determined by the ATF to have come from the United States.[176] Seizures of illicit funds derived from drug trafficking have been low. Some estimate that $20 billion to $25 billion annually in bulk cash flows back to Mexico and its Colombian suppliers from drug sales in the United States. According to an analysis by the *Washington Post* of data from the U.S. and Mexican governments, only about 1% of this cash is recovered despite unprecedented efforts to seize more.[177]

However, there is a lively debate about how large the annual profits from drug trafficking actually are which flow back to Mexico from the United States. Estimates within the U.S. government vary, ranging from $22 billion (U.S. Drug Enforcement Administration) to $19 billion to $29 billion (U.S. Department of Homeland Security) and an even broader range of $8 billion to $25 billion (U.S. State Department).[178] Nongovernmental analysts have calculated considerably lower estimates. The Rand Corporation released a report in 2010 that estimated the amount of drug revenues flowing to Mexico's DTOs annually at $6.6 billion.[179] Independent scholar Alejandro Hope projects total export revenue for Mexico's drug trafficking organizations between $4.7 billion to $8.1 billion, with $6.2 billion as the best estimate.[180] In April 2012, Mexico's Ministry of Finance released a study that estimated total proceeds from organized crime laundered in Mexico in 2011 at approximately $10 billion, with drug trafficking accounting for 41% of the laundered proceeds.[181] Regardless of the total, some analysts remain skeptical that clamping down on money laundering will be the magic bullet for reducing illicit trafficking in Mexico or its associated violence.[182] They argue that other strategies are needed to tackle the problem. U.S. and Mexican government officials assert that one of the most effective ways to dismantle the DTOs is to reduce the criminal proceeds that fund their operations.[183]

Cooperation between Mexico and the United States has markedly increased under the Mérida Initiative. Mexico has demonstrated an increased commitment to control its borders and announced an initiative in September 2010 to control money laundering and disrupt the flow of drug money.[184] In March 2012, the Mexican Attorney General's office created a Specialized Unit for Financial Analysis to increase the government's capacity to prosecute financial crimes including money laundering. In the United States, bilateral cooperation on money laundering cases, including training for Mexican prosecutors, has increased.[185] The United States and Mexico formed a Bilateral Money Laundering Working Group to coordinate the investigation and prosecution of money laundering and bulk cash smuggling.[186] Since 2001, the United States has applied financial sanctions to all the major DTOs in Mexico or individuals heading those DTOs (as well as several smaller organizations) under the Foreign Narcotics Kingpin Designation Act.[187] Between 2008 and April 2011, the U.S. government designated 271 individuals and 135 entities tied to the financial and commercial networks of Mexico's most wanted traffickers under the act.[188]

The brutal violence associated with drug trafficking in Mexico appears to exceed the violence that is intrinsic to narcotics trafficking and organized crime in general. The attack on civil society has been particularly harsh for local government officials and journalists, including the most recent rash of attacks in Veracruz. Beyond the reports of journalists, mayors, and young people being killed described earlier, there have been reports of innocent bystanders increasingly being caught in the violence. On August 25, 2011, 52 people lost their lives in a casino fire allegedly ignited by Los Zetas, the highest number of Mexican civilians killed in a single incident since the beginning of the government's campaign against organized crime.[189] President Calderón decried the incident as the work of "true terrorists."[190] Others have cited this incident as another example of organized crime's involvement in corruption and extortion.[191]

The use of car bombs, simultaneous attacks in different cities, and a couple of incidents of seemingly indiscriminate attacks on civilians (including the aforementioned casino fire) have raised concerns that the DTOs may be using tactics similar to those of insurgent groups or terrorists.[192] The DTOs, however, appear to lack a discernible political goal or ideology, which is one element of a widely recognized definition of terrorism. The U.S. State Department, in its *Country Reports on Terrorism 2011*, published in July 2012, maintains

> No known international terrorist organization had an operational presence in Mexico and no terrorist group targeted U.S. citizens in or from Mexican territory. There was no evidence of ties between Mexican criminal organizations and terrorist groups, nor that the criminal organizations had political or territorial control, aside from seeking to protect and expand the impunity with which they conduct their criminal activity.[193]

The violence has affected the state of democracy in Mexico. For example, the human rights group Freedom House downgraded Mexico in its 2011 ranking as part of its annual evaluation of political rights and civil liberties worldwide. Freedom House ranks countries as free, partly free, or not free. In its *Freedom in the World 2011* report, Mexico was downgraded from "free" in 2010 to "partly free" in 2011 because of a decline in its political rights rating "due to the targeting of local officials by organized crime groups and the government's inability to protect citizens' rights in the face of criminal violence."

For the foreseeable future, current and future Mexican governments will likely have to deal with the DTOs and the violence they generate. The DTOs are having a profound demoralizing and delegitimizing effect on local, state, and federal government in Mexico. It may take years of building stronger institutions before violence is markedly reduced. Notwithstanding the DTO violence, Mexico continues to have one of the lower homicide rates in the region, although the recent escalation in drug trafficking-related deaths has pushed the national homicide rate significantly higher. From a nationwide homicide rate of 11 homicides per 100,000 in 2008, the national homicide rate rose to 14 per 100,000 in 2009.[194] According to a U.N. global study on homicide published last year, Mexico's homicide rate was 18 per 100,000 in 2010. The same study reporting national rates in the region for 2010 shows that Mexico's overall homicide rate is far lower than those of Guatemala (41), El Salvador (66), and Honduras (82). In South America, Colombia, Brazil, and Venezuela's national homicide rates also significantly exceeded Mexico's in recent years.[195] But the violence from organized crime has pushed up Mexico's rate. In 2007, organized crime deaths in Mexico were the cause of slightly less than 32% of all intentional homicides, but by 2010 and 2011 organized crime homicides accounted for more than half of all intentional homicides.[196]

The Mexican public does not appear to credit the government's claim of success in reducing the violence and improving street security. Recent polls have shown Mexicans believe the DTOs are winning the conflict. For example, a survey conducted by Pew Research Center and published in late August 2011 found that less than half (45%) believed the government is making progress in the campaign against the DTOs.[197] However, the Pew study had some interesting additional findings. The Mexican public, while appalled at the violence, has continued to back the use of the Mexican military as part of the Calderón government's antidrug campaign (83% of respondents). This apparent support for the military's role in the antidrug effort comes despite a popular movement protesting abuses by the military, which has gained ground since early 2011 (see below). According to the Pew survey, a larger fraction says they would support American military assistance (38%) than in 2010, with nearly three-quarters of respondents indicating they welcomed U.S. help to train the Mexican police and the military.[198] Another survey, "Citizenship, Democracy, and Drug-related Violence," conducted by several NGOs between May and June 2011 with more than 7,400 interviews of Mexicans from high, intermediate, and low violence states, found that only 26% of respondents believed that the government was "winning the war on drugs." Somewhat paradoxically, this study found that Mexicans supported the government's strategy, but did not believe it was successful.[199] A recent poll conducted by the *Dallas Morning News* and the Mexican newspaper *El Universal* in May 2012 supports this finding. The poll of Mexican voters found 64% approve the Mexican military taking a lead role in the fight against organized crime whereas only 21% said they thought the strategy was working.[200]

President Calderón has confronted a recently emerging peace movement led by Mexican poet Javier Sicilia, whose son was killed by drug gangs in Cuernavaca in March 2011. Sicilia, who now leads the Movement for Peace with Justice and Dignity, has met with the president several times, including in a televised meeting in June 2011. He has led a peace caravan across Mexico, and headed demonstrations in Mexico City. Sicilia has urged the president to abandon his military-led strategy, which some of his supporters believe has caused violence and human rights abuses by security forces. They propose a new approach focused on combating poverty, inequality, and unemployment, which they say are contributing to the rising violence.[201] Sicilia is slated to lead a peace caravan across the United States in August and September 2012.[202]

For many Mexican citizens, Calderón's campaign against organized crime would have been a success if it had significantly reduced violence. But such a goal has eluded the government's current strategy by stimulating DTO rivalries and intra-DTO battles for succession. In addition, the operations of the Mexican security forces have led to complaints of human rights violations that include forced disappearances, torture, and arbitrary detention.[203] The manner in which the violence will be reduced will now depend upon the policy choices of incoming president Enrique Peña Nieto, who will be inaugurated on December 1, 2012.

To reduce the violence will require public support for the government's policy. Thus far, the confrontation with the DTOs and other criminal organizations has failed to bring the violence down, and public backing for the Calderón counterdrug strategy has waned. Some observers have criticized the Calderón government for adopting an aggressive approach (literally declaring war on the drug traffickers) without having a clear definition of success, without understanding the consequences of the policy, and without having the tools necessary to win.[204] Elements of the government's strategy in the Beyond Mérida program that are designed to reduce the violence, such as institutionalizing the rule of law, reforming the justice system, and completing economic and social development programs to combat crime, all have a longer timeframe.[205] It may take years or decades to build effective, efficient legal institutions in Mexico that resist threats and bribery. Yet policy analysts believe these institutions are necessary before the DTOs can be reduced from a national security threat to a law and order problem.

Some observers in Mexico are advocating anti-violence programs modeled on successful strategies used in other Latin American cities, such as Rio de Janeiro in Brazil and Guayaquil in Ecuador, or from programs in the United States.[206] Some analysts have called for a violence reduction strategy to be applied in the near term, while longer-term efforts to reform the police and justice system carry on simultaneously. Drug policy analyst Mark Kleiman and others have endorsed enforcement efforts that concentrate resources on the most violent organizations.[207]

Such a targeted strategy would sequentially focus on groups based on their violence levels or violence behaviors. It would put incentives in place to avoid the designation of being most violent. This strategy has risks associated with it including that such a policy might appear to favor one or more groups by focusing the government's efforts on a particular group (the most violent) or lead to greater disequilibrium among rival organizations.[208] However, the current nonselective or "undifferentiated" strategy seems to have stimulated drug war rivalries, invited succession battles, and continued to ratchet up the violence.

A very new development is significantly increased sharing of intelligence at the federal level by the United States with Mexico, which reflects greater U.S. confidence in Mexican law enforcement capacity and integrity. This development again raises the possibility that identifying and targeting DTO leaders for apprehension and investigation and successfully removing them can work to lower the violence. However, if the long-established pattern of ineffectual attacks and prosecution of DTO leaders continues, the intense violence is likely to endure. If a near-term solution to the violence is not adopted, there could be public pressure in Mexico to resort to the policies of accommodation that worked in the past. Alternatively, some communities may take matters into their own hands and resort to vigilante justice, as some have already.[209]

As noted above, U.S.-Mexico security cooperation has increased significantly with the implementation of the Mérida Initiative, an Administration program that Congress began funding in 2008. The new Beyond Mérida strategy in Mexico is increasingly focused on the challenges of bringing violence under control. The increased use of intelligence-based security operations that has led to successes in taking down the top DTO leaders is now being expanded to disrupt the capacity of the entire organization—not just top leadership and their hired killers, but those that handle the money and acquire the guns.[210]

The goal of the Mexican government's present drug strategy is to reduce the extent and character of the DTOs' activity from a national security threat to a law and order problem and to transfer responsibility from military forces back to the police. While the DTOs have used terrorist tactics, they do not use them to the degree or with the same intentions as did narco traffickers in Colombia.[211] Mexico's challenge remains largely an organized crime or mafia problem, and the most important tools for managing it include long-term institutional reform and the replacement of a culture of illegality with one of rule of law and legality.

APPENDIX. COMPARING MEXICO AND COLOMBIA

Secretary of State Hillary Clinton compared the upsurge in violence in Mexico to the situation in Colombia 20 years ago in her remarks before the Council of Foreign Relations in September 2010.[212] The comparison to Colombia was quickly disavowed by the Mexican government (and reportedly by President Obama), but broadened the debate about the seriousness of the threat posed to Mexico's national security and democracy.

Some analysts employ the Colombia comparison to argue that the successes of Plan Colombia[213] offer appropriate prescriptions for Mexico. Other observers counter that Colombia two decades ago faced a very different challenge than Mexico faces today. The government of Colombia confronted an insurgency of armed guerrillas who were attempting to overthrow the Colombian government, while simultaneously facing a campaign of violence by its drug trafficking organizations. The Revolutionary Armed Forces of Colombia (FARC) and other armed groups in the country had the goal of replacing the Colombian state, which is significantly different from the goal of the DTOs of Mexico, which want impunity to traffic drugs and engage in other illicit activities for profit. While the FARC and other insurgents turned to drug trafficking to help finance their cause, their goal was to overthrow the sovereign state. At the height of their power, the FARC and other insurgents controlled more than a third of the country's municipalities.[214] The degree to which some of Mexico's municipalities are influenced by the DTOs is hard to determine. In Mexico, the goal of the traffickers is to corrupt the police and government at all levels to allow them to pursue illicit profits, but it is not to take control of the apparatus of the state. Thus, it remains a problem of criminality rather than a battle with insurgents or terrorists.

On the other hand, because some of the *characteristics* of the violence in Mexico—political assassinations, car bombs, extreme violence, and the increased killing of innocent bystanders— are similar to the tactics of political insurgents, some analysts have asserted that the violence goes beyond conventional organized crime behavior. These observers maintain that the violence is highly organized and exceptionally brutal, and therefore it is qualitatively different from criminal violence.[215] Some policy analysts have described the Mexican criminal organizations as a "criminal insurgency."[216] John P. Sullivan at the Center for Advanced Studies in Terrorism describes how the response to the government's enforcement crackdown led to the evolution of the conflict and violence: "In Mexico, when faced with a crackdown, the cartels chose to battle each other and the government to maintain a stake in the game. A high level of violence, impunity, and a criminal insurgency were thus an unintended side effect."[217]

From another perspective, Professor Phil Williams argues that the violence is that of traditional organized crime, but taken to new depths or levels of intensity. He suggests that the Mexican drug trafficking-related violence grows out of a "perfect storm" of conditions. The situation in Mexico has precedents and parallels with the growth of criminal organizations in Italy, Russia, Albania, and elsewhere. In addition, there is a feature of "anomie" to Mexico's violence—the homicidal violence has become a feature of everyday life leading to "a degeneration of rules and norms and the emergence of forms of behavior unconstrained by standard notions of what is acceptable."[218]

The Mexican DTOs have no ideology other than a ruthless pursuit of profit, but their corruption and intimidation have challenged the state's monopoly on the use of force and rule of law. In Mexico, the police and court system, historically weak and undercut by corruption, are not equipped, organized, or managed to combat the drug organizations. Most arrests are never prosecuted. However, there have been many arrests, and suspects are usually displayed to the news media.[219] Arrests have only a low chance of turning into successful prosecutions. The rate of impunity (non prosecution) for murder in Mexico is 81% and higher for other types of crime.[220] The violent response of the DTOs to the Calderón government's antidrug campaign, similar to what was seen in smaller municipalities throughout Colombia, has intimidated local, state, and federal authorities. DTO profits, like those made by local FARC commanders in Colombia, are shared with government officials at all levels. Unlike the Colombian FARC, the Mexican traffickers do not seek to replace the government and provide services, but they are committed to manipulating it with bribery and violence to continue their illegal activities without interference.

Some observers argue that parts of the Mexican state have been "captured" similar to the control insurgents once had over large parts of Colombia. These analysts maintain that some states or localities in Mexico are under DTO control.[221] For example, in Michoacán, the LFM organization controlled many local businesses through extortion (taxing businesses or charging them for security services). According to one estimate made in 2010, approximately 85% of legitimate businesses in Michoacán had some type of relationship with the LFM.[222] Another study concerning DTO presence in Mexican local governments was released in late August 2010. That study, entitled "Municipal Government and Organized Crime," prepared for a committee of the Mexican Senate, reportedly found that 195 Mexican municipalities (8% of the total) were completely under control of organized crime, while another 1,536 (63% of the total) were "infiltrated" by organized crime. The study concluded that a majority of Mexican municipalities had organized crime elements capable of controlling the illicit businesses of retail drug trafficking, cultivation and trafficking of drugs, kidnapping, and extortion.[223] The study found that criminal structures operate with logistical support from corrupt municipal police and politicians.[224]

Some analysts contend that Colombia's experience provides valuable lessons for Mexico.[225] The increasing training provided by Colombian security forces to Mexico's army and police in recent years demonstrates that there are operational lessons that Mexican authorities value.[226] Others maintain that Mexico's situation is distinctly complex, which limits the relevance of Colombia as a model. Clearly, there are many lessons learned from studying the U.S. supported successes and failures in Colombia, but their application to Mexico is limited by the countries' very different histories and circumstances.

End Notes

[1] General Charles Jacoby Jr., Commander of U.S. Northern Command, Senate Armed Services Committee, Hearing on the Proposed Fiscal 2013 Defense Authorization as it Relates to the U.S. Southern and Northern Commands (transcript), March 13, 2012.

[2] Robert J. MacCoun and Peter Reuter, *Drug War Heresies: Learning from Other Times, Vices and Places* (New York: Cambridge University Press, 2001); Kevin Jack Riley, *Snow Job? The War Against International Cocaine Trafficking* (New Brunswick: Transactional Publishers, 1996).

[3] For more background on the Mexican elections, see CRS Report R42548, *Mexico's 2012 Elections*, by Clare Ribando Seelke.

[4] While the term "cartel" was commonly applied to Colombian and Mexican organizations and is used frequently in the press and elsewhere, this report favors the use of the term "drug trafficking organizations." Today's Mexican DTOs are not necessarily engaged in price-fixing and other forms of collusive economic activity ascribed to cartels.

[5] William Booth, "Attacks Grow Ever More Gruesome in Mexico," *Washington Post*, May 24, 2012.

[6] For more background, see CRS Report R42548, *Mexico's 2012 Elections*, by Clare Ribando Seelke.

[7] "The Strategies of Peña Nieto's Top Advisor," *LatinNews Daily Report*, August 1, 2012.

[8] Following the murder of a second journalist on the staff at *El Diario* newspaper in Ciudad Juárez, the editor published a plea to the DTOs to consider a truce after asking openly "what do you want of us?" in an editorial September 19, 2010. The Mexican government condemned the idea of a truce, although the editorial was published because the paper said that the authorities could not guarantee the safety of their colleagues.

[9] Dr. Catalina Botero, *Annual Report of the Office of the Special Rapporteur for Freedom of Expression*, Office of the Special Rapporteur for Freedom of Expression, Document 69, Washington, DC, December 30, 2011, http://www.oas.org/en/iachr/expression /docs/reports/annual/ 2012%2003%2021%20 Annual%20Report%20 RELE% 202011 pirnting.pdf.

[10] Sofia Miselem, "Migrant Massacre Challenges Mexico Anti-Crime Strategy," *Agence France Presse*, August 31, 2010; "Drug Cartel Suspected in 72 Migrants' Deaths," *NPR: Morning Edition*, August 26, 2010; Tim Johnson, "Violent Mexican Drug Gang, Zetas, Taking Control of Migrant Smuggling," *Miami Herald*, August, 12, 2011.

[11] CRS interview with DEA officials on August 5, 2011.

[12] Shannon K. O'Neil, "Drug Cartel Fragmentation and Violence," Council on Foreign Relations Blog, August 9, 2011.

[13] Some studies have shown that violence tends to escalate after a government launches a major law enforcement initiative against a DTO or other organized crime group. See, for example, International Centre for Science in Drug Policy, *Effect of Drug Law Enforcement on Drug-Related Violence: Evidence from a Scientific Review*, 2010.

[14] See, for example, Human Rights Watch, *Neither Rights nor Security: Killings, Torture, and Disappearances in Mexico's "War on Drugs,"* November 2011; Catherine Daly, Kimberly Heinle, and David A. Shirk, *Armed with Impunity: Curbing Military Human Rights Abuses in Mexico*, Trans-Border Institute, Special Report, July 2012.

[15] The potential for a rapid and sudden decline in Mexico because of the undermining influence of criminal gangs and DTOs was widely debated. See, for example, United States Joint Forces Command, "The Joint Operating Environment 2008: Challenges and Implications for the Future Joint Force," December 2008.

[16] President Calderón's full statement at the security conference was, "This criminal behavior is what has changed, and become a challenge to the state, an attempt to replace the state." See Tracy Wilkinson and Ken Ellingwood, "Cartels Thrive Despite Calderón's Crackdown; Drug Gangs Have Expanded Their Power and Reach in both Mexico and the United States," *Los Angeles Times*, August 8, 2010.

[17] William Finnegan, "Silver or Lead," *The New Yorker*, May 31, 2010. Mexican crime expert, Edgardo Buscaglia, argues that about one-third of Mexican municipalities are controlled by organized crime. See, "Point Person: Our Q & A with Edgardo Buscaglia," *Dallas Morning News*, April 9, 2010.

[18] "A Conversation with U.S. Secretary of State Hillary Rodham Clinton," Council on Foreign Relations, September 8, 2010. Transcript available at http://www.cfr.org/publication/22896/ conversation_with_us_secretary_of_ state_hillary_rodham_clinton.html.

[19] Assistant Secretary of State Valenzuela and Director of the White House Office of National Drug Control Policy Kerlikowske made remarks at the annual Conference on the Americas qualifying what Secretary of State Clinton had said earlier in the day, September 8, 2010. President Obama was reported to have negated the

comparison of Mexico to Colombia 20 years ago in comments he made to the Spanish language newspaper *La Opinion*. The White House did not provide an English translation of the remarks printed in *La Opinion*. See "Mexico Drug War Not Comparable to Colombia: Obama," *Reuters*, September 10, 2010, at http://www.reuters.com/article/idUSTRE6885TH20100910.

[20] U.S. Department of Justice, National Drug Intelligence Center, *National Drug Threat Assessment: 2011*, August 2011, http://www.justice.gov/ndic/pubs44/44849/44849p.pdf, hereinafter referred to as the NDTA. The NDTA 2011 estimated that the Mexican DTOs maintain drug distribution networks in 1,000 U.S. cities.

[21] The NDTA, 2010, February 2010, states "Direct violence similar to the violence occurring among major DTOs in Mexico is rare in the United States." For a discussion of why the violence has not spread into the United States, see CRS Report R41075, *Southwest Border Violence: Issues in Identifying and Measuring Spillover Violence*, coordinated by Kristin M. Finklea.

[22] For further discussion of corruption of U.S. and Mexican officials charged with securing the border, see CRS Report R41349, *U.S.-Mexican Security Cooperation: The Mérida Initiative and Beyond* , by Clare Ribando Seelke and Kristin M. Finklea.

[23] "Mexico Politics: Whither the War on Drugs?," *Economist Intelligence Unit*, September 2, 2010.

[24] David Luhnow, "Questions Over Tape Face Mexico Politician," *Wall Street Journal*, October 16, 2010. In the U.S. Department of State's 2011 *International Narcotics Control Strategy Report* it identifies the arrest of 38 officials and police in Michoacán in 2009, 37 of whom were released for lack of evidence.

[25] Tracy Wilkinson, "Ex-Mayor of Cancun Released as Case Appears to Collapse," *Los Angeles Times*, July 21, 2011.

[26] Trans-Border Institute (TBI), Justice in Mexico, *June 2011 News Report*.

[27] Luis Astorga and David A. Shirk, *Drug Trafficking Organizations and Counter-Drug Strategies in the U.S.-Mexican Context*, Woodrow Wilson International Center for Scholars Mexico Institute, Working Paper Series on U.S.-Mexico Security Cooperation, April 2010, p. 11.

[28] Ibid. p. 4.

[29] For more on the political history of Mexico, see CRS Report RL32724, *Mexico: Issues for Congress*, by Clare Ribando Seelke.

[30] Astorga and Shirk, *Drug Trafficking Organizations and Counter-Drug Strategies*, p. 5.

[31] Francisco E. Gonzalez, "Mexico's Drug Wars Get Brutal," *Current History*, February 2009.

[32] Shannon O'Neil, "The Real War in Mexico: How Democracy Can Defeat the Drug Cartels," *Foreign Affairs*, vol. 88, no. 4 (July/August 2009).

[33] U.S. Department of State, *2011 International Narcotics Control Strategy Report (INCSR)*, March 2011.

[34] The region where Sinaloa comes together with the states of Chihuahua and Durango is a drug-growing area sometimes called Mexico's "Golden Triangle" after the productive area of Southeast Asia by the same name. In this region, a third of the population is estimated to make their living from the illicit drug trade. See Tim Johnson, "For Mexican Cartels, Marijuana is Still Gold," *San Jose Mercury News*, September 5, 2010.

[35] *STRATFOR* (formerly *Stratfor Global Intelligence*, a subscription database), "Mexico Security Memo: Long Fight Between Military, Gunmen in Sinaloa," May 2, 2012.

[36] IHS Jane's, *Jane's Sentinel Security Assessment–Security, Mexico*, February 6, 2012. The report notes that one reason the illicit crops have increased in Mexico is that eradication by Mexican military has decreased over recent years because those forces have been deployed to combat organized crime.

[37] U.S. Department of State, *INCSR 2011*. The report states notes "While opium poppy cultivation in Mexico is very sparse in comparison to the densities estimated in Burma and Afghanistan, Mexico's share of global poppy production has been increasing in recent years." Mexico only produces 7% of the world's supply of heroin, but is the major supplier of heroin to the United States. However, some authorities in Mexico question the size of the poppy cultivation estimates of the U.S. government and the United Nations. See Steven Dudley, "Raw Feed: Making Sense of Mexico's Heroin Production*," In Sight: Organized Crime in the Americas*, March 7, 2011, at http://insightcrime.org/insightlatest-news/item/649-rawfeed-deciphering-mexicos-rise-in-heroin-productio.

[38] William Booth and Anne-Marie O'Connor, "Mexican Cartels Emerge as Top Source for U.S. Meth," *Washington Post*, November 28, 2010.

[39] Oscar Becerra, "Traffic Report–Battling Mexico's Sinaloa Cartel," *Jane's Information Group*, May 7, 2010. The author describes the networked structure: "The Sinaloa Cartel is not a strictly vertical and hierarchical structure, but instead is a complex organization containing a number of semi-autonomous groups."

[40] Special Agent Camarena was an undercover DEA agent working in Mexico who was kidnapped, tortured, and killed in 1985. The Felix Gallardo network broke up in the wake of the investigation of its role in the murder.

The famous case and ensuing investigation is chronicled on a DEA website honoring Agent Camarena at http://www.justice.gov/ dea/ongoing/red_ribbon/redribbon_history.html.

[41] This turf battle resulted in more than 400 deaths in the final quarter of 2008. See Viridian Rios and Gabriel Aguilera, "Keys to Reducing Violence in Mexico: Targeted Policing and Civic Engagement," *ReVista*, vol. XI, no. 2 (Winter 2012).

[42] Sandra Dibble, "Tijuana Violence Slows, Drops from Spotlight," *San Diego Union Tribune*, April 26, 2010. Following the January 12, 2010 arrest of Teodoro "El Teo" Garcia Simental, on February 8, 2010 his brother, Manuel, and their chief lieutenant Raydel Lopez Uriarte, were arrested. For more information, see testimony of Anthony P. Placido, Assistant Administrator for Intelligence, Drug Enforcement Administration and Kevin L. Perkins, Assistant Director, Criminal Investigative Division, Federal Bureau of Investigation, before the Senate Caucus on International Narcotics Control, May 5, 2010.

[43] Interview with David Shirk, Director of the Trans-Border Institute, University of San Diego, May 13, 2010. For more background on the role of Tijuana authorities in the reduction of violence, see Rios and Aguilera, "Keys to Reducing Violence in Mexico."

[44] *STRATFOR,* "Mexican Drug Wars Update: Targeting the Most Violent Cartels," July 21, 2011.

[45] Patrick Corcoran, "A Survey of Mexico's Trafficking Networks," *In Sight: Organized Crime in the Americas*, June 27, 2011.

[46] "Outsmarted by Sinaloa: Why the Biggest Drug Gang Has Been Least Hit," *Economist*, January 7, 2010.

[47] The son (Jesus Vicente Zambada) and brother (Jesus Zambada García) of Zambada García are in U.S. custody. The son of the Sinaloa cartel leader was arrested in March 2009 and extradited to the United States in 2010, and has alleged in U.S. federal court that he was ineligible for narcotics trafficking charges because of immunity he earned by being an informant for the DEA (a claim rejected by a Chicago Federal Judge in April 2012 in advance of his trial which is slated to begin in October 2012). The brother, who was arrested in Mexico in 2008, was extradited to the United States on April 3, 2012, and faces eight charges of drug trafficking and one of involvement in organized crime. Edward Fox, "Mexican Drug Lord Fails to Prove He Was Informant," *In Sight: Organized Crime in the Americas*, April 6, 2012; "Top Member of Sinaloa Cartel, "El Rey" Zambada, Extradited to United States," TBI, Justice in Mexico, *April 2012 News Report.*

[48] Ibid. See also John Burnett and Marisa Peñaloza, "Mexico's Drug War: A Rigged Fight," *NPR, All Things Considered*, May 18, 2010.

[49] Geoffrey Ramsey, "Colombian Officials Arrest Money Launderer for 'Chapo' Guzman," *In Sight: Organized Crime in the Americas*, August 11, 2011.

[50] TBI, Justice in Mexico, *June 2012 News Report.*

[51] Some analysts trace the origins of the split to a personal feud between "El Chapo" Guzmán of the Sinaloa DTO and former ally Vicente Carillo Fuentes. In 2004, Guzmán allegedly ordered the killing of Rodolfo Carrillo Fuentes, another of Vicente's brothers. Guzmán's son, Edgar, was killed in May 2008 allegedly on orders from Carrillo Fuentes. See Alfredo Corchado, "Juárez Drug Violence Not Likely To Go Away Soon, Authorities Say," *Dallas Morning News*, May 17, 2010.

[52] Molly Molloy, research librarian at New Mexico State University, keeps a tally of homicides as reported in the Juárez media and the official reports from the Chihuahua Attorney General. She and others have reported more than 3,000 deaths in Ciudad Juárez in 2010, and more than 10,000 deaths in the beleaguered city since January 2008. See Frontera List, at http://groups.google and more information about the list at http://fronteralist.org/.

[53] *STRATFOR*, "Mexican Drug Cartels: Two Wars and a Look Southward," December 17, 2009.

[54] Patrick Corcoran, "A Survey of Mexico's Trafficking Networks," *In Sight: Organized Crime in the Americas*, June 27, 2011; *STRATFOR*, "Mexican Drug Wars Update: Targeting the Most Violent Cartels," July 21, 2011.

[55] "Leader of La Linea Sentenced in Texas court for 2010 U.S. Consulate Murders in Ciudad Juárez," TBI, Justice in Mexico, *April 2012 News Report.*

[56] George W. Grayson, *Mexico: Narco-Violence and a Failed State?* (New Brunswick, NJ: Transaction Publishers, 2010), pp. 72-73.

[57] Nacha Cattan, "Killing of Top Mexico Drug Lord 'Tony Tormenta' May Boost Rival Zetas Cartel," *Christian Science Monitor*, November 8, 2010.

[58] Patrick Corcoran, "A Survey of Mexico's Trafficking Networks," *In Sight: Organized Crime in the Americas*, June 27, 2011.

[59] Most reports indicate that Los Zetas were created by a group of 30 lieutenants and sub-lieutenants who deserted from the Mexican military's Special Mobile Force Group (Grupos Aeromóviles de Fuerzas Especiales, GAFES) to join the Gulf Cartel in the late 1990s. See CRS Report RL34215, *Mexico's Drug Cartels*, by Colleen W. Cook.

[60] Scott Stewart and Alex Posey, "Mexico: The War with the Cartels in 2009," *STRATFOR*, December 9, 2009; DEA maintains the split between Los Zetas and the Gulf DTO began in March 2008 at the same time there was growing evidence that Los Zetas had aligned themselves with the BLO. CRS consultation with the Drug Enforcement Administration, December 20, 2010.

[61] William Booth, "Drug War Violence Appears in Mexico's Northeast, Near Texas Border," *Washington Post*, April 21, 2010.

[62] "The War Is Mainly Between the Drug Cartels," *Latin American Security and Strategic Review*, April 2010.

[63] Ibid.

[64] According to one account, Los Zetas are active throughout the Gulf Coast with centers of operation in Veracruz, the southern states of Tabasco, Yucatán, Quintana Roo, and Chiapas, and in the Pacific Coast states of Guerrero and Oaxaca, as well as Aguascalientes and Zacatecas. They are also gaining dominance in Mexico State and Hidalgo, which they are using to gain entree to Mexico City. See chapter "Emerging and New Narco Sects—Los Zetas and La Familia," in George W. Grayson, Mexico: Narco-Violence and a Failed State? (New Brunswick, NJ: Transaction Publishers, 2010.)

[65] Steven S. Dudley, "Drug Trafficking Organizations in Central America: Transportistas, Mexican Cartels and Maras," in *Shared Responsibility: U.S.-Mexico Options for Confronting Organized Crime*, ed. Eric L. Olson, David A. Shirk, and Andrew Selee (Washington, DC: Woodrow Wilson International Center for Scholars and the University of San Diego, 2010).

[66] Patrick Corcoran, "Are the Zetas the Most Dangerous Drug Gang in Mexico?," *In Sight: Organized Crime in the Americas*, August 8, 2011; Geoffrey Ramsey, "Have the Zetas Replaced Sinaloa as Mexico's Most Powerful Cartel?," *In Sight:Organized Crime in the Americas*, January 3, 2012.

[67] James C. McKinley, Jr. "Keeping Resident Close, and Maybe a Cartel Closer, Mexican Mayor's First Months in Office Marked by Scandal, Twists," *Pittsburgh Post-Gazette*, April 25, 2010.

[68] *STRATFOR*, "Mexico: The Cartel Turf War Intensifies," May 9, 2008.

[69] Ivan Moreno, "Mexico City Area Shootout Leads to Arrest of Major Alleged Drug Trafficker," *Associated Press*, April 23, 2010.

[70] The Mexican government's strategy to remove high-value targets or kingpins has been especially productive since the end of 2009 when Arturo Beltrán Leyva was killed. That event was followed in 2010 by the arrest or attempted arrest and killing of several other key leaders or top lieutenants vying for leadership such as Edgar Valdez. At the close of 2010, the pace of the strategy to take out top leaders seemed to be increasing.

[71] Edgar Valdez is an American-born drug smuggler from Laredo, Texas and allegedly started his career in the United States dealing marijuana. His nickname is "La Barbie" because of his fair hair and eyes. Nicholas Casey and Jose de Cordoba, "Alleged Drug Kingpin Is Arrested in Mexico," *Wall Street Journal*, August 31, 2010.

[72] "15 Suspected Drug Cartel Enforcers Captured in Mexico," *EFE News Service*, April 24, 2010; Trans-Border Institute, Justice in Mexico, *February* and *March 2010 News Reports*.

[73] Finnegan, "Silver or Lead." With regard to heroin, LFM has allowed independent traffickers to cultivate opium poppies and to produce heroin for a "tax" in Michoacán, according to a source at the U.S. Embassy in Mexico City.

[74] Robert J. Bunker and John P. Sullivan, "Cartel Evolution Revisited: Third Phase Cartel Potentials and Alternative Futures in Mexico," *Small Wars & Insurgencies*, vol. 21, no. 1 (March 2010), p. 45.

[75] Finnegan, "Silver or Lead."

[76] Samuel Logan and John P. Sullivan, *Mexico's Divine Justice*, ISN Security Watch, August 17, 2009.

[77] Sidney Weintraub and Duncan Wood, *Cooperative Mexican-U.S. Antinarcotics Efforts*, Center for Strategic and International Studies, November 2010.

[78] *STRATFOR*, "Mexican Drug Wars: Bloodiest Year to Date," December 20, 2010.

[79] Ibid.

[80] "Patterned After the Knights Templar, Drug Cartel Issues 'Code of Conduct,'" *Fox News Latino*, July 20, 2011.

[81] *STRATFOR*, "Mexican Drug War Update: Indistinct Battle Lines," April 16, 2012.

[82] Patrick Corcoran, "A Survey of Mexico's Trafficking Networks," *In Sight: Organized Crime in the Americas*, June 27, 2011.

[83] Patrick Corcoran, "Mexico: Upstart Gangs Eat into Cartel Hegemony," *In Sight: Organized Crime in the Americas*, August 4, 2011.

[84] Patrick Corcoran, "Mexico: Upstart Gangs Eat into Cartel Hegemony," *In Sight: Organized Crime in the Americas*, August 4, 2011.

[85] In Colombia's case, successfully targeting the huge and wealthy Medellín and Cali cartels and dismantling them meant that a number of smaller drug trafficking organizations replaced them. One result of Colombia's dismembering these enormous organizations was that they were replaced by smaller organizations ("cartelitos") which have not been as violent and thus the government was seen to have reduced violence in the drug trade. Critically, however, were other factors in Colombia that were not present in Mexico, such as the presence of guerilla insurgents and paramilitaries who became deeply involved in the illegal drug business, and, some would argue, the Colombian cartels of the 1980s and 1990s were structured and managed very differently than their contemporary counterparts in Mexico. (See Appendix).

[86] O'Neil, "Drug Fragmentation and Violence."

[87] *STRATFOR*, "Mexico's Drug Wars: Bloodiest Year to Date," December 20, 2010; *STRATFOR*, "Mexican Drug Wars Update: Targeting the Most Violent Cartels," July 21, 2011.

[88] O'Neil, "Drug Cartel Fragmentation and Violence;" Eduardo Guerrero Guitiérez, "La Raiz de La Violencia," *Nexos en Línea*, June 1, 2011. Guerrero also argues that eliminating leaders has dispersed the violence.

[89] See Alejandro Poiré and Maria Teresa Martinez, "La Caida de los Capos No Muliplica la Violencia: El Caso de Nacho Coronel," *Nexos en Linea*, May 1, 2011. (Alejandro Poiré and Maria Teresa Martinez were officials from the National Public Security Council at the time the article was written. Poiré was since appointed Mexico's Minister of Interior in November 2011).

[90] Mária de la Luz González, "Delitos Aumentan en el País, Alertan," *El Universal*, August 23, 2011. This article cites data from México Evalua that is available in Spanish at http://www.mexicoevalua.org/.

[91] Morris Panner, "Latin American Organized Crime's New Business Model," *ReVista*, vol. XI, no. 2 (Winter 2012). The author comments: "... the business is moving away from monolithic cartels toward a series of mercury-like mini-cartels. Whether diversification is a growth strategy or a survival strategy in the face of shifting narcotics consumption patterns, it is clear that organized crime is pursuing a larger, more extensive agenda."

[92] See for example, Eric L. Olson and Miguel R. Salazar, *A Profile of Mexico's Major Organized Crime Groups*, Woodrow Wilson International Center for Scholars, February 17, 2011.

[93] Often kidnapping and extortion are a mechanism to collect payment for drug deliveries, for example. Weapons trafficking and money laundering are obviously closely tied to drug trafficking. DEA officials suggested in an interview that about 80% of the DTOs income may come from drugs, and they continue to use "DTO" or "cartel" to identify the organizations. CRS interview with DEA officials on August 5, 2011.

[94] William Booth, "Drug War Violence Appears in Mexico's Northeast, Near Texas Border," *Washington Post*, April 21, 2010; Ioan Grillo, "Special Report: Mexico's Zetas Rewrite Drug War in Blood," *Reuters*, May 23, 2012.

[95] President of the United States, *Strategy to Combat Transnational Organized Crime*, July 19, 2011 at http://www.whitehouse.gov/sites/default/files/Strategy_to_Combat_Transnational_ Organized_Crime_July_2011.pdf.

[96] Tim Johnson, "Do U.S., Mexican Officials Favor One Cartel Over Another?," *Miami Herald*, August 24, 2011.

[97] Samuel Logan and James Bosworth, *Beyond 2012*, Southern Pulse, 2012, http://www.southernpulse.com.

[98] Eduardo Guerrero-Gutiérrez, *Security, Drugs, and Violence in Mexico: A Survey*, 7th North American Forum, Washington, DC, October 2011 at http://iis-db.stanford.edu/evnts/6716 /NAF_2011_EG_(Final).pdf.

[99] Eduardo Guerrero-Guitiérrez, *Security, Drugs, and Violence in Mexico: A Survey.*

[100] Olga Rodriguez, "Mexico Drug War's Latest Toll: 49 Headless Bodies," *Washington Times*, May 14, 2012; Tracy Wilkinson, "Mexico Under Siege: Dozens of Bodies Found Dumped; Authorities Suspect a Drug Cartel, and Say Most of Victims Had Been Decapitated," *Los Angeles Times*, May 14, 2012; Jo Tuckman, "Mexican Drug Cartel Massacres have Method in Their Brutal Madness," *Guardian*, May 14, 2012.

[101] Phil Williams, "El Crimen Organizada y la Violencia en Mexico: Una Perspectiva Comparativa," *ISTOR: Revista de Historia International*, 11th Year, Number 42, Fall 2010. Professor Williams argues that the leaders of the DTOs act like medieval barons, "engaged in constant power struggles and fluid alliances," even as their businesses have fully exploited the opportunities of 21st century globalization.

[102] Ibid.

[103] Cory Molzahn, Viridiana Rios, and David A. Shirk, *Drug Violence in Mexico: Data and Analysis Through 2011*, Trans-Border Institute, University of San Diego, March 2012.

[104] Mexican government data for 2007-2010 is available at http://www.presidencia.gob.mx/base- and data for January through September 2011 is available at http://www.pgr.gob.mx/ temas%20relevantes /estadistica /estadisticas.asp.

[105] Molzahn, Rios, and Shirk, *Drug Violence in Mexico: Data and Analysis Through 2011.*

[106] The Mexican government announced in early August 2012 that there had been a 7% decline in homicides overall in Mexico in the first half of 2012, and an almost 15% decline in organized-crime related homicides. However, the government did not release any data to back these claims. See "Calderon Calls for Mexico to Stay the Course," *LatinNews Daily Report*, August 3, 2012; "Calderón Afirma Que Homicidios Cayeron 7% en México en Primera Mitad de 2012," *Univision*, August 2, 2012.

[107] TBI, *Drug Violence in Mexico: Data and Analysis from 2001-2009*, January 2010.

[108] Angelica Duran-Martinez, Gayle Hazard, and Viridiana Rios, *2010 Mid-Year Report on Drug Violence in Mexico*, Trans-Border Institute, August 2010.

[109] For a discussion of how the two sources compare, see Ríos and Shirk, *Drug Violence in Mexico: Data and Analysis Through 2010*, Trans-Border Institute, University of San Diego, February 2011; Molzahn, Rios, and Shirk, *Drug Violence in Mexico: Data and Analysis Through 2011*.

[110] Ibid. According to the report, the agencies involved include the Center for Investigation and National Security (CISEN), the National Center for Information, Analysis and Planning to Fight Crime (CENAPI) with the Office of the Federal Attorney General (PGR), the Public Security Secretariat (SSP), Secretary of National Defense (SEDENA), Secretary of the Navy (SEMAR), and the Secretary of the Interior (Gobernación).

[111] The January 2012 data release is further broken down in four categories: organized crime homicides (79%); Organized Crime-Government Clashes (2%); Organized Crime Direct Attack on Officials (6%); and Organized Crime Clashes (1.3%). For more details on what distinguishes these categories, see Molzahn, Rios, and Shirk, *Drug Violence in Mexico: Data and Analysis Through 2011*.

[112] Ibid.

[113] Ibid, p. 11.

[114] Ibid.

[115] Mike O'Conner, "El Mañana Cedes Battle to Report on Mexican Violence," Committee to Protect Journalists Blog, May 23, 2012, at http://www.cpj.org/blog/2012/05/el-manana-cedes-battle-to-report-on-mexican-violen.php.

[116] TBI, *Justice in Mexico News Monitor*, July 2012.

[117] Molzahn, Rios, and Shirk, *Drug Violence in Mexico: Data and Analysis Through 2011*.

[118] Catherine E. Shoicet, "Mexican Troops Capture a Top Suspect in Slayings of 49," *CNN*, May 21, 2012.

[119] Dora Beszterczey and Shannon O'Neil, "Breaking the Cycle," *Americas Quarterly*, Winter 2011. This source notes that as many as 10,000 businesses have closed down in Ciudad Juárez alone, while the city's unemployment rate soared from "virtually zero" to 20% in the last three years.

[120] Nacha Cattan, "Is Violence in Mexico Affecting Foreign Investment? No, Say Recent Reports," *Christian Science Monitor*, August 8, 2011; Secretaría de Economia, *Subsecretaria de la Inversión Extrajera Directa (IED) a Nivel Nacional y Subnacional: Seguridad y Otros Factores*, July 27, 2011.

[121] Mexican Federal Government, "Información Sobre el Fenómeno Delictivo en México," August 2010; David Shirk, "Mexican Government Reveals Distribution of Drug Violence," *Justice in Mexico* blog, Trans-Border Institute, http://justiceinmexico.org/2010/08/28/.

[122] U.S. Department of State, Bureau of Consular Affairs, *Travel Warning: Mexico*, April 22, 2011, http://travel.state Andrew Rice, "The End of America: Why Mexico's Pain is El Paso's Gain," *New York Times*, July 31, 2011.

[123] U.S. Department of State, Bureau of Consular Affairs, *Travel Warning: Mexico*, February 8, 2012, at http://travel.state. Seguridad, Justicia, y Paz, "San Pedro Sula La Ciudad Más Violenta del Mundo; Juárez, La Segunda," January 11, 2012, at http://www.seguridadjusticiaypaz.org.mx/sala-deprensa/541-san-pedro-sula-la-ciudad-mas-violenta-del-mundo-juarez-la-segunda. According to this Mexican NGO, the most violent city in the world was San Pedro Sula, Honduras, in 2011, with Ciudad Juárez second (although still the most violent in Mexico).

[124] The choice of "silver or lead" (either a bribe or a bullet) is forced on many government officials by Mexico's drug traffickers. See William Finnegan, "Silver or Lead."

[125] TBI, Justice in Mexico, *January 2010 News Report*.

[126] Duran-Martinez, Hazard, and Rios, *2010 Mid-Year Report on Drug Violence in Mexico*.

[127] TBI, Justice in Mexico, *November 2010 News Report*.

[128] Mexican Federal Government, "Información Sobre el Fenómeno Delictivo en México," August 2010; David Shirk, "Mexican Government Reveals Distribution of Drug Violence," *Justice in Mexico* blog, Trans-Border Institute, http://justiceinmexico.org/2010/08/28/.

[129] Eduardo Guerrero Gutiérrez, "Cómo Reducir La Violencia en México," *Nexos en Línea*," November 3, 2010.

[130] Ibid.

[131] Nik Steinberg, "The Monster and Monterrey: The Politics and Cartels of Mexico's Drug War," *The Nation*, May 25, 2011; David Luhnow, "Expats Flee Drug War in Mexico's No. 3 City," *Wall Street Journal*, September 11, 2010.

[132] Molzahn, Ríos, and Shirk, *Drug Violence in Mexico: Data and Analysis Through 2011.*

[133] TBI, *Justice in Mexico: June 2011 News Report.*

[134] For a vivid description of increasing violence in Guadalajara, see William Finnegan, "The Kingpins," *The New Yorker*, July 2, 2012.

[135] *STRATFOR*, "Mexico Security Memo: The Value of Nuevo Laredo," March 7, 2012.

[136] David Luhnow, "Mexico Economy Withstands Drug War," *Wall Street Journal*, November 22, 2011.

[137] "Mexico Denies that Firms Are Leaving Over Security," *LatinNews Daily*, April 5, 2012.

[138] Kenan Christiansen, "Tourism Up, Mexico Aims for Non-U.S. Visitors," *New York Times*, March 4, 2012.

[139] See, for example, *STRATFOR*, "The Evolution of Mexican Drug Cartels' Areas of Influence," April 28, 2011; *STRATFOR*, "Mexican Drug Wars Update: Targeting the Most Violent Cartels," July 21, 2011.

[140] Ibid; Guy Taylor, "Life Stirs Anew in 'Murder Capital' Juarez," *Washington Times*, May 27, 2012.

[141] Rios and Aguilera, "Keys to Reducing Violence in Mexico: Targeted Policing and Civic Engagement."

[142] The State Department does not identify which murders may be attributed to the drug trafficking-related violence or organized crime, although the most recent travel warning does describe the heightened risk caused by transnational criminal organizations (TCOs) in different parts of the country. U.S. Department of State, Bureau of Consular Affairs, *Travel Warning: Mexico*, February 8, 2012, at http://travel.state

[143] Norwegian Refugee Council—Internal Displacement Monitoring Centre, "Briefing Paper on Forced Displacement in Mexico due to Drug Cartel Violence," December 2010.

[144] Norwegian Refugee Council—Internal Displacement Monitoring Centre, *Global Overview 2011: People Internally Displaced by Conflict and Violence*, April 2012, at http://www.unhcr.org/IDMC/IDMC-report.pdf.

[145] For further information, see profile of Mexico on the U.N. High Commissioner for Refugees (UNHCR) website at http://www.unhcr.org/cgi-bin/texis/vtx/page?page=49e492706& submit=GO.

[146] Patricia Giovine, "More Mexicans Fleeing the Drug War Seek U.S. Asylum," *Chicago Tribune*, July 14, 2011.

[147] U.S. Department of Justice, Executive Office for Immigration Review, Office of Planning, Analysis, and Technology, Immigration Courts, FY2011 Asylum Statistics, at http://www.justice.gov /eoir/efoia/FY11AsyStatsCurrent.pdf.

[148] For a fuller discussion of the Mexican government's strategy see CRS Report RL32724, *Mexico: Issues for Congress*, by Clare Ribando Seelke. The report identifies a broad-based strategy that includes (1) carrying out joint police-military operations to support local authorities and citizens; (2) increasing the operational and technical capacities of the state; (3) initiating legal and institutional reforms; (4) strengthening crime prevention and social programs; and (5) strengthening international cooperation (such as the Mérida Initiative and Beyond Mérida, as described below).

[149] Ken Ellingwood, "An Agony of Its Own; Some See a Colombian Parallel to Mexico's Drug Violence. But as the U.S. Considers Its Options, It's the Differences that Will Count," *Los Angeles Times*, September 26, 2010; Randal C. Archibold, "Adding to Unease of a Drug War Alliance," *New York Times*, May 30, 2012; Claire O'Neill McCleskey, "Mexican Generals Charged with Drug Trafficking," *In Sight: Organized Crime in the Americas*, August 1, 2012. The last article notes that the 50,000 troops deployed by President Calderón since 2006 were sent to 14 of Mexico's 32 states.

[150] One former drug operative in Mexico described the dilemma in an interview. "Trying to stop the gangsters 'is like mowing the grass....You can cut it down. But it always grows back.'" See "Under the Volcano," *Economist*, October 16, 2010. See also Daniel Kurtz-Phelan, "The Long War of Genaro Garcia Luna," New York Times, July 13, 2008.

[151] The evolution is described by Luis Astorga and David Shirk as a move from centralized, hierarchical structures to "an increasingly multi-polar constellation of trafficking organizations with varying specializations and capacities in the late 1990s and 2000s." Luis Astorga and David A. Shirk, *Drug Trafficking Organizations and Counter-Drug Strategies in the U.S.-Mexican Context*, Woodrow Wilson International Center for Scholars Mexico Institute, Working Paper Series on U.S.-Mexico Security Cooperation, May 2010, p. 25. See also Juan Carlos Garzón, *Mafia & Co.: The Criminal Networks in Mexico, Brazil, and Colombia*, Woodrow Wilson International Center for Scholars, June 2008. This evolution in the structure of criminal groups to new models is also described in CRS Report R41547, *Organized Crime: An Evolving Challenge for U.S. Law Enforcement*, by Jerome P. Bjelopera and Kristin M. Finklea.

[152] For background on the Mérida Initiative and its successor Beyond Mérida, see CRS Report R41349, *U.S.-Mexican Security Cooperation: The Mérida Initiative and Beyond* , by Clare Ribando Seelke and Kristin M. Finklea.

[153] Estrategia Todos Somos Juárez, http://www.todossomosjuarez.gob.mx/estrategia/index.html

[154] One of the earliest successes of the Calderón counterdrug strategy was the extradition of Osiel Cardenas Guillen (the notorious leader of the Gulf DTO) to the United States in January 2007. Extraditions have increased significantly under President Calderón. For example, in 2009, the Mexican government extradited a record 107 suspects to the United States, 94 in 2010, and 93 in 2011. For more background, see CRS Report R41349, *U.S.-Mexican Security Cooperation: The Mérida Initiative and Beyond* , by Clare Ribando Seelke and Kristin M. Finklea

[155] David Shirk, "Mexican Government Reveals Distribution of Drug Violence," *Justice in Mexico* blog, Trans-Border Institute, http://justiceinmexico.org/2010/08/28/.

[156] "Mexico's President Calls for Legalisation Debate," *LatinNews Daily Report,* August 4, 2010. President Calderón subsequently expressed opposition to a California ballot initiative, Proposition 19, which would have legalized adult use of marijuana. California voters defeated the measure in the November 2010 general election.

[157] "Calderón Calls for Debate on Marijuana," *Latin News Weekly Report,* August 5, 2010.

[158] "The Summit of the Americas and Drug Legalization," *Latin American Security & Strategic Review*, April 2012. At the time, this comment was interpreted to mean that the President was willing to engage in a debate about drug legalization.

[159] "Mexico Politics: Whither the War on Drugs?," *Economist Intelligence Unit,* September 2, 2010.

[160] Randal C. Archibold, "Mexico Holds 3 Generals Said to Aid Drug Cartels," *New York Times*, May 19, 2012; Randal C. Archibold, "Adding to Unease of a Drug War Alliance," *New York Times*, May 30, 2012.

[161] Claire O'Neill McCleskey, "Mexican Generals Charged with Drug Trafficking," *In Sight: Organized Crime in the Americas*, August 1, 2012; Randal C. Archibold, "Mexico: Former Defense Officials Are Accused of Aiding Traffickers," *New York Times*, August 2, 2012. The judge also charged members of the BLO including Hector Valdez (alias "La Barbie") who is thought to have implicated the army officials in his testimony.

[162] Ibid.

[163] Thousands of gang members in both the United States and Mexico serve the Mexican DTOs. In Ciudad Juárez there are an estimated 500 gangs with a combined membership of between 15,000 to 25,000 persons. Eduardo Guerrero Gutiérrez, "Cómo Reducir La Violencia en México."

[164] Ginger Thompson and Mark Mazzetti, "U.S. Drones Fly Deep in Mexico to Fight Drugs," *New York Times*, March 16, 2011.

[165] Ginger Thompson, "U.S. Widens Its Role in Battle Against Mexico's Drug Cartels," *New York Times*, August 7, 2011.

[166] Ibid.

[167] William J. Burns, Deputy Secretary of State, "Roundtable with Mexican Media," U.S. Embassy, Mexico City, August 16, 2011.

[168] Ibid.

[169] Mexican Federal Government, "Información Sobre el Fenómeno Delictivo en México," August 2010; David Shirk, "Mexican Government Reveals Distribution of Drug Violence," *Justice in Mexico* blog, Trans-Border Institute, http://justiceinmexico.org/2010/08/28/.

[170] Ríos and Shirk, *Drug Violence in Mexico: Data and Analysis Through 2010.*

[171] Molzahn, Rios, and Shirk, *Drug Violence in Mexico: Data and Analysis Through 2011.*

[172] TBI, *Drug Violence in Mexico: Data and Analysis from 2001-2009*, January 2010.

[173] Diana Villiers Negroponte, "Measuring Success in the Drug War: Criteria to Determine Progress in Mexico's Efforts to Defeat Narco-traffickers," Brookings Institution, October 19, 2010, at http://www.brookings.edu/opinions/ 2010/0525_mexico_drug_war_ negroponte.aspx.

[174] See *STRATFOR*, "Mexican Drug Cartels: An Update," May 17, 2010. The DEA in various testimony before Congress has predicted that the violence will continue to increase. For example, in testimony before the Senate Caucus on International Narcotics Control, DEA's Anthony Placido said "The fight against Mexican DTOs is at a critical stage and the violence which is the by-product of this contest may get worse before it gets better. As such, we must manage expectations as well. It took decades for these Mexican DTOs to gain the level of power and impunity that they presently enjoy. We're working at breakneck pains with our government of Mexico counterparts to deal with this cancer, but we may have to deal with the chemotherapy in the process." For more see, Statement of Anthony P. Placido, Assistant Administrator for Intelligence, Drug Enforcement

Administration and Kevin L. Perkins, Assistant Director, Criminal Investigative Division, Federal Bureau of Investigation, Hearing before the Senate Caucus on International Narcotics Control, "Drug Trafficking Violence in Mexico: Implications for the United States," May 5, 2010.

[175] For background on the problem of gun trafficking, see CRS Report R40733, *Gun Trafficking and the Southwest Border*, by Vivian S. Chu and William J. Krouse. The Department of Homeland Security (DHS) estimates between $19 to $29 billion generated by illicit drug sales in the United States flows back to Mexico each year. See DHS, Immigration and Customs Enforcement (ICE), *United States-Mexico Criminal Proceeds Study*, June 2010. Analysts have found it difficult to determine how much of these funds are transferred back to the Mexican DTOs through bulk cash flows and how much is laundered through other methods. Douglas Farah, "Money Laundering and Bulk Cash Smuggling: Challenges for the Mérida Initiative," in *Shared Responsibility: U.S.-Mexico Options for Confronting Organized Crime*, ed. Eric L. Olson, David A. Shirk, and Andrew Selee (Washington, DC: Woodrow Wilson International Center for Scholars and the University of San Diego, 2010).

[176] Pete Yost, "ATF: 68,000 Guns in Mexico Traced to U.S.," *Washington Post*, April 27, 2012. See also, Colby Goodman and Michael Marizco, *U.S. Firearms Trafficking to Mexico: New Data and Insights Illuminate Key Trends and Challenges*, Woodrow Wilson International Center for Scholars Mexico Institute, Working Paper on U.S.-Mexico Security Cooperation, September 2010. Analysts contest how many firearms the Mexican government has seized and if the sample of those submitted for tracing to the ATF is representative. The Mexican government and many others have maintained that the increased availability of high-powered weapons, often originating from the United States, provides the tools for more violence.

[177] William Booth and Nick Miroff, "Stepped-up Efforts by U.S., Mexico Fail to Stem Flow of Drug Money South," *Washington Post*, August 25, 2010.

[178] Mollie Laffin-Rose, "'Organized Crime Laundered $10 Bn in Mexico in FY2011,'" *In Sight: Organized Crime in the Americas*, April 20, 2012. This article has links to all the U.S. government studies; see also footnote number 169.

[179] Beau Kilmer, Jonathan P. Caulkins, and Brittany M. Bond et al., *Drug Trafficking Revenues and Violence in Mexico: Would Legalizing Marijuana in California Help?*, RAND Corporation, Los Angeles, CA, 2010.

[180] Eric L. Olson, *Considering New Strategies for Confronting Organized Crime in Mexico*, Woodrow Wilson International Center for Scholars: Mexico Institute, Washington, DC, March 2012.

[181] Mollie Laffin-Rose, "'Organized Crime Laundered $10 Bn in Mexico in FY2011,'" *In Sight: Organized Crime in the Americas*, April 20, 2012.

[182] See for example, Alejandro Hope, "Money Laundering and the Myth of the Ninja Accountant," *In Sight: Organized Crime in the Americas*, October 11, 2011.

[183] See, for example, testimony from Hearing before the U.S. Senate Caucus on International Narcotics Control, "Money Laundering and Bulk Cash Smuggling along the Southwest Border," March 9, 2011. Anti-money laundering efforts including countering bulk cash smuggling are important elements of the National Southwest Border Counternarcotics Strategy available at http://www.whitehouse.gov/sites/default/files/ondcp/policy swb_counternarcotics_strategy11.pdf.

[184] Embassy of Mexico, "Fact Sheet—National Strategy for Preventing and Fighting Money Laundering and the Financing of Terrorism," September 2010.

[185] Joseph Palazzo, "U.S. in New Drug-Money Push," *Wall Street Journal*, September 30, 2010.

[186] For more background, see CRS Report R41349, *U.S.-Mexican Security Cooperation: The Mérida Initiative and Beyond* , by Clare Ribando Seelke and Kristin M. Finklea.

[187] The U.S. Department of the Treasury's Office of Foreign Assets Control (OFAC) targets and blocks financial assets, subject to U.S. jurisdiction, of drug kingpins and related associates and entities. See CRS Report R41215, *Latin America and the Caribbean: Illicit Drug Trafficking and U.S. Counterdrug Programs*, coordinated by Clare Ribando Seelke.

[188] Celina B. Realuyo, *It's All About the Money: Advancing Anti-Money Laundering Efforts in the U.S. and Mexico to Combat Transnational Organized Crime*, Woodrow Wilson International Center for Scholars: Mexico Institute, Washington, DC, May 2012. This report describes both U.S. and Mexican anti-money laundering efforts.

[189] Tracy Wilkinson, "As Fury Builds in Mexico, 5 Arrested in Casino Fire," *Chicago Tribune*, August 30, 2011.

[190] Dudley Althaus, "Calderón: Casino Killers 'Terrorists'," *Houston Chronicle*, August 27, 2011.

[191] "Corruption, not terrorism? Extortion now suspected in casino deaths," *Washington Post*, September 1, 2011.

[192] Mark A. R. Kleiman, Jonathan P. Caukins, and Angela Hawken, *Drugs and Drug Policy: What Everyone Needs to Know* (Oxford University Press, 2011); *Jane's Information Group*, "Jane's Sentinel Security Assessment—

Central America and the Caribbean," February 16, 2011. Of note, some Members of Congress have introduced legislation (H.R. 1270, H.R. 4303) that would direct the U.S. Secretary of State to designate certain Mexican DTOs as foreign terrorist organizations.

193 U.S. Department of State, *Country Reports on Terrorism 2011*, July 31, 2012 at http://www.state

194 *Economist Intelligence Unit*, "Mexico Risk: Security Risk," September 23, 2010.

195 United Nations Office on Drugs and Crime, *Global Study on Homicide: Trends, Contexts, Data*, 2011 at http://www.unodc.org/documents/data-and-analysis/statistics. Rates have been rounded to present nearest whole number.

196 Molzahn, Rios, and Shirk, Drug *Violence in Mexico: Data and Analysis Through 2011.*

197 Pew Research Center, "Crime and Drug Cartels Top Concerns in Mexico," Press Release, August 31, 2011. The study can be accessed at http://pewglobal.org/files/2011/08/Pew-Global-Attitudes-Mexico-Report-FINAL-August-31-2011.pdf.

198 Ibid. See also, Sara Miller Llana, "In Drug War, Mexico Warms to the U.S.," *Christian Science Monitor: Daily News Briefing*, September 2, 2011.

199 CASEDE, USAID, and CEGI et al., *Encuesta Ciudadanía Democracia y Narcoviolencia (CIDENA, 2011): Methodology and Findings*, March 26, 2012. Summary in English at http://csis.org/files/attachments/120326_SIMO_slides.pdf.

200 Alfredo Corchado, "Most Mexicans Want U.S. to Take a Bigger Role in Fighting Violence, Poll Finds," *Dallas Morning News*, May 13, 2012.

201 Candace Vallantin, "Mexicans Campaign to End Drug War; Renowned Poet Puts Down his Pen to Focus on a Caravan For Peace," *Toronto Star*, June 7, 2011.

202 Washington Office on Latin America, "Mexican Peace Movement Announces Upcoming U.S. Caravan for Peace," at http://www.wola.org/highlight/caravan_for_peace "Mexican Activist Gets U.S. Support for Planned Peace Caravan," *EFE News Service*, June 9, 2012.

203 Human Rights Watch, *Neither Rights nor Security*; testimony from Hearing of the Tom Lantos Human Rights Commission, "Human Rights in Mexico," May 10, 2012; Catherine Daly, Kimberly Heinle, and David A. Shirk, *Armed with Impunity: Curbing Military Human Rights Abuses in Mexico*, Trans-Border Institute, Special Report, July 2012.

204 See, for example, Jorge G. Castaneda, "What's Spanish for Quagmire?," *Foreign Policy*, January/February 2010.

205 The United States and Mexico are recognizing that reduction in violence must be a key goal of the Beyond Mérida strategy. For more on the Beyond Mérida strategy, see CRS Report R41349, *U.S.-Mexican Security Cooperation: The Mérida Initiative and Beyond.*

206 Eduardo Guerrero Gutiérrez, "Cómo Reducir La Violencia en México," *Nexos en Línea*," November 3, 2010. Guerrero cites the Boston program "Operation Ceasefire" and the Tri-Agency Resource Gang Enforcement Team (TARGET) of Orange County, California, as two examples of effective programs to reduce violence by applying the principle of concentrating enforcement efforts and reducing violence through credibly communicating to violent offenders that they will be prosecuted.

207 Eric L. Olson, *Considering New Strategies for Confronting Organized Crime in Mexico*; Mark Kleiman, "Surgical Strikes in the Drug Wars: Smarter Policies for Both Sides of the Border," *Foreign Affairs*, vol. 90, no. 5, September/October 2011.

208 Guillermo Vásquez del Mercado Almada, "Five Ps for a Violence Reduction Strategy in Mexico (Part III)," *Small Wars Journal*, March 9, 2012. The author also endorses a violence reduction strategy, but cautions against "sequential" targeting. He backs a strategy with the following tactics: "a) aim for simultaneous rather than sequential targets; b) contain violence; and c) conquer high intensity crime zones."

209 Nick Miroff and William Booth, "In Mexico, a Legal Breakdown Invites Brutal Justice," *Washington Post*, December 9, 2010; Vanda Felbab-Brown, *Calderón's Caldron: Lessons from Mexico's Battle Against Organized Crime and Drug Trafficking in Tijuana, Ciudad Juárez, and Michoacán*, The Brookings Institution, Washington, DC, September 2011. In the Brookings report, see section on "Mexico's Militias."

210 For more on the Mérida Initiative and Beyond Mérida, see CRS Report R41349, *U.S.-Mexican Security Cooperation: The Mérida Initiative and Beyond* , by Clare Ribando Seelke and Kristin M. Finklea.

211 Ken Ellingwood, "Is Mexico a New Colombia? Mexicans May Have Cause to Bristle at U.S. Comparison," *Chicago Tribune*, September 26, 2010. Also see Appendix.

212 "A Conversation with U.S. Secretary of State Hillary Rodham Clinton," Council on Foreign Relations, September 8, 2010. Transcript available at http://www.cfr.org/publication/22896/ conversation_with_us_secretary_of_state_hillary_rodham_clinton.html.

[213] Plan Colombia is a U.S.-supported counterdrug and counterterrorism program that has operated for more than a decade in Colombia. For more background, see CRS Report RL32250, *Colombia: Background, U.S. Relations, and Congressional Interest*, by June S. Beittel.

[214] U.S. General Accounting Office, *Drug Control: Challenges in Implementing Plan Colombia*, Statement of Jess T. Ford, Director, International Affairs and Trade, GAO-01-76T, October 12, 2000.

[215] For example, there have been near simultaneous actions against Mexico's military or police forces, coordinated attacks on different cities, cartel roadblocks throughout cities like Monterrey to prevent responders from reaching firefights or other hot spots, and kidnappings by cartel forces dressed in Mexican police or military uniforms or in close simulations of the official uniforms.

[216] For other analysts using the terminology of "criminal insurgency" see Bob Killebrew and Jennifer Bernal, *Crime Wars: Gangs, Cartels and U.S. National Security*, Center for a New American Security, September 2010.

[217] John P. Sullivan, "Counter-supply and Counter-violence Approaches to Narcotics Trafficking," *Small Wars & Insurgencies*, vol. 21, no. 1 (March 12, 2010), p. 186.

[218] Williams, "El Crimen Organizada y la Violencia en Mexico."

[219] William Booth, "In Mexico, Made-for-TV Confessions," *Washington Post*, August 31, 2011.

[220] Mexico Evalúa, *Seguridad y Justicia Penal en los Estados: 25 Indicadores de Nuestra Debilidad Institucional*, March 2012.

[221] For example, see William Finnegan, "Silver or Lead," *The New Yorker*, May 31, 2010.

[222] Ibid.

[223] "Measuring the Extent of Drug Cartel Control in Mexico," *LatinNews Daily*, September 15, 2010. Ricardo Ravelo, "Los Cárteles Imponen Su Ley," *Proceso*, October 24, 2010.

[224] Ibid.

[225] For example, Robert C. Bonner, "The New Cocaine Cowboys," *Foreign Affairs*, vol. 89 (July/August 2010). Bonner looks to an earlier era for lessons from Colombia, but asserts that "Virtually all the key lessons learned from the defeat of the Colombian cartels in the 1990s are applicable to the current battle against the Mexican cartels."

[226] Juan Forero, "Colombia Stepping Up Anti-Drug Training of Mexico's Army, Police," *Washington Post*, January 22, 2011.

In: Organized Crime
Editors: F. B. Hall and F. C. Martin

ISBN: 978-1-62618-415-2

Chapter 4

STRATEGY TO COMBAT TRANSNATIONAL ORGANIZED CRIME: ADDRESSING CONVERGING THREATS TO NATIONAL SECURITY*

The Staff of the National Security Council

Transnational organized crime refers to those self-perpetuating associations of individuals who operate transnationally for the purpose of obtaining power, influence, monetary and/or commercial gains, wholly or in part by illegal means, while protecting their activities through a pattern of corruption and/ or violence, or while protecting their illegal activities through a transnational organizational structure and the exploitation of transnational commerce or communication mechanisms. There is no single structure under which transnational organized criminals operate; they vary from hierarchies to clans, networks, and cells, and may evolve to other structures. The crimes they commit also vary. Transnational organized criminals act conspiratorially in their criminal activities and possess certain characteristics which may include, but are not limited to:

- In at least part of their activities they commit violence or other acts which are likely to intimidate, or make actual or implicit threats to do so;
- They exploit differences between countries to further their objectives, enriching their organization, expanding its power, and/or avoiding detection/apprehension;
- They attempt to gain influence in government, politics, and commerce through corrupt as well as legitimate means;
- They have economic gain as their primary goal, not only from patently illegal activities but also from investment in legitimate businesses; and
- They attempt to insulate both their leadership and membership from detection, sanction, and/ or prosecution through their organizational structure.

The White House
Washington, July 19, 2011

* This document was released by the Obama Administration, July 2011.

In the National Security Strategy, I committed my Administration to the pursuit of four enduring national interests: security, prosperity, respect for universal values, and the shaping of an international order that can meet the challenges of the 21st century. The expanding size, scope, and influence of transnational organized crime and its impact on U.S. and international security and governance represent one of the most significant of those challenges. During the past 15 years, technological innovation and globalization have proven to be an overwhelming force for good. However, transnational criminal organizations have taken advantage of our increasingly interconnected world to expand their illicit enterprises.

Criminal networks are not only expanding their operations, but they are also diversifying their activities, resulting in a convergence of transnational threats that has evolved to become more complex, volatile, and destabilizing. These networks also threaten U.S. interests by forging alliances with corrupt elements of national governments and using the power and influence of those elements to further their criminal activities. In some cases, national governments exploit these relationships to further their interests to the detriment of the United States. Despite a long and successful history of dismantling criminal organizations and developing common international standards for cooperation against transnational organized crime, not all of our capabilities have kept pace with the expansion of 21st century transnational criminal threats. Therefore, this strategy is organized around a single, unifying principle: to build, balance, and integrate the tools of American power to combat transnational organized crime and related threats to our national security – and to urge our partners to do the same. To this end, this strategy sets out 56 priority actions, starting with ones the United States can take within its own borders to lessen the impact of transnational crime domestically and on our foreign partners. Other actions seek to enhance our intelligence, protect the financial system and strategic markets, strengthen interdiction, investigations, and prosecutions, disrupt the drug trade and its facilitation of other transnational threats, and build international cooperation. While this Strategy is intended to assist the United States Government in combating transnational crime, it also serves as an invitation for enhanced international cooperation. We encourage our partners and allies to echo the commitment we have made here and join in building a new framework for international cooperation to protect all our citizens from the violence, harm, and exploitation wrought by transnational organized crime.

Sincerely,

Executive Summary

The *Strategy to Combat Transnational Organized Crime* applies all elements of national power to protect citizens and U.S. national security interests from the convergence of 21st century transnational criminal threats. This *Strategy* is organized around a single unifying principle: *to build, balance, and integrate the tools of American power to combat transnational organized crime and related threats to national security—and to urge our foreign partners to do the same.*

The end-state we seek is to reduce transnational organized crime (TOC) from a national security threat to a manageable public safety problem in the United States and in strategic regions around the world.

The *Strategy* will achieve this end-state by pursuing five key policy objectives:

1) Protect Americans and our partners from the harm, violence, and exploitation of transnational criminal networks.
2) Help partner countries strengthen governance and transparency, break the corruptive power of transnational criminal networks, and sever state-crime alliances.
3) Break the economic power of transnational criminal networks and protect strategic markets and the U.S. financial system from TOC penetration and abuse.
4) Defeat transnational criminal networks that pose the greatest threat to national security by targeting their infrastructures, depriving them of their enabling means, and preventing the criminal facilitation of terrorist activities.
5) Build international consensus, multilateral cooperation, and public-private partnerships to defeat transnational organized crime.

The *Strategy* also introduces new and innovative capabilities and tools, which will be accomplished by prioritizing within the resources available to affected departments and agencies.

A new Executive Order will establish a sanctions program to block the property of and prohibit transactions with significant transnational criminal networks that threaten national security, foreign policy, or economic interests.

A proposed legislative package will enhance the authorities available to investigate, interdict, and prosecute the activities of top transnational criminal networks.

A new Presidential Proclamation under the Immigration and Nationality Act (INA) will deny entry to transnational criminal aliens and others who have been targeted for financial sanctions.

A new rewards program will replicate the success of narcotics rewards programs in obtaining information that leads to the arrest and conviction of the leaders of transnational criminal organizations that pose the greatest threats to national security.

An interagency Threat Mitigation Working Group will identify those TOC networks that present a sufficiently high national security risk and will ensure the coordination of all elements of national power to combat them.

I. Introduction

> "Combating transnational criminal and trafficking networks requires a multidimensional strategy that safeguards citizens, breaks the financial strength of criminal and terrorist networks, disrupts illicit trafficking networks, defeats transnational criminal organizations, fights government corruption, strengthens the rule of law, bolsters judicial systems, and improves transparency. While these are major challenges, the

> United States will be able to devise and execute a collective strategy with other nations facing the same threats."
>
> — National Security Strategy, May 2010

In January 2010, the United States Government completed a comprehensive review of international organized crime—the first on this topic since 1995. Based on the review and subsequent reporting, the Administration has concluded that, in the intervening years, international —or transnational— organized crime has expanded dramatically in size, scope, and influence and that it poses a significant threat to national and international security. In light of the review's findings, we have adopted the term "transnational organized crime" (TOC) to describe the threats addressed by this *Strategy*. While the term "international organized crime" has been commonly used in the past, "transnational organized crime" more accurately describes the converging threats we face today. As emphasized in the *National Security Strategy*: "...these threats cross borders and undermine the stability of nations, subverting government institutions through corruption and harming citizens worldwide."

In years past, TOC was largely regional in scope, hierarchically structured, and had only occasional links to terrorism. Today's criminal networks are fluid, striking new alliances with other networks around the world and engaging in a wide range of illicit activities, including cybercrime and providing support for terrorism. Virtually every transnational criminal organization and its enterprises are connected and enabled by information systems technologies, making cybercrime a substantially more important concern. TOC threatens U.S. interests by taking advantage of failed states or contested spaces; forging alliances with corrupt foreign government officials and some foreign intelligence services; destabilizing political, financial, and security institutions in fragile states; undermining competition in world strategic markets; using cyber technologies and other methods to perpetrate sophisticated frauds; creating the potential for the transfer of weapons of mass destruction (WMD) to terrorists; and expanding narcotrafficking and human and weapons smuggling networks. Terrorists and insurgents increasingly are turning to criminal networks to generate funding and acquire logistical support. TOC also threatens the interconnected trading, transportation, and transactional systems that move people and commerce throughout the global economy and across our borders.

In October 2010, the national security advisors of 44 nations gathered in Sochi, Russia to discuss trans-national crime. Representing the United States, former National Security Advisor General James L. Jones, USMC, Ret. warned of the TOC threats to international security and urged immediate international action, saying:

> "In a world full of transnational threats, transnational crime is in an ascendant phase... This lethal nexus of organized crime, narco-trafficking, and terrorism is a threat that the United States, Russia and all of us share and should be working together to combat... Today, right now, we have an opportunity for cooperation not just between the United States and Russia, but among all nations represented here today. It's up to us to seize the moment..."

The various elements of this *Strategy* flow from a single unifying principle: we will *build, balance, and integrate the tools of American power to combat TOC and related threats to national security and urge our foreign partners to do the same.* To this end, the *Strategy* recognizes TOC as a significant threat to national and international security and emphasizes U.S. planning, priorities, and activities accordingly. The *Strategy* addresses TOC and drug trafficking as increasingly intertwined threats to maximize the impact of U.S. resources. It also provides a framework to direct U.S. power against those TOC actors, activities, and networks that are determined to pose the greatest threat to national and international security.

This *Strategy* establishes priority actions in several key areas. It starts by taking a hard look at what actions the United States can take within its own borders to lessen the threat and impact of TOC domestically and on our foreign partners. The other priority actions seek to:

- Enhance Intelligence and Information Sharing;
- Protect the Financial System and Strategic Markets Against Transnational Organized Crime;
- Strengthen Interdiction, Investigations, and Prosecutions;
- Disrupt Drug Trafficking and Its Facilitation of Other Transnational Threats; and
- Build International Capacity, Cooperation, and Partnerships.

This *Strategy* complements but does not replicate the work of other major U.S. security initiatives. It is guided by the *National Security Strategy* and interlocks with other U.S. strategies and initiatives, to include the *National Drug Control Strategy*, the *National Strategy for Counterterrorism,* the *International Strategy for Cyberspace*, the *National Strategy to Combat Weapons of Mass Destruction,* the U.S.-Mexico *Merida Initiative,* the *Law Enforcement Strategy to Combat International Organized Crime,* the *National Strategy for Maritime Security, Countering Piracy Off the Horn ofAfrica: Partnership & Action Plan,* and several other U.S. security assistance, counterdrug, and capacity-building efforts around the world.

The Interagency Policy Committee (IPC) on Illicit Drugs and Transnational Criminal Threats will oversee a whole-of-government approach to implementing this *Strategy*. Co-chaired by the National Security Staff and the Office of National Drug Control Policy, this IPC will issue implementation guidance, establish performance measures, and receive regular progress updates from the interagency community. This IPC will be informed by and work with other IPCs such as the Maritime Security IPC. With a new *Strategy to Combat Transnational Organized Crime* and an array of new authorities and tools, this Administration is committing itself to ensuring that we rise to the national security challenges of the 21st century and ensure an international order that protects the safety and well-being of our citizens.

II. Transnational Organized Crime: A Growing Threat to National and International Security

Transnational organized crime (TOC) poses a significant and growing threat to national and international security, with dire implications for public safety, public health, democratic institutions, and economic stability across the globe. Not only are criminal networks expanding, but they also are diversifying their activities, resulting in the convergence of threats that were once distinct and today have explosive and destabilizing effects. This *Strategy* organizes the United States to combat TOC networks that pose a strategic threat to Americans and to U.S. interests in key regions.

Penetration of State Institutions, Corruption, and Threats to Governance

Developing countries with weak rule of law can be particularly susceptible to TOC penetration. TOC penetration of states is deepening, leading to co-option in a few cases and further weakening of governance in many others. The apparent growing nexus in some states among TOC groups and elements of government—including intelligence services—and high-level business figures represents a significant threat to economic growth and democratic institutions. In countries with weak governance, there are corrupt officials who turn a blind eye to TOC activity. TOC networks insinuate themselves into the political process in a variety of ways. This is often accomplished through direct bribery (but also by having members run for office); setting up shadow economies; infiltrating financial and security sectors through coercion or corruption; and positioning themselves as alternate providers of governance, security, services, and livelihoods. As they expand, TOC networks may threaten stability and undermine free markets as they build alliances with political leaders, financial institutions, law enforcement, foreign intelligence, and security agencies. TOC penetration of governments is exacerbating corruption and undermining governance, rule of law, judicial systems, free press, democratic institution-building, and transparency. Further, events in Somalia have shown how criminal control of territory and piracy ransoms generate significant sums of illicit revenue and promote the spread of government instability.

Threats to the Economy, U.S. Competitiveness, and Strategic Markets

TOC threatens U.S. economic interests and can cause significant damage to the world financial system through its subversion, exploitation, and distortion of legitimate markets and economic activity. U.S. business leaders worry that U.S. firms are being put at a competitive disadvantage by TOC and corruption, particularly in emerging markets where many perceive that rule of law is less reliable. The World Bank estimates about $1 trillion is spent each year to bribe public officials, causing an array of economic distortions and damage to legitimate economic activity. The price of doing business in countries affected by TOC is also rising as companies budget for additional security costs, adversely impacting foreign direct investment in many parts of the world. TOC activities can lead to disruption of the global supply chain, which in turn diminishes economic competitiveness and impacts the ability of U.S. industry and transportation sectors to be resilient in the face of such disruption. Further, transnational criminal organizations, leveraging their relationships with state-owned entities, industries, or state-allied actors, could gain influence over key commodities markets such as gas, oil, aluminum, and precious metals, along with potential exploitation of the transportation sector.

With the expansion of the drug trade, illicit drugs have become more lethal over the years. The number of Americans who died each year from accidental overdoses from all drugs, but mostly illicit ones, more than tripled from 1992 to 2007, increasing to 38,000.

Crime-Terror-Insurgency Nexus

Terrorists and insurgents increasingly are turning to TOC to generate funding and acquire logistical support to carry out their violent acts. The Department of Justice reports that 29 of the 63 organizations on its FY 2010 Consolidated Priority Organization Targets list, which includes the most significant international drug trafficking organizations (DTOs) threatening the United States, were associated with terrorist groups. Involvement in the drug trade by the Taliban and the Revolutionary Armed Forces of Colombia (FARC) is critical to the ability of these groups to fund terrorist activity. We are concerned about Hizballah's drug and criminal activities, as well as indications of links between al-Qa`ida in the Lands of the Islamic Maghreb and the drug trade. Further, the terrorist organization al-Shabaab has engaged in criminal activities such as kidnapping for ransom and extortion, and may derive limited fees from extortion or protection of pirates to generate funding for its operations. While the crime-terror nexus is still mostly opportunistic, this nexus is critical nonetheless, especially if it were to involve the successful criminal transfer of WMD material to terrorists or their penetration of human smuggling networks as a means for terrorists to enter the United States.

Expansion of Drug Trafficking

Despite demonstrable counterdrug successes in recent years, particularly against the cocaine trade, illicit drugs remain a serious threat to the health, safety, security, and financial well-being of Americans. The demand for illicit drugs, both in the United States and abroad, fuels the power, impunity, and violence of criminal organizations around the globe. Mexican DTOs are escalating their violence to consolidate their market share within the Western Hemisphere, protect their operations in Mexico, and expand their reach into the United States. In West Africa, Latin American cartels are exploiting local criminal organizations to move cocaine to Western Europe and the Middle East. There have also been instances of Afghan DTOs operating with those in West Africa to smuggle heroin to Europe and the United States. Many of the well-established organized criminal groups that had not been involved in drug trafficking—including those in Russia, China, Italy, and the Balkans—are now establishing ties to drug producers to develop their own distribution networks and markets. The expansion of drug trafficking is often accompanied by dramatic increases in local crime and corruption, as the United Nations has detected in regions such as West Africa and Central America.

Human Smuggling

Human smuggling is the facilitation, transportation, attempted transportation, or illegal entry of a person or persons across an international border, in violation of one or more countries' laws, either clandestinely or through deception, whether with the use of fraudulent documents or through the evasion of legitimate border controls. It is a criminal commercial transaction between willing parties who go their separate ways once they have procured illegal entry into a country.

The vast majority of people who are assisted in illegally entering the United States and other countries are smuggled, rather than trafficked. International human smuggling networks are linked to other trans-national crimes including drug trafficking and the corruption of government officials.

They can move criminals, fugitives, terrorists, and trafficking victims, as well as economic migrants. They undermine the sovereignty of nations and often endanger the lives of those being smuggled.

In its 2010 report *The Globalization of Crime: A Transnational Organized Crime Threat Assessment,* the United Nations Office on Drugs and Crime (UNODC) estimated that the smuggling of persons from Latin America to the United States generated approximately $6.6 billion annually in illicit proceeds for human smuggling networks.

Trafficking in Persons

Trafficking in Persons (TIP), or human trafficking, refers to activities involved when one person obtains or holds another person in compelled service, such as involuntary servitude, slavery, debt bondage, and forced labor.

TIP specifically targets the trafficked person as an object of criminal exploitation—often for labor exploitation or sexual exploitation purposes—and trafficking victims are frequently physically and emotionally abused. Although TIP is generally thought of as an international crime that involves the crossing of borders, TIP victims can also be trafficked within their own countries.

Traffickers can move victims between locations within the same country and often sell them to other trafficking organizations.

Weapons Trafficking

Criminal networks and illicit arms dealers also play important roles in the black markets from which terrorists and drug traffickers procure some of their weapons. As detailed in the 2010 UNODC report *The Globalization of Crime,* "The value of the documented global authorized trade in firearms has been estimated at approximately $1.58 billion in 2006, with unrecorded but licit transactions making up another $100 million or so.

The most commonly cited estimate for the size of the illicit market is 10% - 20% of the licit market." According to the head of UNODC, these "illicit arms fuel the violence that undermines security, development and justice" worldwide. U.S. Federal law enforcement agencies have intercepted large numbers of weapons or related items being smuggled to China, Russia, Mexico, the Philippines, Somalia, Turkmenistan, and Yemen in the last year alone.

Intellectual Property Theft

TOC networks are engaged in the theft of critical U.S. intellectual property, including through intrusions into corporate and proprietary computer networks. Theft of intellectual property ranges from movies, music, and video games to imitations of popular and trusted brand names, to proprietary designs of high-tech devices and manufacturing processes.

This intellectual property theft causes significant business losses, erodes U.S. competitiveness in the world marketplace, and in many cases threatens public health and safety. Between FY 2003 and FY 2010, the yearly domestic value of customs seizures at U.S. port and mail facilities related to intellectual property right (IPR) violations leaped from $94 million to $188 million. Products originating in China accounted for 66% of these IPR seizures in FY 2010.

Cybercrime

TOC networks are increasingly involved in cybercrime, which costs consumers billions of dollars annually, threatens sensitive corporate and government computer networks, and undermines worldwide confidence in the international financial system. Through cybercrime, transnational criminal organizations pose a significant threat to financial and trust systems—banking, stock markets, e-currency, and value and credit card services—on which the world economy depends. For example, some estimates indicate that online frauds perpetrated by Central European cybercrime networks have defrauded U.S. citizens or entities of approximately $1 billion in a single year. According to the U.S. Secret Service, which investigates cybercrimes through its 31 Electronic Crimes Task Forces, financial crimes facilitated by anonymous online criminal fora result in billions of dollars in losses to the Nation's financial infrastructure. The National Cyber Investigative Joint Task Force, led by the Federal Bureau of Investigation (FBI), functions as a domestic focal point for 18 federal departments or agencies to coordinate, integrate, and share information related to cyber threat investigations, as well as make the Internet safer by pursuing terrorists, spies, and criminals who seek to exploit U.S. systems. Pervasive criminal activity in cyberspace not only directly affects its victims, but can imperil citizens'and businesses' faith in these digital systems, which are critical to our society and economy. Computers and the Internet play a role in most transnational crimes today, either as the target or the weapon used in the crime. The use of the Internet, personal computers, and mobile devices all create a trail of digital evidence. Often the proper investigation of this evidence trail requires highly trained personnel. Crimes can occur more quickly, but investigations proceed more slowly due to the critical shortage of investigators with the knowledge and expertise to analyze ever increasing amounts of potential digital evidence.

The Critical Role of Facilitators

Connecting these converging threats are "facilitators," semi- legitimate players such as accountants, attorneys, notaries, bankers, and real estate brokers, who cross both the licit and illicit worlds and provide services to legitimate customers, criminals, and terrorists alike. The range of licit-illicit relationships is broad. At one end, criminals draw on the public reputations of licit actors to maintain facades of propriety for their operations. At the other end are "specialists" with skills or resources who have been completely subsumed into the criminal networks. For example, TOC networks rely on industry experts, both witting and unwitting, to facilitate corrupt transactions and to create the necessary infrastructure to pursue their illicit schemes, such as creating shell corporations, opening offshore bank accounts in the shell corporation's name, and creating front businesses for their illegal activity and money laundering.

Business owners or bankers are enlisted to launder money, and employees of legitimate companies are used to conceal smuggling operations. Human smugglers, human traffickers, arms traffickers, drug traffickers, terrorists, and other criminals depend on secure transportation networks and safe locations from which to stage smuggling activity or to store bulk cash or narcotics for transport. They also depend on fraudulently created or fraudulently obtained documents, such as passports and visas, to move themselves or their clients into the United States and illegally reside here.

Transnational criminal networks such as organized crime groups, drug traffickers, and weapons dealers at times share convergence points—places, businesses, or people—to "launder" or convert their illicit profits into legitimate funds.

Many of these disparate networks also appear to use the same casinos, financial intermediaries, and front companies to plan arms and narcotics deals because they view them as safe intermediaries for doing business. Cash-intensive and high-volume businesses such as casinos are especially attractive, particularly those in jurisdictions that lack the political will and oversight to regulate casino operations or fail to perform due diligence on casino licensees. Illicit networks similarly abuse some of the same financial intermediaries and front companies in regions where government or law enforcement corruption is prevalent, with officials receiving either revenues from the criminal businesses or ownership stakes in the legitimate-appearing commercial entity.

Regional Priorities

TOC—A Global Problem—Manifests Itself in Various Regions in Different Ways

Western Hemisphere

TOC networks—including transnational gangs—have expanded and matured, threatening the security of citizens and the stability of governments throughout the region, with direct security implications for the United States. Central America is a key area of converging threats where illicit trafficking in drugs, people, and weapons—as well as other revenue streams— fuel increased instability. Transnational crime and its accompanying violence are threatening the prosperity of some Central American states and can cost up to eight percent of their gross domestic product, according to the World Bank. The Government of Mexico is waging an historic campaign against transnational criminal organizations, many of which are expanding beyond drug trafficking into human smuggling and trafficking, weapons smuggling, bulk cash smuggling, extortion, and kidnapping for ransom. TOC in Mexico makes the U.S. border more vulnerable because it creates and maintains illicit corridors for border crossings that can be employed by other secondary criminal or terrorist actors or organizations. Farther south, Colombia has achieved remarkable success in reducing cocaine production and countering illegal armed groups, such as the FARC, that engage in TOC. Yet, with the decline of these organizations, new groups are emerging such as criminal bands known in Spanish as *Bandas Criminales,* or *Bacrims*.

Mexico Los Zetas Cartel Leaders Heriberto Lazcano-Lazcano and Miguel Angel Treviño Morales

Colombia: From Recipient to Provider of Assistance

After years of intensive capacity building assistance in Colombia, the United States is working to transfer financial and operational responsibility for institutional development to the Government of Colombia. Colombia now is an exporter of law enforcement and justice sector capabilities, providing assistance and advice for police, prosecutors, protection programs, and judiciary, criminal law, and procedure development. This reality is the result of the success of U.S. assistance in Colombian capacity building, a success the United States aims to replicate with other partner states. On July 2, 2008, the world witnessed the extraordinary courage and capability of Colombian forces during their daring rescue of 15 hostages—including 3 Americans—who had been held captive for years in the jungles by FARC guerrillas. The rescue was accomplished without firing a shot.

INTERPOL Fugitive Dawood Ibrahim, South Asia "Company D"

Afghanistan/Southwest Asia

Nowhere is the convergence of transnational threats more apparent than in Afghanistan and Southwest Asia. The Taliban and other drug-funded terrorist groups threaten the efforts of the Islamic Republic of Afghanistan, the United States, and other international partners to build a peaceful and democratic future for that nation. The insurgency is seen in some areas of Afghanistan as criminally driven—as opposed to ideologically motivated—and in some areas, according to local Afghan officials and U.S. estimates, drug traffickers and the Taliban are becoming indistinguishable. In other instances, ideologically driven insurgent networks are either directly trafficking in narcotics or have linked up with DTOs to finance their criminal actions. The threatening crime-terror-insurgency nexus in this region is illustrated by cases such as that of INTERPOL fugitive Dawood Ibrahim, the reputed leader of South Asia's powerful "D Company." He is wanted in connection with the 1993 Mumbai bombing and is sanctioned under United Nations Security Council Resolution 1267 (Taliban/al-Qa`ida).

Russia/Eurasia

Russian and Eurasian organized crime networks represent a significant threat to economic growth and democratic institutions. Russian organized crime syndicates and criminally linked oligarchs may attempt to collude with state or state-allied actors to undermine competition in strategic markets such as gas, oil, aluminum, and precious metals. At the same time, TOC networks in the region are establishing new ties to global drug trafficking networks. Nuclear material trafficking is an especially prominent concern in the former Soviet Union. The United States will continue to cooperate with Russia and the nations of the region to combat illicit drugs and TOC.

The Balkans

A traditional conduit for smuggling between east and west, the Balkans has become an ideal environment for the cultivation and expansion of TOC. Weak institutions in Albania, Kosovo, and Bosnia and Herzegovina have enabled Balkan-based TOC groups to seize control of key drug and human trafficking routes and Western European markets. The Balkans region has become a new entry point for Latin American cocaine, a source of synthetic drugs, and a transit region for heroin chemical precursors for use in the Caucasus and Afghanistan. Excess weapons are smuggled to countries of concern. Insufficient border controls and the ease of acquiring passports enable the transit of criminals and terrorist figures to Western Europe. Cooperation between the United States and the European Union, as well as bilateral cooperation with the countries in the region to foster legal institution building, economic progress, and good governance in the Balkans will be key to eliminating the environment supporting TOC.

West Africa

West Africa has become a major transit point for illegal drug shipments to Europe and for Southwest Asian heroin to the United States. It has also become both a source of—and transit point for—methamphetamine destined for the Far East. West Africa also serves as a transit route for illicit proceeds flowing back to source countries. TOC exacerbates corruption and undermines the rule of law, democratic processes, and transparent business practices in several African states that already suffer from weak institutions. Due to its lack of law enforcement capabilities, its susceptibility to corruption, its porous borders, and its strategic location, Guinea-Bissau remains a significant hub of narcotics trafficking on the verge of developing into a narco-state. While many officials within the Government of Guinea-Bissau recognize the extent of the drug problem and express a willingness to address it, a crippling lack of resources and capacity remains a hindrance to real progress in combating drug trafficking.

The recent re-appointment of U.S. Treasury-designated drug kingpin Jose Americo Bubo Na Tchuto as Naval Chief of Staff is likely to further entrench drug cartels in the permissive operating conditions prevailing in Guinea-Bissau. In the Gulf of Guinea, maritime criminals operate in areas of weak governance, kidnapping oil workers, stealing oil from pipelines, and causing environmental damage that harms the citizenry.

The United States will work with African governments, European partners, and multilateral institutions to counter this threat to development, democratic processes, and the rule of law in the region.

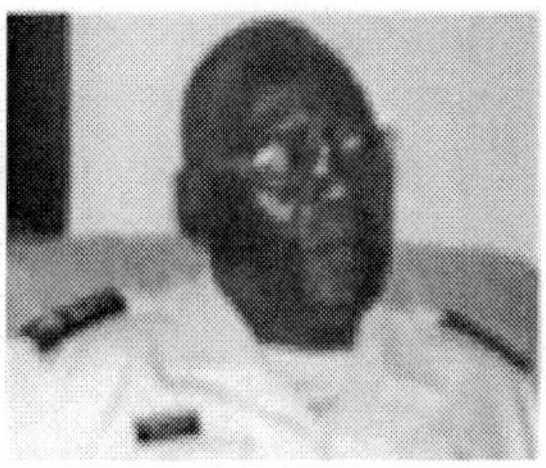

Jose Americo Bubo Na Tchuto,
U.S. Treasury-designated drug kingpin

Asia/Pacific

TOC networks and DTOs are integrating their activities in the Asia/Pacific region. Due to the region's global economic ties, these criminal activities have serious implications worldwide. The economic importance of the region also heightens the threat posed to intellectual property rights, as a large portion of intellectual property theft originates from China and Southeast Asia.

Human trafficking and smuggling remain significant concerns in the Asia/Pacific region, as demonstrated by the case of convicted alien smuggler Cheng Chui Ping, who smuggled more than 1,000 aliens into the United States during the course of her criminal career, sometimes hundreds at a time.

TOC networks in the region are also active in the illegal drug trade, trafficking precursor chemicals for use in illicit drug production. North Korean government entities have likely maintained ties with established crime networks, including those that produce counterfeit U.S. currency, threatening the global integrity of the U.S. dollar. It is unclear whether these links persist.

The United States will continue to improve its understanding of the TOC threats in the Asia/Pacific region and will work with partner nations to develop a comprehensive response.

Cheng Chui Ping, convicted alien smuggler

III. STRATEGY TO COMBAT TRANSNATIONAL ORGANIZED CRIME

For decades, the United States and other countries have dismantled scores of criminal organizations around the world. The U.S. experience with La Cosa Nostra, as well as Colombia's experience with the Medellin and Cali Cartels—and even the FARC—prove that it is possible to constrain, shrink, disrupt and dismantle criminal and insurgent groups once considered to be untouchable.

This *Strategy* builds upon such past experience. Today the threat from TOC is more complicated because criminal networks are more fluid and are using increasingly sophisticated tactics. TOC can exploit the interconnected nature of our modern trading, transportation, and transactional systems that move people and commerce throughout the global economy and across our borders. Countering TOC today requires an integrated and comprehensive approach. This *Strategy* sets out such an approach to *raise international awareness* about the reality of the TOC threat to international security; *galvanize* multilateral action to *constrain* the reach and influence of TOC; *deprive* TOC of its enabling means and infrastructure; *shrink* the threat TOC poses to citizen safety, national security, and governance; and *ultimately defeat* the TOC networks that pose the greatest threat to national security. TOC presents sophisticated and multifaceted threats that cannot be addressed through law enforcement action alone. Accordingly, we will establish an interagency Threat Mitigation Working Group to identify those TOC networks that present a sufficiently high national security threat as to merit the focused use of complementary law enforcement and non-law enforcement assets and that may be vulnerable to whole-of-government responses. The Working Group will ensure the coordination of all elements of national power to effectively protect our borders, people, economy, and financial system from the threats posed by the most dangerous and sophisticated of these transnational criminal networks.

This *Strategy* sets out five overarching policy objectives that are consistent with the vision and priorities of the *National Security Strategy:*

1) **Protect Americans and our partners from the harm, violence, and exploitation of transnational criminal networks.** Our priority is the safety, security, and prosperity of American citizens and the citizens of partner nations. We will target the

networks that pose the gravest threat to citizen safety and security, including those that traffic illicit drugs, arms, and people—especially women and children; sell and distribute substandard, tainted and counterfeit goods; rob Americans of their prosperity; carry out kidnappings for ransom and extortion; and seek to terrorize and intimidate through acts of torture and murder.

2) **Help partner countries strengthen governance and transparency, break the corruptive power of transnational criminal networks, and sever state-crime alliances.** The United States needs willing, reliable and capable partners to combat the corruption and instability generated by TOC and related threats to governance. We will help international partners develop the sustainable capacities necessary to defeat transnational threats; strengthen legitimate and effective public safety, security, and justice institutions; and promote universal values. We will also seek to sever the powerful strategic alliances that form between TOC and states, including those between TOC networks and foreign intelligence services.
3) **Break the economic power of transnational criminal networks and protect strategic markets and the U.S. financial system from TOC penetration and abuse.** TOC networks—using bribery, fraud, and violence—have the capacity to disrupt economic activity and put legitimate businesses at a distinct competitive disadvantage. We will attack the financial underpinnings of the top transnational criminals; strip them of their illicit wealth; sever their access to the financial system; expose their criminal activities hidden behind legitimate fronts; and protect strategic markets and the U.S. financial system.
4) **Defeat transnational criminal networks that pose the greatest threat to national security, by targeting their infrastructures, depriving them of their enabling means, and preventing the criminal facilitation of terrorist activities.** We will target, disrupt, and defeat the TOC networks that pose the greatest threat to the safety and security of Americans and U.S. national security interests. These include criminal networks—including transnational criminal gangs—that traffic drugs, bulk cash, arms, people, sensitive documents, or other contraband. Further, we will seek to prevent collaboration between criminal and terrorist networks and deprive them of their critical resources and infrastructure, such as funding, logistical support for transportation, staging, procurement, safe havens for illicit activities, and the facilitation of services and materiel, which could include WMD material.
5) **Build international consensus, multilateral cooperation, and public-private partnerships to defeat transnational organized crime.** We will build new partnerships—with industry, finance, academia, civil society and non-governmental organizations—to combat TOC networks that operate in the illicit and licit worlds. We will also fight criminal networks with an alliance of legitimate networks, and ensure the freedom of the press so that the media and journalists may safely expose the harms inflicted by TOC. We will expand and deepen our understanding, cooperation, and information sharing at home with State and local agencies, with foreign partners, and with multilateral institutions. Internationally, we will further international norms against tolerating or sponsoring crime in all its forms, including in cyberspace.

Priority Actions

Start at Home: Taking Shared Responsibility for Transnational Organized Crime

> I reiterated that the United States accepts our shared responsibility for the drug violence. So to combat the southbound flow of guns and money, we are screening all southbound rail cargo, seizing many more guns bound for Mexico, and we are putting more gunrunners behind bars. And as part of our new drug control strategy, we are focused on reducing the demand for drugs through education, prevention and treatment... We are very mindful that the battle President Calderón is fighting inside of Mexico is not just his battle; it's also ours. We have to take responsibility just as he's taking responsibility.
>
> —President Barack Obama speaking at a joint press conference with Mexican President Felipe Calderón, March 3, 2011

We must begin our effort to disrupt TOC by looking inward and acknowledging the causes that emanate from within our own borders to fuel and empower TOC. The demand for illegal drugs within the United States fuels a significant share of the global drug trade, which is a primary funding source for TOC networks and a key source of revenue for some terrorist and insurgent networks. Any comprehensive strategy to defeat TOC must seek to reduce the demand for drugs and other illegal goods that finance TOC networks. The President's *National Drug Control Strategy* emphasizes prevention, early intervention, treatment, and innovative criminal justice approaches to drive down drug use, and calls for continued support for the millions of Americans who are in recovery from addiction. Supported by a budget that increases resources for vital prevention and treatment programs, the *National Drug Control Strategy* seeks to reduce the size of the illegal drug market in the United States, depriving TOC networks of revenue while helping more of our citizens break the cycle of drug abuse and reducing the adverse consequences to our communities. We must also stop the illicit flow from the United States of weapons and criminal proceeds that empower TOC networks. The Administration has placed an increased emphasis on stemming these outbound flows, dedicating additional law enforcement, investigative, and prosecution resources to targeting TOC, such as deploying additional U.S. Customs and Border Protection "outbound teams" to our borders, screening outbound rail and vehicle traffic for weapons and bulk currency, and by investing additional resources in the integrated Border Enforcement Security Task Forces along the U.S.-Mexico border to investigate the organizations involved in cross-border crimes. We will also work with Congress to seek ratification or accession to key multilateral instruments related to countering the illicit trafficking of weapons. Further, we will work with our international partners to build their law enforcement capacities, strengthen their judicial institutions, and combat the corrosive threat of corruption, while also recognizing that the United States itself is not immune to public corruption. Continued vigilance is required to ensure the integrity of U.S. officials and institutions as we face the new and converging threats posed by TOC. In addition to the greater vigilance required by our governmental institutions, American businesses and individuals need to inform law enforcement about criminal activity and reduce their vulnerability to fraud schemes, intellectual property theft, and identity theft. Acknowledging our own challenges and aggressively addressing them here at home represent the first essential steps in building the cooperative multilateral approach required to defeat TOC.

Actions

a) Reduce the demand for illicit drugs in the United States, thereby denying funding to illicit trafficking organizations.
b) Continue to attack drug trafficking and distribution networks and their enabling means within the United States to reduce the availability of illicit drugs.
c) Sever the illicit flow across U.S. borders of people, weapons, currency, and other illicit finance through investigations and prosecutions of key TOC leadership, as well as through the targeting of TOC networks'enabling means and infrastructure.
d) Identify and take action against corporate and governmental corruption within the United States.
e) Work with Congress to secure ratification of the Inter American Convention against the Illicit Manufacturing of and Trafficking in Firearms, Ammunition, Explosives and Other Related Materials.
f) Seek accession to the Protocol against the Illicit Manufacturing of and Trafficking in Firearms, their Parts and Components and Ammunition, supplementing the UN Convention against Transnational Organized Crime.

Project Deliverance: Targeting Mexican Drug Trafficking Networks in the United States

On June 9, 2010 the DEA-led interagency Special Operations Division executed a coordinated takedown in support of Project Deliverance, a 22-month multi-agency network of law enforcement investigations targeting the transportation infrastructure of Mexican transnational criminal organizations in the United States, especially along the Southwest border. During the final takedown, 429 arrests took place in 16 states through coordination among more than 3,000 Federal, State, and local law enforcement officers. In total, Project Deliverance has led to 2,266 arrests and the seizure of $154 million, 1,262 pounds of meth-amphetamine, 2.5 tons of cocaine, 1,410 pounds of heroin, 69 tons of marijuana, 501 weapons, and 527 vehicles during the entire course of the operation.

Enhance Intelligence and Information Sharing

A shift in U.S. intelligence collection priorities since the September 11, 2001 attacks left significant gaps in TOC-related intelligence. Meanwhile, the TOC threat has worsened and grown in complexity over the past 15 years. The fluid nature of TOC networks, which includes the use of criminal facilitators, makes targeting TOC increasingly difficult. Enhancing U.S. intelligence collection, analysis, and counterintelligence on TOC is a necessary first step, but should be accompanied by collaboration with law enforcement authorities at Federal, State, local, tribal, and territorial levels and enhanced sharing with foreign counterparts. We will also supplement our understanding of TOC involvement in licit commercial sectors to better enable policymakers to develop specific interventions. Our aim is enhanced intelligence that is broad-based and centered on substantially upgraded signals intelligence (SIGINT), human intelligence (HUMINT) and open sources intelligence (OSINT). This effort will be aided through greater information sharing with foreign partners and closer cooperation among intelligence, law enforcement, and other applicable agencies domestically. We will augment our intelligence in step with the new TOC threats described previously. The Administration will review its current intelligence priorities, including the National Intelligence Priorities Framework, and determine how best to enhance our intelligence against the highest-level TOC threats to national security. Priorities will include:

- Enhancing SIGINT and HUMINT collection on TOC threats, especially taking into account the potential role of TOC to facilitate WMD terrorism;
- Employing the Open Source Center to draw upon "grey" literature, smaller press outlets that cover crime in foreign countries, and social media fora to develop profiles of individuals, companies, and institutions linked to TOC networks;
- Coordinating with the interagency International Organized Crime Intelligence and Operations Center (IOC-2) to utilize existing resources and databases of the Organized Crime Drug Enforcement Task Force (OCDETF) Fusion Center (OFC) and SOD to share intelligence, de-conflict operations, and produce actionable leads for investigators and prosecutors working nationwide;
- Expanding collection and immigration, customs, transportation, and critical infrastructure screening capabilities in TOC "hotspots" around the world;
- Developing protocols to ensure appropriate TOC data flows to agencies conducting screening and interdiction operations to disrupt TOC activities at the border and at critical points of the supply chain;
- Using specialized intelligence centers such as the El Paso Intelligence Center, the Bulk Cash Smuggling Center, the National Export Enforcement Coordination Center, and the Cyber Crimes Center to coordinate the collection and analysis of intelligence regarding various aspects of the TOC threat;
- Using the National Intellectual Property Rights Coordination Center, an interagency and international law enforcement task force established in 2000 and led by ICE, to assist with combating intellectual property theft and maintaining the integrity of public health, public safety, the military, and the U.S. economy; and
- Enhancing Department of Defense support to U.S. law enforcement through the Narcotics and Transnational Crime Support Center.

Actions

a) Enhance U.S. intelligence collection, analysis, and counterintelligence on TOC entities that pose the greatest threat to national security.
b) Develop greater synergies between intelligence analysts, collectors, and counterintelligence personnel; ensure their efforts directly support operational law enforcement needs and screening requirements.

c) Strengthen ties among U.S. intelligence and counterintelligence, law enforcement, and military entities, while strengthening cooperation with international intelligence and law enforcement partners.
d) Develop and foster stronger law enforcement and Intelligence Community relationships among Federal, State, local, tribal, and territorial authorities.
e) Support multilateral senior law enforcement exchanges to promote the sharing of criminal intelligence and enhance cooperation, such as the "Quintet of Attorneys-General" and the "Strategic Alliance Group" fora established with the United Kingdom, Canada, New Zealand, and Australia.
f) Update the National Intelligence Priorities Framework to ensure that it is aligned with current TOC threats.
g) Enhance support to Intelligence Community analysis of TOC by the Office of the Director of National Intelligence, specifically by the National Intelligence Council and the National Intelligence Managers.
h) The National Counterproliferation Center shall develop a plan that assesses the links between TOC and WMD proliferators.
i) Establish a comprehensive and proactive information-sharing mechanism to identify TOC actors and exclude them from the United States or uncover them within the United States.

Information Sharing to Combat Transnational Organized Crime

The Special Operations Division

Established in 1994, the Special Operations Division (SOD) is a DEA-led multi-agency operations coordination center with participation from Federal law enforcement agencies, the Department of Defense, the Intelligence Community, and international law enforcement partners. SOD's mission is to establish strategies and operations to dismantle national and international trafficking organizations by attacking their command and control communications.

Special emphasis is placed on those major drug trafficking and narco-terrorism organizations that operate across jurisdictional boundaries on a regional, national, and international level. SOD provides foreign- and domestic-based law enforcement agents with timely investigative information that enables them to fully exploit Federal law enforcement's investigative authority under Title III of the U.S. Code. SOD coordinates overlapping investigations, ensuring that tactical and operational intelligence is shared among law enforcement agencies.

The Organized Crime Drug Enforcement Task Force Fusion Center

Created in June 2006, the Organized Crime Drug Enforcement Task Force (OCDETF) Fusion Center (OFC) serves as a central data warehouse for drug intelligence, financial intelligence, and related investigative information, and is designed to conduct cross-agency integration and analysis of such data with a view to creating comprehensive intelligence pictures of targeted organizations, including those identified as Consolidated Priority Organization Targets—the United States' most wanted international drug and money laundering targets.

The OFC provides agencies with operational human and financial intelligence, and is staffed with agents and analysts detailed from 14 participating investigative agencies. These personnel conduct analysis to produce investigative leads, develop target profiles, and identify links between drug organizations and other criminal activity in support of drug investigations.

The International Organized Crime Intelligence and Operations Center

In May 2009, Attorney General Eric Holder announced the establishment of the International Organized Crime Intelligence and Operations Center (IOC-2), an entity that marshals the resources and information of U.S. law enforcement agencies and Federal prosecutors to collectively combat the threats posed by international criminal organizations. Understanding that international criminal organizations are profit-driven, IOC-2 also works with investigators and prosecutors to target the criminal proceeds and assets of international criminal organizations.

In recognition of the demonstrated interrelationship between criminal organizations that engage in illicit drug trafficking and those that engage in international organized crime involving a broader range of criminal activity, IOC-2 works in close partnership with the OFC and SOD.

The Bulk Cash Smuggling Center

ICE established the National Bulk Cash Smuggling Center (BCSC) in 2009 to combat bulk cash smuggling.

The BCSC is an operations support facility providing real-time investigative assistance to the Federal, State, and local officers involved in enforcement and interdiction of bulk cash smuggling and the transportation of illicit proceeds.

The BCSC is partnered with the El Paso Intelligence Center to further identify and target the financial infrastructure of drug trafficking organizations.

These organizations seek to avoid traditional financial institutions by repatriating illicit proceeds through commercial and private aircraft, passenger and commercial vehicles, maritime vessels, and pedestrians crossing at our U.S. land borders.

These combined interagency efforts, successful financial investigations, Bank Secrecy Act requirements, and anti-money laundering compliance by financial institutions has strengthened formal financial systems and forced criminal organizations to seek other means to transport illicit funds across our borders.

The EPIC Border Intelligence Fusion Section

The El Paso Intelligence Center (EPIC), managed by the DEA, was established in 1974 to support enforcement efforts against drug and alien smuggling along the Southwest border. EPIC has grown over time to better support Federal, State, local and tribal law enforcement.

The DHS Office of Intelligence and Analysis established the Border Intelligence Fusion Section (BIFS) at EPIC in November 2010 with the objective of providing U.S. law enforcement, border enforcement, and investigative agencies with multi-source intelligence and law enforcement information to support investigations, interdictions, and other law enforcement operations related to the Southwest border.

The BIFS is a joint, collaborative effort of the Department of Homeland Security, Department of Justice, Department of Defense, and partners in the Intelligence Community and, as a multi-source/all threats intelligence section at EPIC, the BIFS will access and analyze intelligence and information received by and developed at EPIC in order to produce a common intelligence picture and common operating picture.

Protect the Financial System and Strategic Markets Against Transnational Organized Crime

Transnational criminals are now more entrepreneurial and sophisticated, and their growing infiltration of licit commerce and economic activity fundamentally threatens the free markets and financial systems that are critical to the stability and efficiency of the global economy. TOC threatens free markets because it disregards the laws and norms that legitimate businesses respect, thereby reaping an unfair competitive advantage. By eroding market integrity, quality, and competitiveness and using financial systems to move, conceal, and increase illicit funds, transnational criminals exploit and undermine not only the interests of the United States but also those of all countries promoting the rule of law.

By carefully following strategic and emerging markets for indicators of criminal interest, the United States can detect, disrupt, and reduce the economic power of TOC. To do so, the United States will work with our international partners to deter or sever crime-state alliances, raise awareness to alert businesses that may be unwitting facilitators for criminal enterprises, and continue to develop appropriate safeguards to protect the legitimate flow of trade and investment.

By targeting criminal assets and opportunities, the United States and its allies can markedly reduce the profitability, growth, and evolution of TOC networks. However, some TOC activity is inherently harder to detect and deter. The United States will place special emphasis on IPR violations and cybercrimes due to their particular impact on the economy and consumer health and safety. The United States remains intent on improving the transparency of the international financial system, including an effort to expose vulnerabilities that could be exploited by terrorist and other illicit financial networks.

At the same time, the United States will enhance and apply our financial tools and sanctions more effectively to close those vulnerabilities, disrupt and dismantle illicit financial networks, and apply pressure on the state entities that directly or indirectly support TOC. We will continue to monitor TOC infiltration of the global economy to better protect the financial system and freeze the assets of criminal networks under expanded Presidential sanctions authorities and/or seize them under existing forfeiture laws.

Actions

a) Implement a new Executive Order to prohibit the transactions and block the assets under U.S. jurisdiction of TOC networks and their associates that threaten critical U.S. interests.
b) Prevent or disrupt criminal involvement in emerging and strategic markets.

c) Increase awareness and provide incentives and alternatives for the private sector to reduce facilitation of TOC.
d) Develop a mechanism that would make unclassified data on TOC available to private sector partners.
e) Implement the Administration's joint strategic plan on intellectual property enforcement to target, investigate, and prosecute intellectual property crimes committed by TOC.
f) Enhance domestic and foreign capabilities to combat the increasing involvement of TOC networks in cybercrime and build international capacity to forensically exploit and judicially process digital evidence.
g) Use authorities under the USA PATRIOT Act to designate foreign jurisdictions, institutions, or classes of transactions as 'primary money-laundering concerns," allowing for the introduction of various restrictive measures on financial dealings by U.S. persons with those entities.
h) Identify foreign kleptocrats who have corrupt relationships with TOC networks and target their assets for freezing, forfeiture, and repatriation to victimized governments.
i) Work with Congress to enact legislation to require disclosure of beneficial ownership information of legal entities at the time of company formation in order to enhance transparency for law enforcement and other purposes.
j) Support the work of the Financial Action Task Force, which sets and enforces global standards to combat both money laundering and the financing of terrorism.

The Mogilevich Organization

Semion Mogilevich is wanted by the United States for fraud, racketeering, and money laundering and was recently added to the FBI's Ten Most Wanted fugitives list.

Mogilevich and several members of his criminal organization were charged in 2003 in the Eastern District of Pennsylvania in a 45-count racketeering indictment with involvement in a sophisticated securities fraud and money-laundering scheme, in which they allegedly used a Pennsylvania company, YBM Magnex, to defraud investors of more than $150 million.

Even after that indictment—and being placed on the FBI's Ten Most Wanted list—Mogilevich has continued to expand his criminal empire.

Mogilevich was arrested by Russian police on tax charges in January 2008 and was released pending trial in July 2009. Other members of his organization remain at large.

Strengthen Interdiction, Investigations, and Prosecutions

This *Strategy* sets priorities and objectives to help law enforcement and other applicable agencies at the Federal, State, local, territorial and tribal levels work together in a collaborative manner to target TOC networks—their leaders as well as their enabling means and infrastructure—in the United States and abroad.

It is equally important that we build strong working relationships with our international partners to harmonize our efforts, and to ensure that they have the capabilities and regulatory and legislative frameworks to prevent, reduce, and eliminate TOC threats.

Building upon the improved information sharing described earlier, the United States will leverage consolidated TOC databases to provide more accurate intelligence on known TOC members and their associates so they can more easily be denied entry to the United States or access to lawful immigration status, employment, or secure facilities.

This *Strategy* pursues TOC through criminal investigations and interdiction focused on both the networks and their leadership. Criminal investigations will use an integrated approach that incorporates financial, weapons, and TOC-related corruption investigations into a comprehensive attack on the entire criminal organization.

Interdiction efforts will focus on depriving TOC networks of their products, proceeds, infrastructure, and enabling means. The use of multi-agency task forces such as the ICE-led Border Enforcement Security Task Forces will remain essential to our efforts to investigate and interdict TOC threats at our borders.

To address recent TOC trends, the Administration will work with Congress on a range of legislative solutions to allow or enhance the prosecution of TOC enterprises and significant TOC activity that affects the United States.

We will also enhance our anti-money laundering and forfeiture authorities to target TOC networks that pose threats to national and international security.

Actions

a) Work with Congress to enhance U.S. authorities to identify, investigate, interdict, and prosecute top transnational criminal networks.
b) Utilize rewards programs to assist in gathering information leading to the arrest or conviction of top transnational criminals.
c) Issue a new Presidential Proclamation under the Immigration and Nationality Act to refuse visas/ deny entry to TOC-affiliated aliens, corrupt foreign officials, and other persons designated for financial sanctions pursuant to the International Emergency Economic Powers Act.
d) Develop a strategy that denies TOC networks and individuals in the United States access to their infrastructure and their enabling means.
e) Deny visas to TOC members and associates and capture top TOC figures who take refuge in the United States or partner countries.
f) Fully integrate financial, weapons, and TOC-related corruption investigations into comprehensive organizational attack activities and operations.
g) Strengthen cooperation with international police organizations, such as Interpol, Europol, Ameripol, and the International Association of Chiefs of Police (IACP), to facilitate cross-border police cooperation.
h) Strengthen efforts to interdict illicit trafficking in the air and maritime domains.
i) Develop and implement a whole-of-government plan to counter kidnapping for ransom in order to disrupt the funding for terrorists, pirates, and other bad actors.
j) Deny TOC access to secure facilities and locations.

The U.S. Secret Service's Cyber Intelligence Efforts

The U.S. Secret Service leverages technology and information obtained through private partnerships to monitor developing technologies and trends in the financial payments industry.

The information obtained is used to enhance the U.S. Secret Service's capabilities to prevent and mitigate attacks against the financial and telecommunications infrastructures. This approach to intelligence collection and sharing has resulted in the successful apprehension of individuals charged with committing some of the world's most advanced cybercrimes during such investigations as those of the Heartland and TJX Intrusions, Maksym Yastremskey, Albert Gonzalez, and others. In FY 2010, the U.S. Secret Service arrested 1,217 suspects for cybercrime related violations, with a fraud loss of $507 million.

Defending U.S. Borders against TOC

In 2006, amidst rising crime on the Southwest border, ICE and CBP worked with other Federal, State, local, and foreign partners to establish the Border Enforcement Security Task Force (BEST), designed to attack TOC networks that exploit our borders and threaten the American public. Since then, this initiative has grown to 21 BESTs arrayed along the Southwest and Northern borders as well as at major seaports. These BESTs have seized more than 36,000 pounds of cocaine, 550 pounds of heroin, 485,000 pounds of marijuana, 4,300 weapons, and $68 million, and led to the arrests of 5,910 individuals.

Disrupt Drug Trafficking and Its Facilitation of Other Transnational Threats

In recent years, new developments in technology and communications equipment have enabled TOC networks involved in drug trafficking and other illicit activities to plan, coordinate, and perpetrate their schemes with increased mobility and anonymity. As a result, many DTOs have developed into versatile, loose networks that cooperate intermittently but maintain their independence. They operate worldwide and employ sophisticated technology and financial savvy. These criminal networks bribe government officials and take advantage of weak border security and ill-equipped law enforcement to facilitate their operations. Along emerging trafficking routes, such as the transit route through West Africa to Europe, criminal networks are spreading corruption and undermining fledgling democratic institutions. Due to the enormous profits associated with drug trafficking, the illegal trade is also a way to finance other transnational criminal and terrorist activities. To diminish these threats, we will continue ongoing efforts to identify and disrupt the leadership, production, intelligence gathering, transportation, and financial infrastructure of major TOC networks. By targeting the human, technology, travel, and communications aspects of these networks, we will be able to monitor and gather intelligence to identify the full scope of the TOC networks, their members, financial assets, and criminal activities. We will continue ongoing efforts to enhance collaboration among domestic law enforcement agencies and our foreign counterparts in order to strengthen our ability to coordinate investigations and share intelligence to combat drug trafficking and TOC. Continued use of economic sanctions under the Foreign Narcotics Kingpin Designation Act (Kingpin Act) to pursue transnational drug organizations will enhance our ability to disrupt and dismantle TOC networks. The Kingpin Act also may be used to prosecute persons involved in illegal activities linked to drug trafficking, such as arms trafficking, bulk cash smuggling, or gang activity. Enhanced intelligence sharing and coordination among law enforcement and intelligence agencies, the military, and our diplomatic community will enable the interagency community to develop aggressive, multi-jurisdictional approaches to dismantle TOC networks involved in drug trafficking. The United States will continue to aggressively target the nexus among TOC networks involved in drug trafficking, terrorist groups, piracy on the high seas, and arms traffickers. In FY 2002, the DEA formally established the Counter-Narco-Terrorism Operations Center (CNTOC) within SOD, which coordinates all DEA investigations and intelligence linked to narco-terrorism and is central to U.S. efforts to disrupt these crime-terror relationships. The United States will utilize its bilateral maritime counterdrug agreements and operational procedures to facilitate cooperation in counterdrug operations. We must attack these organizations as close to the source as we can by forward deploying our law enforcement and intelligence assets. All-source intelligence is used by U.S. Coast Guard assets in the transit zone to extend our borders by interdicting and apprehending traffickers. The United States will continue its longstanding cooperation with the international community in our joint efforts to disrupt the world drug trade through support for drug crop reduction, promotion of alternative livelihoods, and partner nation capacity building. Our counternarcotics efforts will apply all available tools to ensure that improvements are permanent and sustainable by international allies. These efforts will include complementary and comprehensive assistance programs across the prevention, intervention, and enforcement spectrum. By disrupting and dismantling the world's major TOC networks involved in drug trafficking, we will be able to reduce the availability of illicit drugs, inhibit terrorist funding, improve national and international security, and bring TOC networks to justice.

Actions

a) Work with international partners to reduce the global supply of and demand for illegal drugs and thereby deny funding to TOC networks.
b) Sever the links between the international illicit drug and arms trades, especially in strategic regions that are at risk of being destabilized by these interconnected threats.
c) Sustain pressure to disrupt Consolidated Priority Organization Targets, as they often have a particularly corrupting influence or provide support to terrorism.
d) Maximize use of the Kingpin Act to pursue transnational drug organizations.
e) Develop a comprehensive approach to dismantle DTOs with connections to terrorist organizations.
f) Work with international partners to shut down emerging drug transit routes and associated corruption in West Africa.
g) Coordinate with international partners to prevent synthetic drug production, trafficking, and precursor chemical diversion.

Countering Illicit Finance for Drug Traffickers & Terrorists

In February 2011, the U.S. Department of the Treasury, based upon an investigation by the DEA, announced the identification of the Lebanese Canadian Bank (LCB) as a financial institution of primary money laundering concern under Section 311 of the USA PATRIOT Act. The Department of the Treasury found there was reason to believe LCB managers were complicit in facilitating the money-laundering activities of an international narcotics trafficking and money laundering network controlled by Ayman Joumaa who was designated as a drug Kingpin on January 26, 2011 pursuant to the Kingpin Act. This network moved illegal drugs from South America to Europe and the Middle East via West Africa and laundered hundreds of millions of dollars monthly through accounts held at LCB, as well as through trade-based money laundering involving consumer goods throughout the world, including through used car dealerships in the United States. The U.S. Government also found reason to believe there were links between the international narcotics trafficking and money laundering network, LCB, and the terrorist organization Hizballah.

International Drug Enforcement Conference

The annual DEA-led International Drug Enforcement Conference (IDEC), which has been held annually for the past 28 years, is a major contributor to international cooperation and capacity building. The IDEC brings the top drug law enforcement leaders and senior investigators from over 100 nations to a single venue where yearly agendas are set for cooperation, intelligence sharing, and case prioritization. IDEC— the world's largest international drug law enforcement conference—has produced concrete results year after year. During the conferences, DEA and partner nations jointly develop plans to build greater law enforcement and investigatory capacity. In addition, host nation personnel and U.S. law enforcement exchange information on priority investigatory targets.

Build International Capacity, Cooperation, and Partnerships

Sustainable progress against TOC requires both political commitment and effective law enforcement and criminal justice capacities on a worldwide basis. TOC threatens the security and well-being of people around the world and jeopardizes the functioning of the global economy. Not all of these threats are equally visible to international audiences. Absent broad recognition of these shared threats, our collaboration with international partners to confront TOC will be constrained by limited political will. The United States will reach out directly to the international business community and the general public to convey that both nations and individuals share a common enemy in TOC and have a common stake in addressing this threat. For nations that have the will to fulfill their international law enforcement commitments but lack the necessary means, the United States is committed to partnering with them to develop stronger law enforcement and criminal justice institutions necessary for ensuring the rule of law. Over the past decade, important gains have been made in developing criminal justice capacities in key regions of the world. The goal of the United States is to promote the expansion of such achievements on a worldwide basis, to the point where international law enforcement capabilities and cooperation among states are self-sustaining.

Great progress also has been made in developing a common normative framework for international cooperation against TOC threats. The challenge for the United States and other countries over the next decade is to bring the promise of this worldwide regime into practice. The United States will encourage international partners to dedicate the necessary political capital and resources toward making the promise of these commitments a reality. The United States will pursue this through both a renewed commitment to multilateral diplomacy and by leveraging bilateral partnerships to elevate the importance of combating TOC as a key priority of U.S. diplomacy. For example, in February 2011, the United States and the United Kingdom established the Organized Crime Contact Group, to be chaired by the UK Home Secretary and the Assistant to the President for Homeland Security and Counterterrorism. In addition, the United States deploys hundreds of law enforcement attachés to its missions abroad to develop and maintain foreign contacts essential to combating immediate threats to public safety and security. The United States will continue to place a high priority on the provision of international technical assistance through our missions abroad and will continue to improve the coordination of these programs. The United States will leverage all possible areas of cooperation, including legal instruments such as the *UN Convention against Transnational Organized Crime (the Palermo Convention),* the *UN Convention against the Illicit Traffic in Narcotic Drugs and Psychotropic Substances,* and the protocols to which the United States is a party, to obtain the assistance of international partners and to raise international criminal justice, border security, and law enforcement standards and norms. The United States will strengthen its engagement with the United Nations in this regard and leverage the growing role of regional and other multilateral institutions that have risen in significance and influence over the past decade. Additionally, the United States will continue to pursue cooperation with other countries and with partners such as the European Union, the G-8, the G-20, and new inter-regional platforms across the Pacific and Atlantic in developing leading-edge initiatives and political commitments to combat TOC. The United States also will seek to develop informal partnerships with states that share U.S. goals to prevent TOC networks from abusing the benefits of globalization. By promoting flexible networks of law enforcement and diplomatic partners, the United States can leverage the expertise and infrastructure of committed governments and respond more quickly to changing dynamics in transnational criminal threats. The United States convened a meeting of 25 countries and jurisdictions across the Pacific in April 2009 to consider common approaches and strengthen cooperation against transnational criminal networks that span East Asia, the Pacific, and Latin America. The United States hosted a similar event in May 2011 with the European Union to generate enhanced partnerships against trans-Atlantic criminal networks operating across Latin America, West Africa, and Europe. By building cooperative platforms and networks incrementally, the United States will generate greater collective action, joint cases, and common strategic approaches with our international partners to combat transnational criminal threats.

Actions

a) Raise international awareness of TOC and build multilateral cooperation against it.
b) Partner with countries able to contribute key law enforcement resources, other donors, and the United Nations to launch a new International Police Peacekeeping

Operations Support Program to enhance policing and law enforcement capacity in ungoverned spaces.

c) Leverage assets to enhance foreign capabilities, including counterterrorism capacity building, foreign law enforcement cooperation, military cooperation, and the strengthening of justice and interior ministries.
d) Implement a public diplomacy strategy to reduce the demand for illicit goods and services that fuels TOC.
e) Implement the Central American Citizen Security Partnership to strengthen courts, civil society groups and institutions that uphold the rule of law in the region.
f) Implement the State Department's West Africa Citizen Security Initiative to combat transnational criminal threats in the region.
g) Initiate new dialogue in multilateral fora to combat corruption and illicit trade, to include, as part of the Administration's intellectual property enforcement strategy, stemming the flow of dangerous counterfeit products.
h) Build partnerships with other donors, private sector experts, nongovernmental organizations, civil society groups, the media, and academia that focus on supporting political will for criminal justice reform.
i) Increase international scientific research, data collection, and analysis to assess the scope and impact of TOC and the most effective means to combat it.
j) Institutionalize the U.S.-UK Organized Crime Contact Group to deepen bilateral cooperation and galvanize multilateral collaboration against TOC.
k) Finalize the U.S.-Mexico 21st Century Border Action Plan agreements on law enforcement cooperation.
l) Expand cooperation with the United Nations to promote implementation of the United Nations Convention against Transnational Organized Crime, including through the development of an appropriate review mechanism.
m) Strengthen capacities for program management, internal controls, and contract administration to prevent the diversion or improper use of foreign assistance in countries threatened by TOC-related corruption.
n) Increase collaboration with international partners to improve their capacity to support immigration, customs, transportation, and critical infrastructure screening requirements and to harmonize their standards for screening and identification.

Combating Transnational Crime:
The Multilateral Framework

Five major international agreements underpin and provide near global scope to our efforts to combat TOC and corruption: the United Nations Convention against Transnational Organized Crime (UNTOC), its three supplementary protocols against trafficking in persons, migrant smuggling, and illicit trafficking in firearms, and the United Nations Convention against Corruption (UNCAC).

The United States strongly supports the framework provided by these instruments, especially with regard to prosecuting and investigating transnational crime and corruption, engaging in mutual legal assistance, and supplementing bilateral extradition treaties.

These agreements set the point of departure for many of our bilateral law enforcement partnerships around the globe and help bring the international community into agreement with U.S. standards. The key challenge remaining is to promote wider implementation of the Conventions through support for capacity building and by otherwise encouraging international partners to dedicate the necessary political capital and resources toward realizing the potential of these groundbreaking instruments.

INDEX

C

D

E

F

G

H

I

Q

R

S

T